A **Tapestry** of **Relational Child** and **Youth Care Competencies**

A **Tapestry** of **Relational Child** and **Youth Care Competencies**

Theresa Fraser and Mary Ventrella

CANADIAN
SCHOLARS

Toronto | Vancouver

A Tapestry of Relational Child and Youth Care Competencies

By Theresa Fraser and Mary Ventrella

First published in 2019 by
Canadian Scholars, an imprint of CSP Books Inc.
425 Adelaide Street West, Suite 200
Toronto, Ontario
M5V 3C1

www.canadianscholars.ca

Library and Archives Canada Cataloguing in Publication
Title: A tapestry of relational child and youth care competencies / Theresa Fraser and Mary Ventrella.
Names: Fraser, Theresa Ann, 1962- author. | Ventrella, Mary, 1971- author.
Description: Includes index.
Identifiers: Canadiana (print) 20190142944 | Canadiana (ebook) 20190142995 |
    ISBN 9781773380339 (softcover) | ISBN 9781773380353 (ebook) | ISBN 9781773380346 (PDF)
Subjects: LCSH: Youth workers.
Classification: LCC HV1421 .F73 2019 | DDC 362.7—dc23

Page layout by S4Carlisle
Cover design by Rafael Chimicatti

Printed and bound in Ontario, Canada

Canada

Dedication

To our life partners, who always support our next learning ventures, and our children, who teach us every day what it means to be to be in relationship.

To our CYCP elders, who provided us with the courage to proudly call ourselves CYCPs. Thank you to all the children, youth, and families who had the courage to share their stories and experiences and allow us to walk with them. They are our greatest teachers.

We'd also like to thank all our students that we have taught and our Winter 2019 seminar students at Georgian College Orillia Campus, whose feedback helped us improve the book. Their insights on Case Study 8 are reflected here.

We thank Dorita Peer for her endless editorial support without judgment and for making words dance. We thank editors Nick Hilton and Ashley Rayner and are grateful for their editing, passion, and flexibility and for keeping us on schedule. Thank you for allowing us to work with you in collaboration and creativity.

Theresa: I need to thank Jane Clifton, Pat Ferbyack, Grace Nostbakken, and Michael Owens. These are my CYCP elders, who modelled CYC practice and planted seeds that, at the time, I did not think could grow but did. My CYCP identity began as they shared the narrative of their CYCP lived experiences, which I then added to my tapestry of identity. With love, respect, and appreciation for your relational caring.

I also need to honour my parents, John and Darlene, who birthed me at 17 and went on to parent eight more children. Neither finished high school nor had lots of external supports, but both worked hard throughout their lives to be the parents they felt they needed to be. My longtime friend Mike Murphy (who trained at Thistletown Regional Centre in Etobicoke) is always willing to share his praxis connecting current field directions with past wisdom. Kristina Arena, Peter Hoag (the grandparents of the Sheridan CYC program), Julie Jaglowitz, and Deb Megens, you have all assisted Mary and me to look at competencies from a different lens. Thank you all for the pieces that contribute to my fabric of knowing. I fondly express appreciation to my students, who passionately contributed to our co-constructed classrooms, and to my beloved husband, Kevin, who is a CYCP in his heart. You encourage and support me to do anything I feel led to do. My work is our work. Thank you, Ev, Aidan, Chris, Kyle, Carolina, Eric, Shavante, and Landen for being you and calling me Mom.

Mary: To my partner, John, and my three sons, Angelo, Juliano, and Michael, who are the heartbeat of this book for me. You teach me everyday how to be a better person and have shown me how adventurous parenting can be. Your love, acceptance, laughter, and continuous affirmation are why I have purpose and am filled with so much love that I can share with children, youth, and families. Thank you for picking up chores, waiting while I worked on the book, and understanding when I asked you to wait a few minutes. My love for you is deep and endless. Love to dedicate this to my mother, Vittoria, who had the courage to immigrate to Canada with $17 and a baby on the way. She had the determination to provide us with opportunity and choice. Forever grateful for my mom's courage and resliency. To my father, Pasquale, who was alive when I started this book and who I now miss every day. He encouraged me to write and while offered to play with my children. He continues to support me through his values of family, friends, happiness, and work ethics. I miss you, but know you are proud. To my in-laws, Maria and Angelo, for your endless support, encouragement, and dedication to allow me to write and follow my dreams. To my siblings, Nancy, Frank, Tony, Auriela and Milena and Benny, Tony and Terry, and cousins (all of you, too many to mention), who are always supporting me every step I take. Thank you for always being willing to babysit my kids, so that I can write. To my oldest friend, Sonia Sacco, who has been there for me every step of the way. I am forever grateful to you for keeping things real, making me laugh, for your endless support, and for camping with me when you'd rather be in a hotel. I'd like to thank Carol Nichol and Jan King for being creative and finding a way to both supervisee me. Thank you, Carol, for teaching me about myself and what I bring to the relationship. My gratitude and love is deep. To Paul Vella and Julius Cicer for your integrity and modelling how a CYCP walks, engages, and celebrates relationships. (Special thanks to Julius for saving me by the campfire while I was pregnant.) Brenda Webb, Heather Snell, Julie Jaglowitz, Kristine Arena, Peter Hoag, Deb Megens, Katherine Sloss, Howard Bloom, Gisele Beausoleil, Kathleen Cameron, Ira, Erika, Katherine Kelly, and Paula continue to challenge and support my teaching and inspire me every day to provide the best education for our future CYCPs. My colleagues and those of the CYC Board Member Association, Allan Brinkert, Rachel Thomas, Esme McMonagle, Tima Gandhi, Dr. Vani, Dr. Fantus, Patti MaKenna, and Stephanie Collins, taught me how to work collaborative with other disciplines. Administrators Virginia, Grace, and Amy have such a wealth of knowledge and support everyday events. Programs cannot function without you. To all the children, youth, and families who have allowed me the privilege and priceless gift to be in your presence and welcome me in your school, community, and homes. I dedicate this to all of you and every person who had the courage to take steps so that I can have choice, forever grateful for all those that walked before me and made a path for me to make my dreams come true.

Contents

About the Book   *viii*

Foreword   *ix*

Chapter 1   History of Child and Youth Care Practice Settings, Themes, and Education   1

Chapter 2   Professionalism   15

Chapter 3   Cultural and Human Diversity   55

Chapter 4   Applied Human Development   83

Chapter 5   Relationship and Communication   101

Chapter 6   Developmental Practice Methods   139

Chapter 7   Nurturing Creativity in Child and Youth Care Practice   185

Chapter 8   Competency Case Studies   211

Chapter 9   Supervision: Integrating Competencies   219

Chapter 10   The Growing Edge of the Child and Youth Care Practitioner and Profession   239

Appendix A: Table of National Child and Youth Care Certification Board Competencies   *245*

Appendix B: The LEAP Skills   *260*

Author Biographies   *261*

Glossary   *262*

About the Book

This book reviews the child and youth care competencies as published by the National Child and Youth Care Certification Board (CYCCB). Each competency (identified by a number and letter) is explained by the authors with a case example. Readers are then invited to engage in a discussion of a field example. This book is a teaching tool for the novice to seasoned Child and Youth Care Practitioner to support the development of self-awareness, skills, knowledge, and relational practices. This book can be used with students in child and youth care programs, teams for professional development, and organizations/agencies who facilitate their own staff training.

For more information about the Child and Youth Care Certification Board, please visit www.cyccb.org.

A NOTE ON PRONOUNS

Throughout the book, we have tried to use inclusive pronouns so more readers will see themselves reflected in the text. In some cases, we have provided a variety of pronouns; in others, we've selected just one. This isn't a perfect solution, as there are probably pronouns we've missed! We hope that teachers and students will take this as an opportunity to open up discussion about inclusive language and the importance of making everyone not just feel welcome but included in the spaces CYCPs learn, work, and share with the children, youth, families, and communities they walk alongside.

CULTURE

Culture is unique to the individual and can include ancestors and current family experiences. How we walk in the world, see the world, and engage in the world reveals our cultural experience.

> Culture comprises a society's philosophy about the nature of reality, the values that flow from this philosophy, and the social customs that embody these values. Any individual within a culture is going to have his or her own personal interpretation of the collective cultural code; however, the individual's worldview has its roots in the culture—that is, in the society's shared philosophy, values, and customs. (Little Bear, 2014, p. 2)

A day-treatment classroom celebrates culture by inviting parents to cook cultural food and share stories of traditions, food, and festivities. Aaron is proud to share latkes with his peers.

Discussion Opportunity 1:2

Discuss cultural experiences that were meaningful to your family, community, or culture. How do these experiences support building connections and relationships?

DIVERSITY

Human beings are all unique; even our fingerprints vary from one person to another.

Diversity is not one attribute; rather, it is the intersection of multiple factors, such as ethnicity, race, age, gender, sexual orientation, gender identity, ability, socioeconomic status, religious beliefs, educational background, political beliefs, military experiences, work experience, geographic location, and language (Southern Illinois University, Office of Associate Chancellor for Diversity, 2018). Getting to know each person, including all their attributes, celebrates their uniqueness.

Randi is taking four teens to visit Prince Edward Island, and Ronan is very excited to see the geometric traffic signals for drivers who may be colour blind. Ronan is determined to write a proposal so her town considers geometric traffic signs in the future. "All individuals regardless of life contexts can have the same opportunity for success, for voice and for inclusion" (Batasar-Johnie, 2017, pp. 8–9). Celebrating diversity means we all benefit from the experience of others.

Discussion Opportunity 1:3

Share some examples of celebrating diversity that you have witnessed or engaged in while in your own community.

LIFE SPACE

CYCPs relate with children/youth/families in their **life space** and make meaning from these relationships (Harder, Knorth, & Kalverboer, 2013).

The CYCPs Jolene and Frank drive to an inner city bridge and meet two youth and their mother in a box that serves as housing (life space). After this meeting, shelter and other supports are arranged. This is a clear example of the value of working in the life space and in the moment (Phelan, 2010) to support the needs of those we walk beside.

MEANING MAKING

We define **meaning making** as how each person understands an interaction or experience, recognizing that we each attach our own meaning to these experiences (Garfat, 2004; Michael, 2005; Steckley & Smart, 2005). We walk alongside families, communities, elders, multidisciplinary teams, and systems.

A CYCP will facilitate a grief and loss group in an Indigenous community, but only after she has tea with Elders. She knows that having tea and listening to stories of loss is not only honouring ancestors but also developing a relationship and gaining consent for her presence from the Elders. Meaning making recognizes that sharing a cup of tea is about more than just the tea.

Discussion Opportunity 1:4

Can you give an example of an interaction that you shared in a school setting where you attached a different meaning to the interaction than those who shared in it with you? How did you determine that you had attached different meanings to the situation? Do you think it is important that people share the same meaning in interactions, or is it acceptable and part of growth that people have their own perspective from their experiences?

DEVELOPMENT

We consider the **development** of each person. We consider always how the relationship will meet the needs of the children, youth, and families we walk beside (Fulcher & Garfat, 2008; Maier, 1987; Small & Fulcher, 2006). We look at functioning versus chronological expectations.

Prior to attending a movie, Marissa and her CYCP practise how to order popcorn, pay, and order tickets. In the moment, Marissa became nervous, but with the CYCP walking beside her and supporting her, she was able to celebrate success. The development of the relationship between Marissa and the CYCP is enhanced by the shared experience.

LOVE

We **love**—because we know that love is the prerequisite of healthy development (Smith, 2006). Love impacts our development. Mr. Fred Rogers said the greatest thing we can do is help somebody know they are loved and capable of loving (Neville, Ma, & Capotosto, 2018).

Kindness is a value that revolves around notions of love, easy-goingness, praise, and gratefulness. If love and good feelings pervade the group, then balance, harmony, and beauty result. This is a positive rather than a negative approach to social control. If individuals are appropriately and immediately given recognition for upholding strength, honesty, and kindness, then a "good" order will be maintained, and the good of the group will continue to be the goal of all the members of the Society. (Little Bear, 2014, p. 4)

Every Monday, Jang-Mi brings homemade Korean *japchae* noodles to the attendance centre where she helps youth who have been released from closed custody. She knows that many youth come to school hungry after a weekend in the community. Jang-Mi's kindness demonstrates to the youth that they are loved. She creates safety for the group while meeting their needs.

STRENGTH-BASED

CYC practice is **strength-based**. Freeman (2013) indicates the primary responsibility of the CYCP is to highlight the strengths of others at all times and in all spaces. This means that the CYCP reframes interactions and actions in the moment.

For example, Akila is asked to follow a Grade 4 student who runs from the classroom when conflict arises. Akila reflects that it is a strength to know when you are feeling unsafe in the moment and helps the student find a place of safety within the school milieu. Akila then helps other school professionals understand that supporting the child in finding safety is more productive than focusing on the behaviour.

Discussion Opportunity 1:5

Can you share an example of a time when you observed an adult summarizing the strengths they observed in a child/youth? How did the youth react to this approach?

SYSTEMIC RELATIONSHIPS

Children develop directly and indirectly within a complex system of **systemic relationships** within various levels of their life spaces (Fenske, 2005). We are interconnected, interrelated, and interdependent.

Therefore, the CYCP knowledge base includes an understanding of these relational practices, the importance of self as part of the intervention, life span development, strength-based practice, making meaning "in the moment," inclusion, culture and diversity, and empowering children, youth, and families in communities. Child and youth care practice is a way of being in the world relationally with others in all of our life spaces (Garfat & Fulcher, 2012).

Josh enters a shelter after living on the streets for two years. Maurice, the shelter CYCP, asks about his family. Josh indicates that he has not spoken to them for two years, although he deeply misses them. Maurice offers to support Josh in making a phone call to reconnect. Although Josh has not had family contact, it is obvious to Maurice that these relationships still impact him.

The mindfulness theory forms the basis of relational practices and is an invaluable resource for both CYCPs and children, youth, and families. Mindfulness can be viewed as one end of a continuum, with the other end representing mindlessness. Mindlessness is exemplified in a person taking shortcuts, behaving without conscious control, or acting in habitual, unquestioned ways (Langer, 1989). The expectation for CYCPs is then obvious, as care must come from a place of mindfulness, not mindlessness. Change has a reciprocal effect on both parties in a relationship (Krueger & Stuart, 1999). A mindful state enhances awareness, openness, curiosity, and creativity. Applying the mindfulness theory and relational practices are reciprocal skills that increase awareness and acceptance without judgment.

Mindfulness encourages both CYCPs and children, youth, and families to pay attention to how they feel in a given moment. Through heightened observation, CYCPs can add important information to their relationships and draw new meanings from their experiences (Ventrella, 2017). Mindfulness can also support CYCPs and children, youth, and families to regulate their emotions, thoughts, and reactions (Ventrella, 2017). Slavik (2014) implemented mindfulness practices in university classrooms, and the result reported a positive impact on students' ability to concentrate, and process and engage with new information. It was also found that it decreased stress and anxiety and increased creativity.

Mindfulness practices can be implemented in any relationship and can allow us to be the following:

- present in the moment
- aware of ourselves and what we bring to the relationship
- aware of others
- aware of the relationship between two or more persons
- aware of cultural diversity
- aware of our beliefs, values, and ethics
- aware of our thoughts, feelings, reactions, and sensations
- better listeners without judgment
- more empathic and compassionate to ourselves and others
- comfortable with silence

PRACTICE SETTINGS/MILIEUS

In various parts of North America, child and youth work began in the residential milieu. Children/youth required 24-hour care, and Child and Youth Care Practitioners lived with the children (Stuart, 2013; Vachon, 2017). (CYCPs often learn on the job.)

Four core settings of child and youth care practice have evolved: residential, education, community, and justice.

A **residential setting** is anywhere a child has a bed to sleep in. This can include group homes, foster homes, in-patient hospital units, and open/closed custody. Practitioners may live in or out of the residential setting.

An **educational setting** is anywhere a child/youth or adult is learning skills and competencies, such as primary and secondary schools.

A **community setting** is a space where the CYCP engages with the child, youth, family, or community where they are at. This can include homes, street work, recreation centres, parks, overnight/day camps, out-patient hospital programs, places of worship, and so on.

A **justice setting** includes custody when a youth is sentenced to be in a space for a specific, court-ordered period. It also includes follow-up spaces such as probation offices or attendance centres, where youth need to report and visit as a follow-up to their sentencing (Ontario Association of Child and Youth Care [OACYC], 2015).

Several of these settings are interconnected; for example, youth may be in a justice setting, but it is also a residential setting because the youth live there. A youth may be in an in-patient hospital setting and then, upon discharge, becomes a regular attendee of the out-patient skills-building program.

The setting becomes a **milieu** when the physical, emotional, social, cultural, and ideological needs of children/youth/families and communities are addressed (Burns, 2006; Stuart, 2013).

Burns (2006) states that:

- Physical needs include providing the basic necessities (food, clothing, shelter) of the child/youth/family and community.
- Emotional needs include creating and supporting a safe and nurturing environment that supports the child, youth, family, and community in the milieu.
- Social needs include ensuring that children/youth/families/communities have space to gather, share interests, and engage.
- Cultural needs include identifying and celebrating the intersection of culture of the child/youth/family and community.
- Ideological needs include supporting and learning about the values, ethics, and beliefs that the child, youth, family, and community hold.

Within these sectors, CYCPs take on various roles (Freeman, 2014). Child and youth care work, unlike other human service fields, recognizes that the children/youth are the focus of our interventions. Our goal of service is to work with the children, youth, and families to holistically and developmentally address needs in the various **life spaces** to support current functioning and future growth. The child and youth care field accepts and adapts the milieu to meet the needs of children, youth, families, and communities (VanderVen, 1991).

Discussion Opportunity 1:6

Discuss what setting (milieu) you are most drawn to, and share with others what attracts you to this setting.

Discuss what setting you are most disconnected from, and share with others what thoughts, feelings, and reactions you have about this space.

ACCREDITATION AND CERTIFICATION PROCESS

The child and youth care profession is moving toward **regulation** in some Canadian provinces, but, in other provinces, educational **certification** and **accreditation** opportunities are limited. CYCs in Alberta were invited to join the College of Counselling Therapy of Alberta when, on December 11, 2018, Bill 30, the Mental Health Services Protection Act, received royal assent (FACT—Alberta, 2019). In the United States, CYCPs often come to the work after completing a degree, then gain on-the-job training with the agency that employs them. There has been a diligent group of educators seeking accreditation consistency for Canada (Child and Youth Care Education Accreditation Board of Canada, n.d.). They state that accreditation will ensure high-quality education is a result of sound evaluation and continuous improvement.

> Accreditation is a process for regular, rigorous review of program goals, pedagogies, and outcomes. It facilitates dialogue and education within and across CYCP programs about innovation and quality, assisting with decision-making about where and how to situate a School, Department, or Program. Accreditation contributes to high quality education and consistently high standards of professional practice in a variety of manners through the potential functions it may perform:
> 1.   a vehicle for organizational change;
> 2.   a method to achieve sound quality assurance practices;
> 3.   a system for demonstrating accountability to
>   a.   children, youth, and families,
>   b.   students,
>   c.   and child and youth care educators;
> 4.   a mechanism to create a community of practice among child and youth care education programs.
> (Child and Youth Care Education Accreditation Board of Canada, n.d.)

CERTIFICATION

Certification contributes to professionalization as a CYCP. However, professionalization is valued by some and disregarded by others (Vachon, 2015). Skott-Myhre and Skott-Myhre (2011) state that certification in the CYC field may create a hierarchical and expertise-driven professional space in which those tested and certified define the terms of "good work." On the contrary, VanderVen (1991) indicates that it is time that the growing number of those committed to the value of child and youth care gather together and work proactively to advance their field as a profession. Many human services positions must be filled with educated, informed child and youth workers, who bring their unique approach into the life space of children's lives.

Frankly, both authors of this text also had initial reservations about the certification process, as we had both engaged in CYCP-specific postsecondary educational programs that involved highly supervised work and integrated learning experiences that were facilitated by CYC elders. We feared that there is a risk the certification process could be used as a backdoor that might allow entry to those without the foundational knowledge gained through CYC education and experience (Fraser, 2016).

Additionally, no one can deny that the field has grown beyond doing "what is right" because the CYCP intuitively knows what to do (Krueger, 2003; Maier, 1987; Murphy, personal communication, October 1, 2017) to now doing what is right according to CYC

praxis. The underpinning of interventions is now grounded in theory and **evidence-based** (researched), if not emerging, best practice. Therefore, an ongoing need in our unique discipline is to cultivate and foster more CYC research, given many years we have been dependent on the research of the fields of psychology and sociology. Remember, tapestries may seem to resemble other types of artwork, such as paintings on canvas, murals, large drawings, or printed fabrics (Mallory, 2014), but a tapestry is its own unique artistry.

THE CERTIFICATION PROCESS WITH THE NATIONAL CHILD AND YOUTH CARE CERTIFICATION BOARD

The certification process involves an application, references, a proctored exam, and a self-evaluation. The self-evaluation reviews competencies as outlined by the Child and Youth Care Certification Board (CYCCB). You can refer to the Child and Youth Care Certification Board's website for certification completion information.

Discussion Opportunity 1:7

Discuss the certification process after reviewing the CYCCB website. What pieces of certification can you work on from now until you complete the current CYC training in which you are enrolled?

COMPETENCIES

This book presents itself as an opportunity for new and seasoned CYCPs to review all of the elements of performance in the competency domains as identified by the CYCCB. These **competencies** were derived from the work of many CYCs, including a draft document entitled *Proposed Competencies for Child and Youth Work Personnel*, which has been widely circulated (Mattingly, Stuart, & VenderVen, 2001) for community consultation. The final document was published by principal researchers Bill Carty and Carol Stuart with the support of the School of Child and Youth Care program at Ryerson University in Toronto in 2006.

Even as the CYCCB updates or changes competencies, this book will still be valuable, because it ties the competencies to discussion examples. Learning and development happen through discussion, reflection, collaborative teamwork, and taking the initiative and responsibility to listen, question, and think critically within the community of fellow learners and teams (Briegel, 2017). The greatest education a CYCP can obtain is that of example or the tapestry of the lived experiences of those we are honoured to work with. These examples, in addition to the lived experiences shared by the supervisors and colleagues who work with us, create the tapestry of learning.

Each domain of practice chapter (professionalism, culture and human diversity, applied human development, relationship and communication, and developmental practice methods) identifies various competencies. These can be viewed as objectives (actions) or elements of performance that demonstrate the **domain of practice**. The competencies are applied to a variety of relevant and engaging case illustrations, hereafter called discussion opportunities, of children, youth, families, and/or communities. You will notice that similar competencies are identified under different domains of practice. This is because you will view the competency from different perspectives, such as the lens of professionalism or relationship and communication. The milieu that the CYCP works in will be identified in examples. Readers will be encouraged to reflect on and, with curiosity, ponder whether each of these competencies presents a strength or an opportunity for development for themselves and/or their staff team. This book will also address creativity applied to child and youth care practice, as well as a culmination of competencies (since we use many competencies in every interaction we share) in a case study chapter, and supervision in child and youth care. The final chapter, "The Growing Edge of Our CYC Profession," addresses how we provide evidence of our growth as we move forward in our development.

Our CYC practice is a complex tapestry. There is no one way of working that will be successful for everyone. Yet the simplest of interactions can hold richness in the moment that is transferred to other aspects of both the CYCP and the child/youth/family's lives. We make meaning (Garfat, 2002; Stuart, 2013) or experience *meaning making* (Garfat, 1998, 2004; Krueger, 1994, 1998; VanderVen, 1992) in these interactions. They are teachable moments and become part of the fabric of the **relational process**, beginning with noticing and ending with curiosity. Havighurst (1952) defines a **teachable moment** as being a developmental task that is learned at a specific point and makes achievement of subsequent tasks possible. When the timing is right, the ability to learn a particular task is possible. This is the "teachable moment." It is important to keep in mind that unless the time is right, learning will not occur. Hence, it is imperative to repeat important points whenever possible, so that when a student's teachable moment occurs, he/she/they/ze can benefit from the skills or knowledge (Havighurst, 1952).

Teachable moments are the foundation for the belief that we plant seeds for future learning. In so many of our milieus (with the children/youth, families, and communities that we work alongside), we may not witness the process of change. But in these moments, we are planting seeds so when the child/youth or family is ready, and there is care provided, the seeds will germinate. We also remember that those we walk alongside plant seeds in us, and so the relational learning and stories are reciprocal.

Our CYC tapestries tell stories. The narrative often reflects the experience of those that have come before and the seeds that have been planted to help us grow. Our field and practice is an ever-evolving story.

We hope the seeds planted in this book will germinate for you as you grow in your CYCP identity. We hope the narratives you hear and engage contribute to mindful development of your rich, colourful, creative, and strong tapestry of CYC praxis.

CONTEXT

As Child and Youth Care Practitioners, it is important for us to take into consideration the **context** of the individual and family that may impact and influence the child, youth, and family. Each person will have an experience that will be different due to his/her/zir/

their different context. For example, you'll want to consider culture, developmental factors, social systems, mental and physical well-being, government, social media, age, gender, social economics, where the person lives, parenting styles, family structure (single- or two-parent family, blended family), how many siblings are in a family, friendships, and pets—the list goes on and on. We can never respond to a person or family in the same way as another because their context will always be different. It is important to explore how our own reactions change when the context is different.

Let's explore context. After reading each scenario, sit in silence for a few minutes and become aware of how your own beliefs, values, ethics, thoughts, feelings, and **body sensations** change when the context changes.

1. A woman walks into a convenience store and steals a loaf of bread and a jar of peanut butter.
2. A woman walks into a convenience store and spreads peanut butter on some bread in the store.
3. A woman walks into a convenience store, grabs a loaf of bread and peanut butter, then walks out while saying "thank you."
4. A woman walks into a convenience store, singing, and does not appear to notice anyone around her. She opens up several chocolate bars and eats them. She continues as the store manager approaches her. The store owner gives her a hug and makes a phone call.
5. A woman walks into a place that offers food to all who visit. She opens up a box and allows her child to eat a handful of cereal.

Now that you are aware of your beliefs, values, ethics, thoughts, feelings, or body sensation, let's consider context. Consider the following contexts for the above scenarios.

1. The woman and her children were very hungry. Last month, she was laid off from work. She has been applying to jobs but has not been offered employment.
2. The woman lives on the street. She is very hungry.
3. The woman is self-employed and is waiting for a payment that is late. The woman has worked out with the convenience store owner that she can pay her bill at the end of each month. The convenience store owner is a family friend.
4. The woman lives in a very small town, and the local emergency hospital is four hours away. The woman struggles with mental health issues and is not able to afford her medication. Her family is supportive; however, they struggle with responding to their adult child's needs. The community has been supportive to this youth and family.
5. The woman walked into her parent's house, and her nine-year-old child loves to eat dry cereal.

Now that you are aware of the context of each situation, did your reactions change or stay the same? All the examples provided are similar, but the context is different. Understanding context assists the CYCP in identifying the needs of the child/youth/family/community in relation to the context of the need (Garfat, Freeman, Gharabaghi, & Fulcher, 2018).

Chapter 1 Learning Outcomes Evaluation

- After learning about CYC settings, consider which CYC setting(s) would be a good match for your interests and skills.
- Can you define some current CYC relational practices?
- Discuss what accreditation is.
- Discuss the certification process for the Child and Youth Care Practitioner.

REFERENCES

Batasar-Johnie, S. (2017). A response to "why are we so white": A west-Indian/Indo-Caribbean Canadian practitioner. *CYC-Online: E-journal of the International Child and Youth Care Network (CYC-Net)*, (221). Retrieved January 5, 2018, from https://www.cyc-net.org/cyc-online/jul2017.pdf

Briegel, M. (2017). Re-thinking the professional development of child and youth care practitioners. *Relational Child and Youth Care Practice, 30*(3), 10–24.

Burns, M. (2006). *Healing spaces: The therapeutic milieu in child and youth work.* Kingston, ON: Child Care Press.

Child and Youth Care Accreditation Board of Canada. (n.d.). CYCP accreditation. Retrieved June 20, 2018, from http://www.cycaccreditation.ca

FACT—Alberta. (2019). Update on regulation of counselling therapists, addictions counsellors, and child and youth care counsellors in Alberta. Edmonton, AB: Author. Retrieved April 19, 2019, from https://www.fact-alberta.org/files/Regulation%20Update%20Document_Final.pdf

Fenske, P. (2005). People in children's lives: Adults who promote resilience in children who have experienced abuse. *Relational Child and Youth Care Practice, 18*(3), 50–55.

Fewster, G. (1990). *Being in child care: A journey into self.* New York, NY: Haworth.

Fraser, T. (2016). Preparing child and youth care practitioners for the field. *CYC-Online: E-journal of the International Child and Youth Care Network (CYC-Net)*, (212), 23–32. Retrieved June 1, 2018, from http://www.cyc-net.org/cyc-online/oct2016.pdf#page=23

Freeman, J. (2013). Recognition and naming of human strengths. *Child and Youth Care Online, 177,* 7–11.

Freeman, J. (2014). *The field of child and youth care: Are we there yet?* London, UK: Routledge Taylor & Francis. doi:10.1080/0145935X.2013.785875

Fulcher, L. C., & Garfat, T. (2008). *Quality care in a family setting: A practical guide for foster carers.* Cape Town, South Africa: Pretext.

Gannon, B. (2004). The improbable relationship. *CYC-Online: E-journal of the International Child and Youth Care Network (CYC-Net)*, (67). Retrieved December 31, 2010, from http://www.cyc-net.org/cyc-online/cycol-0408-gannon.html

Garfat, T. (1998). The effective child and youth care intervention. *Journal of Child and Youth Care, 12*(1–2).

Garfat, T. (2002). "But that's not what I meant": Meaning-making in foster care. *Irish Journal of Applied Social Studies, 3*(1), 113–124.

Garfat, T. (2004). Meaning-making and intervention in child and youth care practice. *Scottish Journal of Residential Child Care, 3*(1), 9–10.

Garfat, T., Freeman, J., Gharabaghi, K., & Fulcher, L. (2018). Characteristics of a relational child and youth care approach revisited. *CYC-Online: E-journal of the International Child and Youth Care Network (CYC-Net)*, (236), 7–45. Retrieved March 17, 2019, from https://www.cyc-net.org/cyc-online/oct2018.pdf

Garfat, T. & Fulcher, L. C. (2012). Characteristics of a child and youth care approach. In L. C. Fulcher & T. Garfat (Eds.), *Child and youth care in practice* (pp. 5–24). Cape Town, South Africa: CYC Press.

Harder, A., Knorth, E., & Kalverboer, M. (2013). A secure base? The adolescent–staff relationship in secure residential youth care. *The Journal of Child and Family Social Work, 18*(3), 305–317. doi:10.1111/j.1365-2206.2012.00846.x

Havighurst, R. J. (1952). *Human development and education.* New York, NY: Longmans Green.

Krueger, M. (1994). Rhythm and presence: Connecting with children on the edge. *Journal of Emotional and Behavioral Problems, 3*(1), 49–51.

Krueger, M. (1998). *Interactive youth work practice.* Washington, DC: CWLA.

Krueger, M. (2003). Learning child and youth work in context: A case example. *CYC-Online: E-journal of the International Child and Youth Care Network (CYC-Net)*, (51). Retrieved May 31, 2018, from http://www.cyc-net.org/cyc-online/cycol-0403-krueger2.html

Little Bear, L. (2014). *Walking together: First Nations, Métis, and Inuit perspectives in curriculum.* Edmonton, AB: Government of Alberta. Retrieved from http://www.learnalberta.ca/content/aswt/worldviews/documents/jagged_worldviews_colliding.pdf

Maier, H. (1987). *Developmental group care of children and youth.* New York, NY: Haworth.

Mallory, S. (2014). Making of a tapestry: How did they do that? [Blog]. Metropolitan Museum of Art. Retrieved from https://www.metmuseum.org/blogs/now-at-the-met/2014/making-a-tapestry

Mattingly, M., Stuart, C., & VanderVen, K. (2001). North American Certification Project (NACP): Competencies for professional child and youth work practitioners. *Journal of Child and Youth Care Work, 17*, 16–49.

Michael, J. (2005). Life-space supervision in child and youth care practice. In T. Garfat & B. Gannon (Eds.), *Aspects of child and youth care practice in the South African context* (pp. 49–62). Cape Town, South Africa: Pretext.

Neville, M., Ma, N., & Capotosto, C. (Producers), & Neville, M. (Director). (2018). *Won't you be my neighbor?* [Motion picture]. United States: Tremolo Productions.

Ontario Association of Child and Youth Care (OACYC). (2015). *Safeguarding the other 23 hours.* Toronto, ON: Author.

Phelan, J. (2010). What does a CYC practitioner look like? *CYC-Online: E-journal of the International Child and and Youth Care Network (CYC-Net)*, (133). Retrieved from http://www.cyc-net.org/cyc-online/cyconline-mar2010-phelan.html

Skott-Myhre, K., & Skott-Myhre, H. (2011). Theorizing and applying child and youth care praxis as politics of care. *Relational Child & Youth Care Practice, 24*(1–2), 42–43.

Small, R. W., & Fulcher, L. C. (2006). Developing social competencies in group care practice. In L. C. Fulcher & F. Ainsworth (Eds.), *Group care practice with children and young people revisited* (pp. 51–74). New York, NY: Haworth.

Smith, M. (2006). Act justly, love tenderly, walk humbly. *Relational Child and Youth Care Practice, 19*(4), 5–16.

Southern Illinois University, Office of Associate Chancellor for Diversity. (2018). How do we define diversity? Retrieved March 6, 2019, from https://oacd.siu.edu/glossary.php

Steckley, L., & Smart, M. (2005). Two days in Carberry: A step towards a community of practice. *Scottish Journal of Residential Child Care, 4*(2), 53–54.

Stuart, C. (2013). *Foundations of child and youth care.* Dubuque, IA: Kendall Hunt.

Stuart, C., & Carty, B. (2006). *The role of competence in outcomes for children and youth: An approach for mental health.* Toronto, ON: Ryerson University.

Vachon., W. (Producer). (2012, July 5). The self in child and youth care: A conversation with Mike Burns [Audio Podcast]. Retrieved from https://www.podbean.com/media/share/pb-itewf-2cc760

Vachon, W. (Producer). (2015, September 30). Four perspectives on CYC professionalization: A panel discussion [Audio Podcast]. Retrieved from https://www.podbean.com/media/share/pb-32u98-58fee1

Vachon, W. (Producer). (2017, August 30). Closing keynote for OACYC, 2017 Conference [Audio Podcast]. Retrieved from: http://www.cycpodcast.org/?s=Theresa+Fraser

VanderVen, K. (1991). How is child and youth care work unique—and different—from other fields? *Journal of Child and Youth Care, 5*(1), 15–19.

VanderVen, K. (1992). From the side of the swimming pool and the evolving story of child and youth care work. *Journal of Child and Youth Care Work, 8*, 5–6.

CHAPTER 2

Professionalism

Learning Outcomes

This chapter will help you to meet the following objectives:

- Review the professional domain of CYC practice.
- Apply the domain and competencies to field examples.
- Engage in discussion about the domain and competencies.
- Identify areas of strength and development.

This chapter will review the competencies under the professional domain identified by the Child and Youth Care Certification Board (CYCCB).

The CYCCB (2016a) states that:

> Professional practitioners are generative and flexible; they are self-directed and have a high degree of personal initiative. Their performance is consistently reliable. They function effectively both independently and as a team member. Professional practitioners are knowledgeable about what constitutes a profession, and engage in professional and personal development and self-care. The professional practitioner is aware of the function of professional ethics and uses professional ethics to guide and enhance practice and advocates effectively for children, youth, families, and the profession.

The CYCCB (2016b) breaks down the professionalism domain into six key areas:

- Awareness of the profession
- Professional development and behaviour

- Personal development and self-care
- Professional ethics
- Awareness of law and regulations
- Advocacy

1. Awareness of the Profession

a. access the professional literature
b. access information about local and national professional activities
c. stay informed about current professional issues, future trends, and challenges in one's area of special interest
d. contribute to the ongoing development of the field

Child and youth care practice is explicitly built on the fundamental principles of **relational practices**, **life space intervention**, and ecological and developmental perspectives (Ontario Residential Services Review Panel, 2016). In comparison to other professions such as teaching or nursing, the child and youth care profession is quite young and in the early stages of development (Gilmour-Barrett & Pratt, 1977). In Canada, since 1974, the Ontario provincial association (Ontario Association of Child and Youth Care [OACYC]) has been advocating for legislation of child and youth care practitioners via a regulated provincial college (Gilmour-Barratt & Pratt, 1977). The province of Alberta's Bill 30, the Mental Health Services Protection Act, received royal assent on December 11, 2018, and went into effect January 1, 2019. With this new law in place, the profession of child and youth care work in Alberta is now regulated. As with other regulatory colleges across Canada, portability is imminent now that one province has paved the way (Canadian Counselling and Guidance Association, 2014).

Whether we practise in Canada, the United States, Mexico, New Zealand, Ireland, England, Scotland, Africa, or another country, child and youth care practitioners have at least one thing in common: we work **in relationship** with children, youth, families, and their communities.

In Canada, we talk about four settings (milieus) where CYCPs can be employed. These are education, community, justice, and residential. Residential settings include foster care and group care. James (2011) discusses group care as a living option that three government child-serving systems utilize, and these are juvenile justice, mental health settings, and child welfare. Mental health beds in hospitals can be included here as well. Often in these units there is a bed provided for each child or youth that they utilize while they are getting treatment. In the United States, approximately 24,000 children and youth in the child welfare system were in a group home (U.S. Department of Health and Human Services [DHHS], 2013). In Canada, it is estimated there were 30,000 foster kids according to the 2011 National Household Survey (NHS). That is a lot of children and youth in government care. The 2016 NHS enumerated 28,030 children, aged 0 to 14, in the care of a child welfare agency (Statistics Canada, 2016). In 2016, there were 4,300 Indigenous children under the age of four in foster care across Canada, according to government statistics. While 7 percent of children across Canada are Aboriginal, they account for nearly half of all the foster children in the country (Kassam, 2017).

Reflect on how these statistics impact children, youth, families, and communities. These figures confirm that we have many children separated from families and communities. Consider how these statistics impact CYC practices. When we support children and families who have cultures different than our own, how do we honour, respect, learn, and integrate **cultural values** and beliefs? (We will address this in more detail in Chapter 3.)

Our geographical and ecological systems (Bronfenbrenner, 1979) may vary, but, if we intend to work with vulnerable populations, it is important to maintain our awareness of our profession and how we do our work (Garfat & Fulcher, 2012; Gilmour-Barrett & Pratt, 1977; OACYC, 2015; Stuart, 2013). Therefore, we need to be cognizant of the child and youth care professional literature available to us (Gharabaghi, 2016) so we can stay informed about the themes impacting those we work with.

Some examples of relevant themes include:

- How do we define family?
- What relational practices meet child, youth, and family needs in their community?
- What new policies are school boards or government agencies making?
- What community resources are accessible for marginalized populations?
- What is the research saying about psychotropic medication?
- What are the costs and benefits of the CYC field becoming a professionalized body?
- How do we best engage children/youth so their voices are not only heard but also facilitate change?
- What is research saying about funding for youth exiting out of state-managed or purchased care?
- What developmental practice methods are considered best practice for children/youth and families?
- What changes need to be made to increase inclusion, equity, and advocacy?
- What are the current themes voiced by stakeholders? (A selection of resource agencies is noted below in Table 1.)

As CYCPs, we need to be aware of themes/issues that impact not only the profession but also children/youth/families/communities. CYCPs need to both stay informed and advocate about issues that require further attention locally (such as bed bugs or the closing of an advocate office) and globally (sex trafficking). It is not easy to find time to review current events, issues, or themes when we work shifts, have student responsibilities, or we're new to the field or a community. Emerging or employed CYCPs can look to their local associations, read peer-reviewed journals, and become involved in stakeholder committees. These are all great strategies to ensure that a practitioner stays current with what is happening in the world of those they work alongside of, and, in doing so, demonstrate

Table 1: Examples of stakeholder agencies that publish professional reports and journals

Geographical Area	Agency	Population Service	Contact Information
British Columbia, Canada	Representative for Children and Youth	"Since 2007, British Columbia's Representative for Children and Youth has supported our province's young people and their families in dealing with the provincial child and youth welfare system. The Representative also provides oversight to this system and makes recommendations to improve it. The Representative is a non-partisan, independent officer of the Legislature, reporting directly to the Legislative Assembly and not a government ministry." (Representative for Children and Youth, 2019)	https://www.rcybc.ca/
Ontario, Canada	The Office of the Provincial Advocate for Children and Youth*	Guided by the principles of the United Nations Convention on the Rights of the Child. "The children and youth who fall within the mandate of the Advocate's Office include those who are seeking or receiving services from the children's services sector in areas such as child welfare, youth justice, children's mental health, developmental services and children's treatment services. The jurisdiction of the Office also includes students of the provincial and demonstration schools, youth in court holding cells or being transported to and from court holding cells, First Nations children and youth, and children and youth with special needs. The Provincial Advocate derives authority from the *Provincial Advocate for Children and Youth Act, 2007*." (Office of the Provincial Advocate for Children and Youth, n.d.)	https://provincialadvocate.on.ca/main/en/about/aboutus.cfm
United States	National Children's Advocacy Center (NCAC)	"The NCAC models, promotes, and delivers excellence in child abuse response and prevention through service, education, and leadership." (NCAC, 2019)	http://www.nationalcac.org/

Geographical Area	Agency	Population Service	Contact Information
International	International Child and Youth Care Network (CYC-Net)	An international organization serving Child and Youth Care Practitioners and students. CYC-Net operates CYC-Net Press and publishes several journals, including *Relational Child and Youth Care* and the open-access *E-journal of the International Child and Youth Care Network (CYC-Net).*	www.cyc-net.org
	Child and Youth Care Forum	A journal currently published by Springer, focusing on CYC practice and highlighting research in the field.	https://link.springer.com/journal/10566
	The International Journal on Children's Rights	A resource that represents the voices of youth, currently published by Brill.	https://brill.com/view/journals/chil/chil-overview.xml

* On November 15, 2018, the Government of Ontario announced that they would repeal the *Provincial Advocate for Children and Youth Act, 2007* and close the Provincial Advocate Office. At time of printing, this office is still open and is still sharing resources online.

the importance of informed professional practice. Conferences are another valuable way to learn about emerging or evidenced-based practices. These also provide the CYCP with opportunities to join with youth, students, colleagues, mentors, and supervisors while building community.

Alternative ways to stay informed and to practise professionalism are by connecting with social media. In the technological world, this means that, in addition to going to conferences, one can watch YouTube videos and listen to podcasts or join social media groups administered by respected CYCP organizations. You will notice that podcasts are referenced throughout this text. Many CYC supervisors will discuss such resources in order to help students and CYCPs become more aware of the CYC profession and the issues that are integral to **efficacy-based** (effective) or emerging (promising) practice.

The profession develops in new methods every day. Remembering CYC roots as well as looking to the future forges a commitment to lifelong learning and professional practice. Sharing an understanding of this with colleagues by becoming a supervisor, authoring articles, or facilitating workshops are specific ways that practitioners can contribute to the field. Lastly, the most important way CYCPs can learn about what is going on in the worlds of the children/youth/families and communities they work alongside of is to *ask them*. If you can develop a safe and trusting relationship, you may be lucky enough to have their wisdom shared with you.

Discussion Opportunity 2:1

Jonah is a second-year CYCP student who experienced bullying as a high school student after he publicly identified as being queer. After sharing his story during peer presentations in a CYCP class, his professor encouraged him to share his story within the community. Jonah decided to write a presentation proposal about anti-bullying and human rights for LGBTQ2+ students at his old high school. His proposal is accepted, he successfully presents to students in his former high school community, and he receives additional requests from other high schools within the same school board for similar presentations.

In creating his presentation, Jonah shares experiences of LGBTQ2+ teens and also sources articles from the International Child and Youth Care Network (CYC-Net) and references peer-reviewed journals regarding up-to-date research and service delivery.

Do you have a supervisor, mentor, or professional relationship with someone who increases your awareness about the CYC profession? How does this new awareness influence your practices toward self, children, youth, families, and program?

2. Professional Development and Behaviour

a. Value orientation

1. State personal and professional values and their implications for practice, including how personal and professional beliefs, values, and attitudes influence interactions.

Beliefs, values, and attitudes influence our professional development and behaviours of practice. **Beliefs** represent our personal truth we hold at our core. What beliefs do you hold to be true about children and youth? The more awareness CYCPs have about their beliefs, the greater understanding they have about what they bring to the relationship. For example, all children desire love and a safe place to live their full potential. Therefore, demonstrating love (Ranahan, 1999; Thumbadoo, 2011; Vincent, 2016), caring, and expressive ways of being is part of what the CYCP brings to the relationship.

Values help us to understand what is important to us. Values are informed by our education and life experiences (both what we observe in others and ourselves) impact how we decide to live and work in our many life spaces. Values drive both the choices we make and how we make those decisions (Legault, 2003).

Attitude is an enduring evaluation—positive or negative—of people, objects, and ideas. Thus, attitudes are evaluative statements or judgments concerning objects, people, or events. Attitude has three components—cognition, affection, and behaviour. A particular attitude of a person can be based on one component or the other.

There is an essential interaction between the way individuals feel and behave and the way they construe their world, themselves, and prospects for the future (Freeman, 1987, p. 19).

Attitudes can be reflected in behaviour but do not always predict how a person will act (LaPiere, 1934).

What personal and professional values do you hold that influence relationships and practice?

What we believe, value, think, and feel about something contributes to our positive or negative attitude about the person, event, or experience. For example, if I have had three

CYCPs work with me at a school and they leave without saying goodbye, I may develop an attitude that CYCPs are rude. My belief is that people should be acknowledged. My value is that it is important to acknowledge when you depart from a relationship. My subsequent behaviour may result in me avoiding contact with others or being rude to a new CYCPs who are attempting to develop a relationship with me. I may feel it's better to avoid connection if you are going to disconnect from me without warning.

CYCPs bring their own beliefs, values, and attitudes from previous life experiences to their work. With these experiences come formed or emerging beliefs, values, and attitude systems that CYCPs choose to integrate into their work lives. They then can reflectively connect theory to practice because they have experience with children/youth/families and communities (Fraser, 2016).

Discussion Opportunity 2:2

Chava grew up in a strict Orthodox Jewish household. She values *shomer negiah*, a belief of Orthodox members of the Jewish community that says members of the opposite sex cannot touch each other unless they are close family (Leviticus 18:6; Leviticus 18:19). In school meetings, Chava is sometimes invited to shake hands as part of professional introductions. As colleagues develop a relationship with her, they begin to understand this cultural/spiritual practice. Children initially struggled with her hesitancy to touch; however, with the support of her supervisor, Chava is able to use this example in her role of teaching children how to set and respect physical boundaries with each other.

Discussion Opportunity 2:3

Patrice, a second-year CYCP student, is in the same school practicum site as Chava. Patrice grew up in an urban centre with a checkered past and uses a colourful vocabulary. On occasion, she jokes with Chava and the teaching staff in the staff lunchroom. When nervous, Patrice makes statements like "I laughed so hard, I peed my pants." Patrice requires feedback from Chava. Patrice discusses her experience with Chava with her college supervisor. She perceives Chava's comments as conflictual and as a communication of distaste for her as a person, rather than concern about behaviour.

It is truly important to know what your personal, familial, cultural, generational, spiritual, community, and professional values are. These are what ground you, challenge your thinking, and, sometimes, cause you conflict in your work personas, interactions, or roles. Once we understand our beliefs, values, and attitudes, many doors open. With no other place to go, we walk freely through the doorways. Once past my place of unknowing, I find a world full of choice and decision (Scrivens, 2001).

Pick three beliefs and/or values that you hold that are not shared by other practitioners or the children/youth/families that you work with. Write them down in the space provided.

1.

2.

3.

How do your beliefs and values impact your attitudes and relational practices?

2. State a philosophy of practice that provides guiding principles for the design, delivery, and management of services.

CYCPs design programs while considering for whom the program is intended. They ascertain whose needs are being met (child, youth, family, or community?). They have to determine where the program will be delivered (the context), what the activity will be (cost and planning involved), who will deliver the program (which CYCP[s]), and, lastly, how success will be evaluated. One process of activity planning, called the Magic Formula, was designed by Peter Hoag.

Discussion Opportunity 2:4

Antonio loves his human growth and development course, taken in the first year of his CYCP program. Learning about John Bowlby's attachment theory made a lot of sense to him. It helps him to see why the foster children that his family took care of will have challenges in their peer and adult relationships. He discovers that this theory underpins his belief and philosophy about relationship development and commitment.

His second-year field practicum is working with teens who are about to age out of foster care. The teens are in an independent living program with a mentor present in the apartment, but the teens are responsible for getting themselves to school, appointments, and so on. Practicum students are to assist with life skills practice such as shopping, paying bills, organizing appointments, and so on. One youth sees a therapist weekly and is responsible for getting to the appointment independently. She is often suspended from school and hangs around the mall during the day, because she cannot hang around the house when the mentor is at work. Antonio believes the staff can ensure that the youth gets to her appointments. He also believes that, considering she misses appointments on days she is suspended, alternate programming for her needs to occur. The program manager explains that the whole purpose of the program is independent living, and, if the youth misses her appointments, she needs to find solutions with staff and CYCP student support. Antonio realizes that his philosophy is very different than the philosophy of the program, and he takes this into consideration when picking his third-year practicum. He is determined to ask more questions about what philosophies underpin program management.

b. Reflection on one's practice and performance

1. Evaluate own performance to identify needs for professional growth.

Professionals can only improve if they stop and practice being reflective (Sauvé-Griffin, 2009). CYCPs learn the importance of self-reflection during their education. Intentional self-reflection continues throughout our careers during the supervision process, on our own, and with colleagues. Reflection happens during (**reflection-in-action**) or after (**reflection-on-action**) an event or experience (Schön, 1983). Reflection increases CYCP awareness for effective practice through a constant process of review in the context of the relationship, event, and experience. In the simplest of terms, reflective practice involves the cycle of *Experience–Reflection–Action*. More formally, Reid (1993) stated that "reflection is a process of reviewing an experience of practice in order to describe, analyse, evaluate and so inform learning about practice" (p. 305). A strategy to record your professional growth and development is to utilize SMART goals (Doran, Miller, & Cunningham, 1981).

SMART GOALS

SMART goals are a systematic way to ensure that a goal is specific (so the person knows what they are trying to achieve), measureable (so we know exactly what we will see, hear, taste, feel, touch), attainable (so we are ensuring the goal is developmental), realistic (so we are setting up the person for success), and timely (so the person knows how much time they need to strive to meet the goal).

SMART components remind us of what needs to be included in child, youth, and family goals to support them in meeting these goals. SMART goals also are utilized by the CYCP to identify areas for self-improvement.

Reflect on a SMART goal you have for yourself in relation to CYC work overall. This goal can be in relation to any domain of competency. Just ensure that your goal is specific, measurable, attainable, realistic, and timely (Healthy Families BC, 2013).

SMART goal example from the CYCCB competencies

Professional Domain

3.b.1 Incorporate "wellness" practices into own lifestyle

Table 2: SMART Goal Example

Specific	I will take a daily walk of a minimum 30 minutes.
Measurable	I will time my walks and record the length of each in my phone calendar.
Attainable	It is possible for me to schedule 30 minutes of walking in my day.
Realistic	I am physically able to walk for 30 minutes and can do so before or after work.
Timely	I will reassess this goal monthly.

The goal statement is: I will walk for a minimum of 30 minutes daily and document the actual time walked in my phone calendar so I can review my success monthly.

Try it: SMART goal example from the CYCCB competencies

Choose another competency and create a SMART goal for it. Identify the competency number and write out competency language using the SMART goal format below.

Competency:

Table 3: SMART Goal

Specific

Measurable

Attainable

Realistic

Timely

The goal statement is:

When you read an assessment or CYCP document, SMART goals are not written in components (as you completed in Table 3). CYCPs need to be able to document *a* **goal statement**, ensuring that each of the components have been included.

If you are learning how to write a goal, use the SMART format to ensure you are including all parts. You should *also* include a one-sentence statement that identifies the goal with all parts of SMART.

Review the following goals and identify which goals include all components of the SMART goal format. For those that do not include all components of the SMART system, identify the missing component.

Example 1

The CYCP will be successful at their placement.

Use a check mark to identify which components are present in the goal statement above.

Table 4: SMART Goal

Specific	
Measurable	
Attainable	
Realistic	
Timely	

Identify any missing components:

Rewrite the goal statement so it includes all components of the SMART format.

Example 2

The CYCP will document "in-the-moment" interventions after each shift for two weeks and bring the recording to supervision.

Use a check mark to identify which components are present in the goal statement above.

Table 5: SMART Goal

Specific	
Measurable	
Attainable	
Realistic	
Timely	

Identify any missing components:

Rewrite the goal statement so it includes all SMART goal components.

Refer to the Wellness Pie (Figure 1) on p. 38. If you haven't already, identify wellness practices and begin developing SMART goals related to them.

Create a SMART goal statement for yourself that addresses all the SMART components, as well as identifying wellness practices that need improvement.

The goal statement is:

Discussion Opportunity 2:5

Shaniqua's first practicum is so much fun! She gets to work with children in a community-based setting after school and into the evenings. She did not anticipate that she would enjoy the six-to-nine age group as much as she has, given they require so much adult supervision. She experiences, instead, that they are often interested in whatever activity she plans and preps. They are open to expressive arts and will share stories about their days at school, their families, and their hopes and dreams. When they enter the activity room, they will run to her to hug her and to tell her how happy they are to see her.

In January, Shaniqua co-facilitates a girls' anger management group. Some of the youth have probation orders that mandate them to attend a group. One of these girls comes into group and sits in the corner with her arms folded. It takes until Week 5 for this youth to engage with other group members, and, when Shaniqua talks to her, the girl rolls her eyes or makes the motions of kissing her teeth. She is definitely not happy to see Shaniqua.

Shaniqua begins to feel hurt about these incidents. She also feels angry that this teen does not see all the work Shaniqua is putting into planning the group every week. In supervision, Shaniqua spends much time complaining about the teen's rejecting behaviour. Shaniqua's supervisor points out that choosing to come to a program versus being told to come naturally impacts someone's motivation. Wisely, the supervisor directs Shaniqua to research about mandated clients and to ponder what life experiences the teen might have that influence her ability to trust anyone (let alone a group facilitator who might not be much older than she is). Shaniqua is asked to read Laursen's (2002) article about reclaiming relationships.

After following through, Shaniqua identifies that she needs to work on depersonalizing behaviour, as well as gaining more of an understanding of mandated clients, group development, and anger management as they relate to communication. She notes this in her reflective journal, shares it at her meeting with her supervisor, and subsequently creates some SMART goals to accomplish this (Doran, Miller, & Cunningham, 1981).

2. Give and receive constructive feedback.

Providing constructive feedback is the skill of giving feedback in a way that is transparent but also respects a person's dignity. It is respectful and addresses the person's competencies and not the person themselves.

As an example, imagine you are going to a placement interview, and you ask your friend how you look. Your friend looks at you closely and tells you that your shirt buttons are not buttoned correctly. This is very different than her saying something like "Didn't your mother teach you how to button your shirt properly?"

You appreciate this feedback because you want to look prepared for the job and thank her. You then fix your shirt.

However, if you and your mother are criticized about how you dressed, you may respond with something different than "thank you."

Feedback and evaluation are interconnected but serve different functions and purposes. The focus of feedback is to provide specific information on the supervisee's performance to assist them in learning (Wade & Jones, 2015). Promoting child and youth feedback promotes learning and then development. Development within the life space is a central feature of CYC work, a **developmental/ecological perspective** that can be employed when planning for CYC personnel preparation and ongoing improvement (Curry, Lawler, Schneider-Munoz, & Fox, 2011).

Receiving constructive feedback requires that the CYCP is open to learning. Modelling how to receive feedback is important as well. If we believe that those we walk beside can have a voice, then we need to be open to hearing their experience, concerns, and sometimes complaints, about the "service" they are receiving or specifically *your work*. We need to invite input and honest participation from children, youth, families, communities, and colleagues, which means we need to also invite feedback. Receiving ongoing feedback benefits the CYCP's ongoing development.

Discussion Opportunity 2:6

After Patrice uses colourful language at practicum, Chava discusses her reactions to what she hears with her practicum supervisor. Chava knows that she needs to say something, but she is uncomfortable with conflict and perceives Patrice as an outspoken individual. Chava's supervisor initiates role play using "I" statements to demonstrate how Chava can provide feedback to Patrice.

Chava states that she doesn't want to book a formal meeting with Patrice—she would rather provide the feedback informally. She subsequently meets with Patrice over a cup of tea and initiates a general conversation about language. Following this, she talks about the impact of curse words. Patrice apologizes and states that curbing her use of colourful language is one of her SMART goals. Patrice then invites Chava to provide her with feedback if, in future, Chava ever feels uncomfortable.

Giving and receiving feedback is not as easy as just having a conversation. There are many factors that need to be taken into consideration by the CYCP, including where, when, and how feedback is shared. How do we provide **in-the-moment feedback** that is respectful yet encourages learning, development, and empowerment? We also need to consider how we receive and model accepting feedback.

If we can do this effectively, we open ourselves up to learning and subsequent effective relational practice (Garfat, 2003). We have to be responsible about how we hear and integrate received information. Feedback has two parts: what we send and what we receive.

CYCPs need to be cognizant of the social location of both parties communicating so that both are aware of the power dynamics that occur practitioner to practitioner; practitioner to child, youth, or family; or practitioner to supervisor or supervisor to practitioner. For example, if a supervisor provides feedback to a student on their first day of practicum, it is important to be aware of the impact the feedback will have on a new student.

As CYCPs develop, they often become more comfortable in conflict situations. Disagreement (respectfully communicated) can help relationships become stronger and even safer. Many new practitioners may have previously avoided conflict and need experience verbalizing what may be perceived as an opposing view. Conflict does not have to be argumentative and divisive.

1. Provide an example of a time you have provided challenging feedback. How did it work out for you and the person you communicated with?
2. Can you provide the feedback differently now? How so?
3. How do you receive difficult feedback?
4. How do people you are in relationship with feel that you receive feedback? Ask . . . and then reflect on their answers. Reflection means that you think about what you hear from others and be curious about the meaning, then reflect again.

c. Performance of organizational duties

1. Demonstrate productive work habits.

What is a productive work habit in the CYC profession? Who decides this? How is it evaluated? When alumni CYCPs are asked (Survey Monkey Survey, 2016) to define productive work habits, they identify that it is important to look at grounding their work in theory/research to ensure they are practising in an evidenced-based manner. However, **productive work habits** are the things you do on a daily (or shift-by-shift) basis that support your work (e.g., completing a shift log for the next shift team), so those you work with can count on you.

a. Know and conform to workplace expectations relating to attendance, punctuality, sick and vacation time, and workload management

This area of competency is important to team members and the children, youth, and families that CYCPs work with. When a CYCP is expected to pick children up at school or to take someone to a family visit and the CYCP is late, everyone is impacted. Many supervisors suggest employees and students arrive at least 15 minutes before the start of a shift. Shift change occurs, and all team members are ready to start together to ensure clear communication occurs about expectations, roles, and responsibilities.

Illness, stress, and wellness are part of an important discussion to share with a supervisor. Depending on the population that the CYCP works with, coming to work with a cold could impact the health of everyone (especially if the CYCP is working with children, youth, or families that have low immune systems, or if the CYCP works in a setting such as a hospital, which has specific policies in place around fevers, communicable diseases, and so on). On the other hand, if a CYCP works with a program that does not have relief staff or part-time staff, employees or students who call in sick with a cold could impact service provision in their absence. Continuity of service is important for those we work with; illness, stress, and self-care policies/procedures and practices are worth a discussion in advance.

Workload management comes easy for some CYCPs. Workload management tools such as a computer, a smartphone calendar, or an agenda are used on a daily basis. Some CYCPs may be great with managing due dates and timelines without these tools, but others need to work on how they manage and organize their workloads. We practise these organizational skills in the college classroom learning environment, as well as during **work-integrated learning opportunities** such as placement/practicum.

Discussion Opportunity 2:7

Enrico works a part-time job and attends school. He states that he does not write anything down, because he had lots of practice as a waiter and can manage multiple tasks at once. He does find that he is challenged once he begins work-integrated learning, especially when he is upset about issues that are occurring in his placement. During his trauma class, he learns that, when upset, his memorization skills are impacted due to the cortisol hormone increasing in his brain (Kuhlmann, Piel, & Wolf, 2005). He then begins to use his smartphone to document assignment and report due dates so he will not lose marks. He then integrates more **self-care strategies** into his daily routine.

1. When do you struggle with being on time for activities or commitments?
2. If being on time is a challenge, how can you change this for yourself?
3. If this is not a challenge for you, how do you support or manage people around you when they are late for commitments or events?
4. Can you say no? Why or why not?
5. How do you balance your many commitments?

b. Personal appearance and behaviour reflect an awareness of self as a professional as well as a representative of the organization

Have you heard the phrase "It takes one look to make a bad impression"? CYCPs know we represent our agency and those we work with on the way to work/placement, at work/placement, and after leaving work/placement. Our presentation to the world includes cleanliness, use or lack of makeup, piercings, visible tattoos, choice of clothing, and so on. This does not mean that a CYCP does not wear makeup or have piercings—just that when we share these with the world, it is done with thoughtful intention.

Our behaviour communicates so much to others. Are we inclusive? Do we demonstrate that we strive to work in and contribute to collaborative environments? Do we invite those we walk beside to work with us to share their ideas and concerns? Do we walk the walk and talk the talk? Professional CYCPs balance relational connections while adhering to their professional code and ethics.

Discussion Opportunity 2:8

Jewel comes from a rural community and moves to a city to attend college. Her first work-integrated learning experience is in a community centre in the heart of the downtown. She is a young CYCP student and is worried about presenting too professionally, so that the youth see her as both an authority figure and an outsider. With that in mind, she arrives to her placement on the first day wearing jeans, a t-shirt, and a red scarf. She is quite surprised when her supervisor sends her home, warning her that she is putting herself at risk by wearing gang colours in this community.

1. How do you make meaning of the supervisor's response?
2. Have you ever received feedback about your appearance or professional presentation that surprised you? Did you incorporate the feedback? If yes, how?
3. Why did you choose to integrate or not integrate this feedback?
4. How might your professional wardrobe change according to the milieu you're working in?
5. How can a CYCP maintain freedom of expression with how they dress and still follow a given program's professional conduct?

d. Professional boundaries

1. Recognize and assess own needs and feelings and keep them in perspective when professionally engaged.

Being able to recognize and assess your own needs and feelings and keep these in perspective when professionally engaging in a CYCP role is not always easy, but it is essential for understanding, learning, and professionalism. Practitioners can be triggered by an experience but may not be immediately aware of its impact on their beliefs, values, thoughts, feelings, body sensation, and subsequent actions. Journalling, reflective practice activities, and actively using the supervision process cannot be underestimated as helpful tools in the development of a CYCP.

We also need to give ourselves permission to be human. It is hard to keep our personal and professional parts separated, yet we always need to be cognizant that our presence in the relationship is not to have the child/youth or family meet our own needs. Again, this makes a wonderful colleague and supervisor discussion.

Discussion Opportunity 2:9

Marina has just ended her engagement with Franklin. She believed that they could grow old together. Marina is upset, and she is experiencing physical symptoms, including vomiting and headaches. She wants to call in sick, but one of the residents at her group home will be discharged in two days. It is Marina's job to arrange the leaving party.

Marina puts on her best smile and goes to work. As she climbs the stairs, she hears screaming coming from the second floor. One of the female residents is complaining that it is not fair that she cannot go to a party that all of her other friends are allowed to attend. Marina observes day staff talking to the teen, so she goes to the kitchen to check out what has been started for dinner. She finds her shift partner stirring sauce and explaining to another resident why it is important to let sauce simmer all day. She and her shift partner make eye contact, so Marina goes to the games room and observes two teens playing cards. Marina hears two more teens in the laundry room arguing about who gets to put in the first load. All six kids are accounted for, and, once shift change occurs, the day staff members can leave. Marina's cellphone starts to blink; there are text messages from Franklin asking to meet for dinner. She texts quickly, telling him that she is working. He then tries to suggest a meeting after work and then for breakfast. She becomes irritated. She is at work; Franklin knows that she cannot use her phone at work, but the texts kept coming. The laundry room teens get louder, and Marina starts yelling at them. They look up at her in shock; Marina never yells. Marina tells them to stop arguing about laundry and to just do it. She goes to the bathroom and cries, realizing that she could have taken a day off to ground herself. She could plan the party from home. Marina later apologizes to the teens in the laundry room for losing her temper but reminds them that arguing over who gets to use the machines every day is not helpful.

What else could Marina have done to balance work and home expectations?

2. Model appropriate interpersonal boundaries.

CYCPS are specifically trained to focus on building therapeutic relationships with children and youth and their families (Harder, Knorth, & Kalverboer, 2013). In these relationships, we consider many ways of engaging, including how to set **boundaries**. For example, new CYCPs sometimes believe that they need to be viewed as friends by the children and youth that they work with (Garfat, 2008).

The role of being a CYCP requires different boundaries than when we are taking on the role of being a friend. For example, you might discuss personal relationships challenges with your friends but not a youth that you spend time with at the community centre.

Another example of the demonstration of professional boundaries in educational settings is the importance of using proper salutations in emails to professors instead of "hey you" or "hon" or "yo sir."

Hugging children, youth, or families that you work with may be very appropriate when working in a residential setting but less so in a school community. Setting boundaries is an important conversation to have with your work-integrated learning supervisor as an ongoing reflective and iterative practice (Davidson, 2004; Phelan, 1990, 2003).

Discussion Opportunity 2:10

Darya didn't get her choice of placement during the school year, so she volunteers for one day a week in the summer at a day-treatment program so she can gain additional work experience. The program appreciates having an extra pair of hands and eyes on days when the youth go on field trips. On one such field trip, one of the youth puts arm around Darya's shoulder. She is stunned; she does not know what to say to him but is flattered that he is talking to her about what he likes at the zoo.

After a few minutes, one of the male staff tells the youth to take his arm away and then explains to Darya that she needs to be clear about her role with the youth. He gives her clear feedback about how she can respond if this occurs again. Darya is embarrassed about her lack of response to the youth but tells staff that she very much appreciates their feedback. She is more comfortable setting boundaries going forward. The example of other staff is helpful.

How would you have responded to the youth and staff person?

e. Staying current
1. Keep up-to-date with developments in foundational and specialized areas of expertise.

Continuous development is a lifelong process. Keeping up-to-date means reading, talking to other CYCPs and clinicians from other disciplines, and seeking out learning opportunities that are available. Some programs will pay for training, but many CYCPs attend conferences during vacation periods and must pay their own way. **CYCP conferences** are more than just training! They are an opportunity to connect with colleagues locally and from far away. Some CYCPs will participate in **association committees** not only to share expertise but also to network with others sharing the same professional interests. Such gatherings are opportunity to learn, to challenge current practices, and to develop personally and professionally.

2. Identify and participate in education and training opportunities.

Participating in education and training opportunities is important for the continuous development of a CYCP. CYCP conferences are educational, but so are conferences supported by children's mental health centres or justice service organizations. Sometimes, local community services will band together to host educational opportunities for students and practitioners. CYCP students and practitioners can also visit websites that cater to CYCPs so they can see what international learning opportunities are available. Professionals often appreciate attending workshops where students present their expertise about the field. What is important is that CYCPs seek local, provincial, and international training in order to continue learning and building on their child and youth care development and identity. Today, online professional development training is an option for agencies and CYCPs to continue training and development needs while at the same time keeping costs low (Briegel, 2017).

Discussion Opportunity 2:11

1. Go online and find a child and youth care conference happening somewhere in the world. You will be expected to share this with your classroom colleagues in a quick classroom presentation.
2. Find a conference that is not sponsored by a child and youth care group but could be of interest to students and practitioners. You will also be expected to share this information with classroom colleagues in a quick classroom presentation.

3. Personal Development and Self-Care

a. Self-awareness

1. Recognize personal strengths and limitations, feelings, and needs.

When we are practising self-awareness, we are cognizant of our personal strengths, limitations, feelings, and needs. All of these contribute to understanding what we need to practise **self-care** and **personal development**.

Strengths

Strengths are important for the development of all CYCPs. When attending an interview (for a placement or a job), a common question asked of the applicant is "What are your strengths?" Therefore, all CYCPs need to continually reflect on what is in their "tool kit." Using the language of the competencies is a great place to start. What are the strengths from your culture? It is important that CYCPs recognize their own strengths, create a **team culture** that focuses on strengths, and have supervisors who broaden the CYCP repertoire of strengths. They then can apply their creativity in new ways to meet the needs of children/youth/families, co-workers, the program, and themselves (Gilberg & Charles, 2002).

The competencies utilize the word *limitations*; however, given we strive to be strength-based, let us instead use the language "challenges and opportunities." **Challenges**

and opportunities are the skills and knowledge we hope to develop. Once we identify what skills or knowledge we need to develop, we can utilize this information to identify goals. Developing SMART goals (Doran, Miller, & Cunningham, 1981) is an opportunity to further your development. Learning about yourself, further developing skills, increasing your knowledge, and exploring opportunities to synthesize your strengths contribute to personal development and self-care.

Feelings

Recognizing what you are feeling in the moment; what beliefs, values, or thoughts are precipitating these feelings; and what purpose the feeling is serving is an important dynamic for a CYCP to review. If we cannot identify our **primary emotions**, it is difficult to understand why we are feeling these in the moment, and this is a barrier to joining with others or changing how emotions impact us and subsequently drive our behaviour and interactions with others (Linehan, 2014). Being aware and observing your thoughts and feelings allows you to identify how they are coming into the space and how they impact the relationship that you create with those you work with. Sometimes your thoughts and feelings are congruent with those of the people you work with, and sometimes they are different. The differences can lead to stimulating conversation, learning, a new awareness, interactions, or conflict. Recognizing what our feelings are is the first step to having honest and open dialogue between ourselves and those we are in relationship with. This includes children/youth/families/communities, team members, and supervisors.

Needs

It is important to identify your professional, personal, emotional, spiritual, and physical **needs** so you can continually develop your CYCP tool kit. Relationship is our most important tool (Smart & Digney, 2016). Our ability to be in relationship is impacted by our needs. It is also important to identify self-care needs as a way to ensure you are ready and able to meet the needs of others. CYCPs need to be comfortable setting boundaries and verbalizing professional needs. It is important to be able to say no at times to additional duties, shifts, or experiences. Anyone who has travelled on a plane needs to sit through the safety presentation where the flight attendant explains the importance of putting the oxygen mask on yourself before putting one on a vulnerable passenger. In the same way, it is important for the CYCP to recognize their needs so that they can do their job effectively and support those around them.

We also need to model and teach the skill of meeting our own needs to children/youth/families and communities. Children "catch" more from what is modelled in the relationship than what they are taught verbally. More is caught than taught (Foraker-Thompson & Edmunds, 2001). It is important that this is a developmental teaching. For example, teaching a young person that it is okay to not hug relatives at family events lays the foundation for teaching about future sexual consent. We want those we work with to have a voice and use this voice, even if it means they are pushing against institutional norms or us. This may include expressing and demonstrating non-compliance in the face of the rules and institutional practices that have resulted from colonization (Gharabaghi, 2018).

On an ongoing basis, all CYCP professionals reflect on how their tool kit (Smart & Digney, 2014) of needs, thoughts, feelings, challenges, and strengths (limitations) has been impacted, directly or vicariously, by experiencing the challenging life experiences of those we walk beside (**vicarious trauma**).

CYCPs can visit the Professional Quality of Life website (http://www.proqol.org) to download a self-report assessment that helps them to recognize symptoms of vicarious trauma. Each person can self-score their own assessment and even revisit their score at different intervals in their CYC practice. The outcome of this reflective activity is wonderful conversation for supervision. This website also offers research articles and a handy self-care card. Vicarious trauma can impact our current and emerging skill set of strengths and needs. We need to be prepared to adapt our self-care plan to accommodate these ongoing experiences.

Identify Your Strengths

Please review the checklist in Appendix A. What competencies are areas of strength for you? Identify at least three under each domain of practice. You may want to note these on your resume, reflecting on examples of why these specific competencies are strengths. Being able to share examples will help you in future placement or job interviews.

Discussion Opportunity 2:12

Damien is assigned male at birth (AMAB) but has identified as female as long as she can remember. As a little person, she wore feminine clothing, wanted her ears pierced, and wanted to use makeup. Her mother reports that Damien, at as young as six years of age, would wake up from dreams stating that she could wish away her male genitalia. Damien's father is a minister, and Damien's first work-integrated learning experience (placement) is in a church. She is now completing her third-year practicum in a residential justice facility and has finally received a referral to an endocrinologist for hormone therapy. She is conflicted, as she needs to begin transitioning since the resources are now available, but she is worried that the teens and staff at her practicum will reject her journey and identity. She knows that this is not going to be easy professionally, especially since she has already experienced rejection from her family of origin.

Damien brings her worries to supervision. She and her supervisor come up with a plan to introduce her to the community under her new name, Diane, before the second semester. The supervisor also asks Diane to review the student learning contract and to spend some time looking at goals under the relationship and communication domain. Will a new identity coupled with new life challenges impact Diane's work relationships and previous ways of interacting with others? Diane has a lot to think about over the break. Her supervisor also provides her with a lot of great feedback underscoring the strengths that she still has, no matter how she presents to the world. Diane spends time reflecting on the supervision experience and her new goals, and she is proud of herself for not putting off her own needs for fear of how they will impact her professional identity.

2. Separate personal from professional issues.

Reflective practice is required in order to identify personal from professional issues. All CYCPs need to work at separating issues based on the many hats that we wear. Reacting to a situation from the perspective of a parent is very different than from the perspective of a wounded person who has some experience with the event, from which they are trying to heal (Phelan, 2009; Smart & Dingney, 2016). Knowing how one's experiences, values, and belief systems impact practice and relationships is vital. When you become a reflective practitioner, you create awareness and empower your own practices (Rundell, 2007).

Practitioners are encouraged to utilize colleagues, supervisors, mentors, elders, and support systems to gain greater awareness in understanding how their personal beliefs and values influence their professional practice. Seek feedback. We learn from each other. For example, "it is customary for older people to act like Elders and to be treated as such, and the effective modeling of one generation inspires the future conduct of the next" (Cooke-Dallin, Rosborough, & Underwood, 2000).

These resources can help the new and emerging CYCP to create plans that will assist them in increasing their awareness of personal and professional values and of their impact on practice, as well as the creation of subsequent developmental goals. This ensures that their values and beliefs are not imposed nor detrimental to their relational practices (see Discussion Opportunity 2:12).

Diane, as an example of this, will undoubtedly experience judgment and perhaps anger from others who will also need time to come to terms with her transition. Some of these experiences will be appropriate to debrief and unpack in supervision, and some of these issues may be appropriate to unpack with another support person outside of the professional arena.

Discussion Opportunity 2:13

Flora is a 40-year-old, second-career CYCP who emigrated from the south part of the middle belt of Nigeria. As a proud Christian woman, she has seen the conflict between Muslims and Christians. She personally witnessed the work of the Boko Haram, a group of militants that hurt people she loved. She felt lucky to come to Canada and often shares with residents what it is like to have little money, food, and personal **resources**. The staff spent considerable time in team meetings, reviewing policy. One day, they discuss providing all residents with money to buy their own hygiene products so they have personal choice and practice with budgeting and life skills. Flora thinks these are unreasonable resources to give these teens. In her mind, they need to know how to survive with little. They also need to learn how to be independent, given that they are all **Crown wards** (who would likely age out of the system with little money). Flora voices concern that it seems unfair to show the youth an unsustainable view of life.

Flora's supervisor discusses this point of view with Flora and makes attempts to help Flora separate her experience from that of the teens she works with. Flora has many wonderful experiences and skills to share with the residents but is still adapting to living in a new culture herself. The team discussion reflects the difference in values.

Do you think programs can provide resources that youth may or may not be able to sustain? What experiences inform your beliefs? What value system do you have from your family of origin that might conflict with a milieu that you have experience in?

b. Self-care

1. Incorporate "wellness" practices into own lifestyle.

Wellness practices need to be part of our personal and work cultures. This enables us to model and participate in wellness practices with those we walk alongside. Wellness needs to include balance between the physical, emotional, intellectual, social, and spiritual realms, which then results in a CYCP having a sense of accomplishment, satisfaction, and belonging (Eckleberry-Hunt, Van Dyke, & Tucciarone, 2009). Think of a bank account. Withdrawals cannot be made if there is no balance there. It is important that CYCPs incorporate wellness practices into their lives so their "wellness accounts" aren't drained. These practices will be different for every person and could include everything from exercise and mindfulness to hobbies, to faith practices.

Postsecondary students often hear from professors that they need to practise self-care; the question is, how do we continue after graduation? Each of us will define wellness differently. Some will identify that wellness strategies can include sleep, mindfulness, time with friends, hobbies, and exercise (Stuart & Carty 2006). Consider Maslow's (1943) theory of **needs** to structure wellness practices that we can apply to ourselves. When our needs are being met and wellness practices are integrated as part of our regular routine, we are able to meet the needs of others.

Wellness can also include setting boundaries around how many days in a row one works or how many overtime shifts are accepted. Each practitioner needs to ascertain what wellness practices they will incorporate into their lifestyle and then figure out how to balance the many aspects of their life, so that pursuing wellness practices is ongoing and not just a response to stressful situations or during specific periods.

Discussion Opportunity 2:14

Abidemi was pleased to be hired as a relief worker as soon as he graduated from his CYCP program. He is happy to be making money given that he has a substantial student loan. He had only been working two months when he was asked to apply for a contract position for a two-month parenting leave. The only catch is that the job is for overnight staff, but Abidemi needs to spend time with his two children during the day when his partner works. He thinks that the night shift might be perfect, because it will give him time to read materials for the online university course he is taking right now. He applied and got the job, but, within a few weeks, he recognizes that he struggles with staying up from

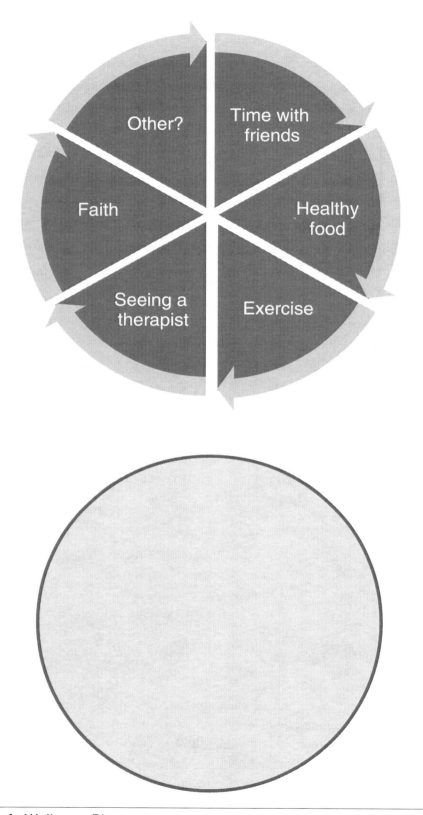

Figure 1: Wellness Pie

9 p.m. to 12 p.m. His partner had pleaded with him to reconsider taking the job, but financial incentives strongly contributed to his decision. He ends up falling asleep at work on many occasions, and this is not well received by his shift partner.

The two months could not end quickly enough for Abidemi; he is relieved when the contract is complete. He returns to being a relief worker, only accepting the shifts that fit with his family schedule.

As helping professionals, understanding that our ability to assist people in their lives only goes as far as we are able to deal effectively with our own lives will lead to maximum therapeutic benefits for the clients with whom we work (Kostouros & McLean, 2006).

It seems that Abidemi is experiencing a conflict between meeting the needs of his life partner and shift partner. Have you ever struggled with meeting the expectations of your work being in conflict with your personal life? How does this then impact your wellness?

Using the circle above and a different coloured pen or marker, please divide the pie in sections that represent wellness prevention and practices that you engage in. Be aware of how big or small the slices are to ensure that they are representative of your current use of wellness practices.

Discussion Opportunity 2:15

1. What wellness practices do you currently use? Do you see these as prevention or maintenance?
2. Review your pie (above) and reflect on the size of the various slices. Discuss these with a partner.
3. What wellness practices would you like to learn more about or incorporate into your lifestyle?

2. Practise stress management.

Stress is a normal psychological and physical reaction to the demands that we experience. When we experience threat, our bodies are designed to release specific hormones (parasympathetic response) that enable a fight-or-flight (or freeze) response to the threat (Roelofs, 2017). Sometimes people experience abuse or trauma that teaches their body that they need to be ready to self-protect at a moment's notice. Consistently activated stress hormones can cause physical harm, so all human beings (particularly those that work in high-stress environments) need to practise stress management (Centers for Disease Control and Prevention, 2005).

CYCPs that work in foster homes (perhaps as therapeutic foster parents) need to work and live not only with the children/youth but also with various systems. They will identify that work with such systems can be stressful. Knowing how to balance all responsibilities is an active state of balance. Throughout your career, practising **stress management strategies** is essential to wellness. This may require you to be able to say "no" sometimes without feeling guilty. It is also important to identify and maintain wellness practices for current and future health. We all deserve to live and work in environments that do not cause us harm. Those we walk alongside deserve our best. They also benefit from the modelling of a healthy lifestyle.

Discussion Opportunity 2:16

1. What strategies do you implement when you are feeling stress?
2. How do you know when you are experiencing stress? What are stress symptoms for you?
3. How do others (who know you) know that you are experiencing stress?
4. How can you decrease stress to increase effective practices?

3. Build and use a support network.

Building a support network means having relationships with others from different ecological systems, and this network is constantly changing. Networking opens new doors and creates relationships that support new creative opportunities, personal development, collaborative research, policy activism, evidence-based practice, and more (Goolsby & DuBois, 2017). CYCP practice is relational (Bellefeuille & Jamieson, 2008). Figuring out where supports are available is part of creating and maintaining a wellness plan. We need to use our supportive **networks** to maintain wellness.

CYCPs need to assess and foster supportive networks that benefit children, youth, and families, as well as their own development.

Practitioners who work in isolation lose the opportunity to build connections and relationships that will foster their development (e.g., peer supervision, collaborating on projects, and more). Practising as part of a team means that other team members will understand their own struggles and achievements as well as the struggles and achievements of the children/youth and families you work with. (Note sharing is encouraged as long as confidentiality is adhered to.)

Given the ease of sharing on social media platforms, practitioners need to be cautious about talking about their practicums (placements) or workplaces while online and on social media like Facebook. For example, a group home in a large metro area was shut down until new staff members could be hired, because the funding government agency discovered that staff members were sharing client information online. In an Eastern Canadian province, a team of nurses and CYCPs celebrated a co-worker's birthday. The birthday cake photo is shared on a team member's Facebook page. Unfortunately, a patient's file could be seen on the desk behind the cake. This inadvertent confidentiality breach hurt the patient's right to privacy. Team members were also disciplined.

Discussion Opportunity 2:17

On a bus, two CYC students were talking about youth in their practicum. Unknown to them, the grandmother of one of the youth reported the conversation to the agency that is the service provider. Both students were terminated from their work-integrated learning practicums.

Not only is this breach of confidentiality unethical, but it can also be hurtful for all stakeholders. How do you ensure that you maintain ethical confidentiality in social media, community, and employment? This is a question we all need to ask ourselves.

4. Professional Ethics

a. Describe the functions of professional ethics

The Child and Youth Care Code of Ethics contains the clause "I have the right and obligation to share in the maintenance of the ethics of my profession" (Winfield, 2003). The function of **ethics** for any profession guides professional expectations and behaviour. This means that each professional is responsible to ensure that they are updated with their discipline's **code of ethics**. Where can you find yours?

Discussion Opportunity 2:18

After reading your code, reflect on what your ethical code means for practice. How does it support you to make effective decisions in the workplace?

b. Apply the process of ethical decision making in a proactive manner

When a practitioner signs our code of ethics, he/she/ze/they make a commitment. This means that ethics drive their interventions and professional actions. It is very important, when in a supervisory relationship, that both supervisor and supervisee discuss the ethical code each professional adheres to. In many service settings, a supervisor may not be a CYCP; he/she/ze/they may be a member of another regulated college, so early discussions regarding how tough scenarios will be unpacked is paramount. We also need to consider the code of ethics that applies to our own geographical area (e.g., province, state, country).

Discussion Opportunity 2:19

Jonah began supervision in his educational milieu practicum in September. He did not have a formal meeting with his supervisor until his college supervisor visited in mid-October. At this meeting, he learned that his supervisor was a teacher who didn't understand the role of a CYCP learning professional. The college supervisor encouraged Jonah to talk directly to his supervisor to request supervision. He also suggested that Jonah share his college practicum manual, which explains the role of the CYCP learning professional. Additionally, he directed Jonah to share his CYCP Code of Ethics with his supervisor so the supervisor can understand how a CYCP learning professional approaches issues and concerns differently than a practice teacher.

c. Integrate specific principles and standards from relevant to specific professional problems

The Canadian Child and Youth Care Code of Ethics

At the Annual General Meeting of the Ontario Association of Child and Youth Care in June 2014, the membership voted to adopt the Code of Ethics of the International Leadership Coalition of Professional Child and Youth Care. The Council of Canadian Child and Youth Care Associations adopted this Code of Ethics at the Annual Council meeting in October 2008 and noted the following:

> The Ethics document resulted from the work of Martha A. Mattingly (1995) of the Program in Child Development and Child Care, University of Pittsburgh, who conducted a meta-analysis of existing codes and consulted widely through the child and youth care associations of the day. Her work is viewed as comprehensive and inclusive by the Council rendering any attempt to craft an alternative [as] an exercise in replication. (Council of Canadian Child and Youth Care Associations, n.d.).

d. Carries out work tasks in a way that conforms to professional ethical principles and standards

CYCPs adhere to professional ethics and standards in all aspects of their work. This means that when a report is being written, for example, we consult with the child/youth/family. Our CYC **best practices** and principles provide a foundation for our relationship building. They form the boundaries that we work within. We all need to know these "rules" or "best practices," and it is our responsibility to support each other in adhering to our basic and foundational standards.

Informing others about CYC ethical principles and standards is part of a CYCP's professional responsibility. According to Fox (2014), professionalizing the field means that we have to adjust our practices to meet our goals and truly serve those who are entrusted to us in the ways that work for them, not the agency. This is important to ensure that the needs of those we walk with are the priority.

5. Awareness of Law and Regulations

a. Access and apply relevant local, state/provincial, and federal laws; licensing regulations; and public policy

Most CYCP postsecondary education programs will inform students about the relevant **legislation** that impacts CYC practice. Laws change and get updated, and, on occasion, new legislation becomes law. CYCPs need to ensure currency by familiarizing themselves with the most current laws and regulations in the geographical areas in which they work.

For example, in Ontario, Canada, as of January 2018, youth up to the age of 21 can reside in a foster home or residence under the guidance of a child protection agency. Previously, youth could only reside in these settings up to the age of 18. This doesn't mean that a child over 16 can be apprehended against their wishes, but basic care can be provided to them if they are in agreement of needing protection (Government of Ontario, 2017).

b. Describe the legal responsibility for reporting child abuse and neglect and the consequences of failure to report

Every geographical area in North America has a **child welfare agency** responsible for child protection. CYCPs need to identify this organization, identify the laws surrounding the report of child abuse/neglect, and, in some geographical locations, identify when children are exposed to domestic violence, which is recognized as a negative experience for children and their development (Cunningham & Baker, 2004; Holt, 2015). CYCPs are professionals, even though they are not a regulated profession at time of writing, except in Alberta. In North America, most codes of ethics value and encourage members to report concerns to the body responsible for investigating concerns.

Most child protection agencies will offer consultation if CYCPs are unsure of the appropriate response. CYCP students engaged in work-integrated learning opportunities are encouraged to share concerns (without identifying information) with their school supervisors as well as with their work-integrated learning supervisors. On some occasions, students may be confused about whose duty it is to report and may not feel that they are safe to do so. In these instances, it may be helpful to discuss concerns with the supervisors of supervisors, as well as to document the specific concerns and steps taken to address these concerns.

Where can you find reporting policies for your agency? Where can you find reporting policies with your local, government-appointed child advocate? This is a question to ask of your supervisor, as well as professors or instructors.

c. Describe the meaning of informed consent and its application to a specific practice setting

Informed consent is important to discuss in child and youth work. **Informed consent** is the invisible activity of evaluating information and making a decision and the visible act of signifying the decision for all the parties involved (Alderson & Morrow, 2011). This means that CYCPs discuss with children, youth, and families the benefits and challenges of potential interventions. CYCPs also advocate on behalf of the children, youth, and families they work with to ensure that other members of the team, including medical personnel, provide informed consent about the interventions they intend to provide. It is recommended that the CYCP document when informed consent is provided. They can also document the challenges and benefits of the interventions that were communicated to the child/youth and family. For example, engaging in life space practice can impact a youth, as they may remember a time that is upsetting from their past. We need to report this potential outcome to children/youth/families when sharing informed consent.

d. Use the proper procedures for reporting and correcting non-compliance

Each agency has their own procedures for reporting; it is your responsibility to comply with the standards. When an incorrect medication has been dispensed or a medication is forgotten, this is **non-compliance**. Most agencies have specific critical incident forms that need to be completed to report such errors. We also need to self-report if we have breached confidentiality or made a procedural error.

Each agency has specific forms to be filled out (such an incident reports or even serious occurrence reports) that can then be followed up in supervision, as well as tracked in "the client's" file, especially given the child or youth may have a challenging incident or day as a result of missed medication.

6. Advocacy

a. Demonstrate knowledge and skills in use of advocacy

Advocacy results in CYCP actions of speaking on behalf or right beside someone else or pleading a cause for another, often to ensure just treatment (Meyers, Sweeney, & White, 2002). Advocacy for the child and youth worker becomes part of daily practice. Advocate roles requires competence in eight attributes: collaboration, communication, scholarly practice, management, professionalism, passion, perseverance, and humility (Kelland, Hoe, McGuire, Andreoli, Yu, & Nixon, 2014). CYCPs advocate for the services that children/youth and families need now and for the services they will need in the future. Advocacy also needs to include reducing the risk of harm and oppression. A youth group defines advocacy as a form of expression through various art forms to influence decision making that will create positive change for people and their environment. Advocacy is how we transform public attitudes into action (Heart and Stroke Foundation, n.d., p. 6). Provide examples of daily, monthly, and yearly advocacy CYCPs can engage in with different populations or in different milieus. We have a responsibility to advocate in all different systems.

b. Access information on the rights of children, youth, and families, including the United Nations Convention on the Rights of the Child

> The **Convention on the Rights of the Child** is an international treaty that recognizes the human rights of children, defined as persons up to the age of 18 years. The Convention establishes in international law that States Parties must ensure that all children—without discrimination in any form—benefit from special protection measures and assistance; have access to services such as education and health care; can develop their personalities, abilities and talents to the fullest potential; grow up in an environment of happiness, love and understanding; and are informed about and participate in, achieving their rights in an accessible and active manner. . . . The Convention on the Rights of the Child is the most widely and rapidly ratified human rights treaty in history. Only two countries, Somalia and the United States, have not ratified this celebrated agreement. . . . By signing the Convention, the United States has signaled its intention to ratify—but has yet to do so. (UNICEF, 2005; emphasis added)

> A "child rights approach" is one which furthers the realization of the rights of all children as set out in the Convention by developing the capacity of duty-bearers to meet their obligations to respect, protect and fulfill rights (Article 4) and the capacity of rights-holders to claim their rights: guided at all times by the rights to non-discrimination (Article 2), consideration of the best interests of the child (Article 3.1), life, survival and development (Article 6), and respect for the views of the child (Article 12). Children also have the right to be directed and guided in the exercise of their rights by caregivers, parents and community members, in line with children's evolving capacities (Article 5). (UNICEF, 2017)

c. Describe the rights of children, youth, and families in relevant settings and systems advocate for the rights of children, youth, and families in relevant settings and systems

The **rights** of those we walk alongside can be identified in every setting, and these can be discussed transparently with CYCPs, children, youth, families, and communities. You can't advocate for the respect of rights if you do not know your rights. If you are working in a milieu where these are not clear, it is important to ask this question of your supervisor. Rights can include the right to attend court or the right to contact family or the right to read reports that are written about you.

The primary goal of child advocacy is to create space for the voice of children/youth and families if they feel that their rights are not being honoured. "Do not speak about us, without us." This phrase means not assuming what children/youth/communities or families need without consulting them. "They are the experts in their own lives. It is hoped that change happens as a result of advocacy. So advocacy targets, provokes, and influences change and therefore *is* the process. The outcome of these actions, the *change*, is the product" (Office of the Provincial Advocate for Children and Youth, 2011; emphasis added).

Children in care are vulnerable given that decisions about them are often made by a committee of people they have never met (Fraser, 2014). Involving children/youth in discussion or participation can benefit CYCPs, in that their participation will promote and improve child protection or other service delivery. The child/youth can also benefit from communication and decision-making experiences that enhance their self-esteem and help them to feel empowered (Sinclair & Franklin, 2000).

CYCPs are always striving toward helping the children/youth and families that they work with to recognize what changes they want to make (self-determination) versus having the CYCP take responsibility and ownership for *making meaning* in the life space (Garfat, 1998; Krueger, 1998).

Discussion Opportunity 2:20

Kevin is a CYCP who worked with foster families providing long-term care to Crown wards.

Rhonda has been a foster parent to Marty for over two years. Marty (aged nine) has settled into her home and is developing a strong relationship with Rhonda and her other family members. Marty always struggled in school at the beginning of the school year and after holiday breaks. She had trouble reintegrating into her classroom community and communicated this behaviourally by having emotional meltdowns and by defying routines and structure within the school milieu. The school often responded to this behaviour by sending Marty home, unofficially or by suspension. This is often experienced by Marty as rejection.

Kevin offered to attend a school meeting with Rhonda to talk about the reactions Marty demonstrated that were trauma-based. He reiterated to the school that if they intended to send Marty home, this had to be within a formal suspension process so there was a paper trail. He also asked if there were any staff at the school who could meet with Marty on a daily basis before and following extended breaks. This person could review strategies that Marty could use when feeling unsafe or ill-prepared for scheduling changes.

The CYCP worked not only with the child but also with their care provider. The CYCP did this by advocating not only for the child's rights but also for the system to create a preventative plan instead of reactionary supports and services.

d. Describe and advocate for safeguards for protection from abuse, including institutional abuse

Institutional abuse is defined as "damaging acts occurring in institutional settings and/or policies of institutions with responsibility for children" (Rimer & Prager, 2015, p. 10). CYCPs may encounter institutional abuse within their workplace and should adhere to their code of ethics to advocate for protection from such abuse.

In the school, as he was walking past the school office, Kevin heard the vice-principal (VP) screaming at a child. This is a tough position for the CYCP. The VP has a more powerful role in the institution than the CYCP. The VP and teachers have more influential roles in the institution than the CYCP students completing work-integrated learning hours within the school. The same can happen when working in a group home: a CYCP student might hear another staff member berating a child, or, when working in community centre, a CYCP student might see community centre staff not allowing a transgender child to use the bathroom of their choice. These are examples of incidents where a CYCP student has to speak up about the abuse or neglect happening in institutions or settings when others know of their occurrence but do not address them.

The rights of children and youth are usually outlined in legislation in every geographical area. Within legislation, reporting steps are outlined. CYCPs are encouraged to discuss, with their supervisors (whether on for a work-integrated learning placement or a college/university supervisor), occasions where they believe they have observed abuse/neglect or domestic violence. Institutional abuse is allowed to continue when it is observed but witnesses do not take professional steps to address it.

An important strategy to safeguard against institutional abuse is to educate the children/youth/families and communities that we work with about what institutional abuse is, what it looks like systemically, and what it looks like in the behaviour of those around us. We also need to educate our colleagues, including teachers, social workers, foster parents, other CYCPs, and others that we experience harm if we do not speak up and express felt vulnerability (Bernstein, 2016).

e. Describe and advocate for safeguards for protection from abuse, including organizational or workplace abuse

Every agency that supports and works with vulnerable youth should have regularly reviewed **policies and procedures**. These policies and procedures can include the reporting of expectations and investigative practices when allegations are made against staff members, students, or other individuals in a caregiving role over vulnerable persons (Snow, 2009).

We need to advocate for **safeguards** and protection from abuse, including **organizational and workplace abuse**, whether we are students or employees. This includes oppression that might exist in educational and work spaces. Things are changing in CYC in many levels and systems. CYCPs are addressing their own cultural privileges and oppression. We need to continue to take action to ensure that safeguards are in place for us now and for seven generations to come (Clarkson, Morrissette, & Regallet,1991). CYCPs believe policies can change. Hiring can change. Conferences can change. CYC can change (Vachon, 2018), so let's challenge ourselves to promote change. We all need to advocate.

f. Advocate for protection of children from systemic abuse, mistreatment, and exploitation

(This includes the impact of all parts of the child's system, including social media.)

In our CYCP training programs, we learn about the legislation that defines abuse within our geographical areas. For example, neglect is a precipitating factor for apprehension in the provinces of Nova Scotia (Government of Nova Scotia, 2017) and Ontario (Government of Ontario, 2017). Neglect is not a reason for child welfare involvement in Yukon if the family is experiencing poverty (Government of Yukon, 2016).

We also learn what our **duty to report** is both in the student and employee roles. This is an ongoing expectation, task, and mission as a CYCP. We are all responsible to stand up against abuse of children in all forms, including sex trafficking and online bullying. Once one is an advocate, it colours their view of the world and of their work, and it becomes part of their tapestry of praxis. Advocacy becomes part of who they are in all of their life spaces (Office of the Provincial Advocate for Children and Youth, 2011).

Discussion Opportunity 2:21

1. How can CYCPs advocate for the protection of children from abuse, maltreatment, or exploitation directly and indirectly?
2. How can CYCPs use social media to advocate for the needs of children/youth/families and communities?
3. What supports may CYCP students need in order to advocate effectively?

Discussion Opportunity 2:22

1. What are important topics to discuss in supervision?
2. Develop questions, successes, concerns, or stories that you can bring to supervision.
3. Explore how these questions can support your professional development.

Chapter 2 Learning Outcomes Evaluation

- Which competency areas are strengths that you have under the professional domain?
- Which competency areas are opportunities that you want to focus on as you proceed through your CYCP development?
- What opportunities (work/school/volunteer) will allow you to develop these skills?
- Create one SMART goal statement that incorporates a competency identified under the professional domain of practice. You can find all of the competencies noted under each domain in Appendix A.

REFERENCES

Alderson, P., & Morrow, V. (2011). *The ethics of research with children and young people. A practical handbook*. London, UK: Sage.

Bellefeuille, G., & Jamieson, D. (2008). Relational-centred planning: A turn toward creative potential and possibilities. In G. Bellefeuille & F. Ricks (Eds.), S*tanding on the precipice: Inquiry into the creative potential of child and youth care practice* (pp. 35–72). Edmonton, AB: McEwan Press.

Bernstein, M. M. (2016, January). Changing the Canadian culture to make children's rights more visible and accessible to children and youth. The role of education in diminishing child exploitation. *7th Annual Meeting of the Children's Rights Academic Network (CRAN)* (pp. 8–12). Retrieved March 6, 2019, from https://carleton.ca/landonpearsoncentre/wp-content/uploads/CRAN2016-.pdf

Briegel, M. (2017). Rethinking professional developmental of child and youth care practitioners. *Relational Child and Youth Care Practice*, 10–24.

Bronfenbrenner, U. (1979). *The ecology of human development: Experiments by nature and design*. Cambridge, MA: Harvard University Press.

Canadian Counselling and Psychotherapy Association (CCPA). (2014). *Statutory regulation in Canada*. Ottawa, ON: Author.

Centers for Disease Control and Prevention (CDC). (2005). *Surviving field stress for first responders*. Atlanta, GA: Author.

Child and Youth Care Certification Board (CYCCB). (2016a). *Professionalism*. College Station, TX: Author. Retrieved from https://www.cyccb.org/competencies/professionalism

Child and Youth Care Certification Board (CYCCB). (2016b). *Competencies*. College Station, TX: Author. Retrieved from https://www.cyccb.org/competencies

Clarkson, L., Morrissette, V., & Regallet, G. (1991). *Our responsibility to the seventh generation Indigenous peoples and sustainable development*. Winnipeg, MB: International Institute for Sustainable Development.

Cooke-Dallin, B., Rosborough, T., & Underwood, L. (2000). The role of elders in child and youth care education. *Canadian Journal of Native Education, 24*(2), 82–91.

Council of Canadian Child and Youth Care Associations. (n.d.). Code of ethics. Retrieved March 17, 2019, from http://www.garthgoodwin.info/cccycodeofethics.htm

Cunningham, A., & Baker, L. (2004). *What about me! Seeking to understand a child's view of violence in the family*. London, ON: Centre for Children & Families in the Justice System.

Curry, D., Lawler, J. M., Schneider-Munoz, J. A., & Fox. L. (2011). A child and youth approach to professional development and training. *Relational Child and Youth Care Practices, 24*(1–2), 148–161.

Davidson, J. C. (2004). Where do we draw the lines? Professional relationship boundaries and child and youth care practitioners. *Journal of Child and Youth Care Work, 19*(1), 31–42.

Doran, G., Miller, A., & Cunningham, M. (1981). There's a S. M. A. R. T. way to write management goals and objectives. *Management Review, 70*(11), 35–36.

Eckleberry-Hunt, J., Van Dyke, A., Lick, D., & Tucciarone, J. (2009). Changing the conversation from burnout to wellness: Physician well-being in residency training programs. *Journal of Graduate Medical Education, 1*(2), 225–230. doi:10.4300/JGME-D-09-00026.1

Foraker-Thompson, J., & Edmunds, M. (2001). More is "caught" than taught. *CYC-Online: E-journal of the International Child and Youth Care Network (CYC-Net),* (32). Retrieved June 8, 2018, from http://www.cyc-net.org/cyc-online/cycol-0901-thompson.html

Fraser, T. (2014). Home can be where your story begins. *Relational Child and Youth Care Practice, 27*(1), 27–34.

Fraser, T. (2016). Preparing child and youth care practitioners for the field. *CYC-Online: E-journal of the International Child and Youth Care Network (CYC-Net),* (212), 23–30.

Freeman, A. (1987). Cognitive therapy: An overview. In A. Freeman & V. Greenwood (Eds.), *Cognitive therapy: Applications in psychiatric and medical settings* (pp. 19–35). New York, NY: Human Sciences Press.

Fox, L. E. (2014). What I think I know now (unfortunately). *Relational Child and Youth Care Practice, 27*(2), 13–15.

Garfat, T. (1998). The effective child and youth care intervention. *Journal of Child and Youth Care, 12*(1–2), 1–168.

Garfat, T. (2003). Four parts magic: The anatomy of a child and youth care intervention. *CYC-Online: E-journal of the International Child and Youth Care Network (CYC-Net),* (50). Retrieved June 8, 2018, from https://www.cyc-net.org/cyc-online/cycol-0303-thom.html

Garfat, T. (2008). Characteristics of a child and youth care approach: An exploration of their possible relevance and their contextualization in the South African reality. *CYC-Online: E-journal of the International Child and Youth Care Network (CYC-Net),* (115). Retrieved from http://www.cyc-net.org/cyc-online/cyconline-sep2008-sbo.html

Garfat, T., & Fulcher, L. C. (2012). Characteristics of a relational child and youth care approach. In T. Garfat & L. C. Fulcher (Eds.), *Child and youth care practice* (pp. 5–24). Cape Town, South Africa: CYC-Net Press.

Garfat, T., & Fulcher, L. (2012). *Child and youth care in practice.* Cape Town, South Africa: CYC-Net Press.

Garfat, T., & Fulcher, L. (2013). Characteristics of a child and youth care approach. *Relational Child & Youth Care Practice, 24*(1), 7–19.

Gharabaghi, K. (2016). A brief response to Theresa Fraser. *CYC-Online: E-journal of the International Child and Youth Care Network (CYC-Net),* (212), 30–32. Retrieved from http://www.cyc-net.org/cyc-online/oct2016.pdf

Gharabaghi, K. (2018). Promoting reflective non-compliance. *CYC-Online: E-journal of the International Child and Youth Care Network (CYC-Net),* (232), 22–26. Retrieved from http://www.cyc-net.org/cyc-online/june2018.pdf

Gharabaghi, K., & Anderson-Nathe, B. (2012). The problems and prospects of culture. *Child & Youth Services, 33*, 89–91.

Gilberg, S., & Charles, G. (2002). Child and youth care practice: The foundation for great supervision. *Journal of Child and Youth Care, 15*(2), 23–31.

Gilmour-Barrett, R., & Pratt, S. (1977). A new profession. In J. Shamsie (Ed.), *Experience and experiment*. Toronto, ON: Canadian Mental Health Association.

Goolsby, M., & DuBois, C. J. (2017). Professional organization membership: Advancing the nurse practitioner. *Journal of the American Nurse Practitioner, 29*(8), 434–440. doi:10.1002/2327-6924.12483

Government of Nova Scotia. (2017). Child and family services act. Retrieved March 17, 2019, from https://nslegislature.ca/sites/default/files/legc/statutes/children%20and%20family%20services.pdf

Government of Ontario. (2017). Child and family services act. Retrieved June 24, 2018, from https://www.ontario.ca/laws/statute/17c14

Government of Yukon. (2016). Child and family services act. Retrieved March 17, 2019, from http://www.gov.yk.ca/legislation/acts/chfase_c.pdf

Harder, A., Knorth, E., & Kalverboer, M. (2012). A secure base? The adolescent–staff relationship in secure residential youth care. *The Journal of Child and Family Social Work, 18*(3), 305–317. doi:10.1111/j.1365-2206.2012.00846.x

Healthy Families BC. (2013). Set SMART goals. Retrieved April 14, 2019, from https://www.healthyfamiliesbc.ca/home/articles/set-smart-goals

Heart and Stroke Foundation. (n.d.). Believe in I'm possible, spark change your style: Youth advocacy toolkit. Ottawa, ON: Heart and Stroke Foundation Canada.

Holt, S. L. (2015). An exploration of the impacts that experiencing domestic violence can have on a child's primary school education: View of educational staff. *British Journal of Community Justice, 13*(2), 7–26.

James, S. (2011). What works in group care?—A structured review of treatment models for group homes and residential care. *Children and Youth Services Review, 33*(2), 308–321. doi:10.1016/j.childyouth.2010.09.014

Kassam, A. (2017, November 4). Ratio of Indigenous children in Canada welfare system is "humanitarian crisis." *The Guardian*. Retrieved from https://www.theguardian.com/world/2017/nov/04/indigenous-children-canada-welfare-system-humanitarian-crisis

Kelland, K., Hoe, E., McGuire, M. J., Yu, J., Andreoli, A., & Nixon, S. A. (2014). Excelling in the role of advocate: A qualitative study exploring advocacy as an essential physiotherapy competency. *Physiotherapy Canada, 66*(1), 74–80. doi:10.3138/ptc.2013-05

Kostouros, P., & McLean, S. (2006). The importance of self-care. *CYC-Online: E-journal of the International Child and Youth Care Network (CYC-Net)*, (89). Retrieved July 2, 2017, from http://www.cyc-net.org/cyc-online/cycol-0606-mclean.html

Krueger, M. (1998). *Interactive youth work practice*. Washington, DC: CWLA.

Kuhlmann, S., Piel, M., & Wolf, O. T. (2005). Impaired memory retrieval after psychosocial stress in healthy young men. *Journal of Neuroscience, 25*(11), 2977–2982. doi:10.1523/jneurosci.5139-04.2005

LaPiere, R. T. (1934). Attitudes vs. actions. *Social Forces, 13*(2), 230–237. doi:10.2307/2570339

Laursen, E. K. (2002). Seven habits of reclaiming relationships. *Reclaiming Children and Youth, 11*(1), 10–14.

Legault, T. (2003). Care workers: Values. *CYC-Online: E-journal of the International Child and Youth Care Network (CYC-Net),* (53). Retrieved January 1, 2018, from http://www.cyc-net.org/cyc-online/cycol-0603-values.html

Linehan, M. (2014). *DBT skills training manual.* New York, NY: Guilford Press.

Maslow, A. (1943). A theory of human motivation. *Psychological Review, 50*(4), 370–396.

Mattingly, M. A. (1995). Developing professional ethics for child and youth care work: Assuming responsibility for the quality of care. *Child & Youth Care Forum, 24*(6), 379–391.

Meyers, J. E., Sweeney, T. J., & White, V. E. (2002). Advocacy for counseling and counselors: A professional imperative. *Journal of Counseling & Development, 80*(4), 394–402. doi:10.1002/j.1556-6678.2002.tb00205.x

Ontario Association of Child and Youth Care (OACYC). (2015). *Safeguarding the other 23 hours.* Toronto, ON: Author.

Ontario Association of Child and Youth Care (OACYC). (n.d.). *Code of ethics.* Retrieved June 24, 2018, from http://www.oacyc.org/code-of-ethics

Ontario Residential Services Review Panel. (2016). *Because young people matter.* Retrieved from http://www.children.gov.on.ca/htdocs/English/professionals/childwelfare/residential/residential-review-panel-report/index.aspx

Office of the Provincial Advocate for Children and Youth. (2011). *Media presentation to Ontario Association of Social Workers and Social Service Workers.* Toronto, ON: Author.

Phelan, J. (1990). Child care supervision: The neglected skill of evaluation. In J. Anglin, C. Denholm, & A. Pence (Eds.), *Perspectives in professional child and youth care.* New York, NY: Haworth.

Phelan, J. (2003). The relationship boundaries that control programming. *Relational Child and Youth Care Practice, 16*(1), 51–56.

Phelan, J. (2009). The wounded healer as helper and help: A CYC model. *CYC-Online: E-journal of the International Child and Youth Care Network (CYC-Net),* (121). Retrieved April 25, 2018, from https://www.cyc-net.org/cyc-online/cyconline-july2009-phelan.html

Ranahan, P. (1999). Reaching beyond caring to loving in child and youth care practice. *Journal of Child and Youth Care, 13*(4), 55–65.

Reid, B. (1993). "But we're doing it already!" Exploring a response to the concept of reflective practice in order to improve its facilitation. *Nurse Education Today, 13*, 305–309.

Rimer, P., & Prager, B. (2015). Reaching out: Working together to identify and respond to child victims of abuse. Scarborough, ON: Nelson College Indigenous.

Roelofs, K. (2017). Freeze for action: Neurobiological mechanisms in animal and human freezing. *Philosophical Transactions of the Royal Society of London. Series B, Biological Sciences, 372*(1718), 20160206. doi:10.1098/rstb.2016.0206

Rundell, F. (2007). "Re-story-ing" our restorative practices. *Reclaiming Children and Youth, 16*(2), 52–59.

Sauvé-Griffin, J. (2009). When we stop and ask why: Reflective practice in action. *Relational Child and Youth Care Practice, 22*(3).

Schön, D. (1983). *The reflective practitioner: How professionals think in action*. London, UK: Temple Smith.

Scrivens, V. (2001). Values. *Journal of Child and Youth Care, 14*(3), 39–47.

Sinclair, R., & Franklin, A. (2000). *A Quality Protects Research Briefing: Young people's participation*. London, UK: Department of Health.

Snow, K. (2009). Vulnerable citizens. *CYC-Online: E-journal of the International Child and Youth Care Network (CYC-Net)*, (130). Retrieved from http://www.cyc-net.org/cyc-online/cycon-line-dec2009-snow.html

Smart, M., & Digney, J. (2014). Now and then. *CYC-Online: E-Journal of the International Journal of Child and Youth Care Network (CYC-Net)*, (185), 26–29. Retrieved from http://www.cyc-net.org/cyc-online/jul2014.pdf

Smart, M., & Digney, J. (2016). How wounded are our healers? *CYC-Online: E-journal of the International Child and Youth Care Network (CYC-Net)*, (212), 34–39. Retrieved June 15, 2018, from http://www.cyc-net.org/cyc-online/oct2016.pdf

Statistics Canada. (2016). *Portrait of a child's life in Canada*. Ottawa, ON: Queen's Printer.

Stuart, C. (2013). *Foundations of child and youth care*. Dubuque, IA: Kendall Hunt Publishing.

Stuart, C., & Carty, B. (2006). *The role of competence in outcomes for children and youth: An approach for mental health*. Toronto ON: Ryerson University.

Thumbadoo, Z. (2011). Isibindi: Love in caring with a child and youth care approach. *Relational Child and Youth Care Practice, 24*(1–2), 193–198.

UNICEF. (2005). Convention on the rights of the child: Frequently asked questions. Retrieved from https://www.unicef.org/crc/index_30229.html

UNICEF. (2017). CRE web toolkit. Retrieved April 23, 2019, from https://www.unicef.org/crc/files/UNICEF_CRE_Toolkit_FINAL_web_version170414.pdf

United Nations Human Rights Office of the High Commissioner. (1989). Convention on the rights of the child. Retrieved June 24, 2018, from https://www.ohchr.org/EN/ProfessionalInterest/Pages/CRC.aspx

U.S. Department of Health and Human Services (DHHS), Administration on Children, Youth and Families. (2013). Trends in foster care and adoption. Washington, DC: U.S. Government Printing Office.

Vachon, W. (2018). Child and youth care fragility. *CYC-Online: E-journal of the International Child and Youth Care Network (CYC-Net)*, (232), 14–18. Retrieved from http://www.cyc-net.org/cyc-online/june2018.pdf

Vincent, J. (2016). Perspectives on love as a component of professional practice. [Joint Special Issue, Love in Professional Practice] *Scottish Journal of Residential Child Care, 15*(3) and *International Journal of Social Pedagogy, 5*(1), 6–21.

Wade, J. C., & Jones, J. E. (2015). Strength-based clinical supervision: A positive psychology approach to clinical training. New York, NY: Springer Publishing Company.

Winfield, J. (2003). Taking care of our professional code of ethics. *Child and Youth Care, 21*(10), 23.

CHAPTER 3

Cultural and Human Diversity

Learning Outcomes

This chapter will help you to meet the following objectives:

- Review the cultural and human diversity domain of CYC practice.
- Apply the domain and competencies to field examples.
- Engage in discussion with colleagues about the domain and competencies.
- Identify areas of strength and development.

Cultural and human diversity issues in CYC professional environments is a foundational domain. CYCPs need to actively promote, acknowledge, and demonstrate respect for cultural and human diversity. The CYCP seeks self-understanding and has the ability to access and evaluate information related to cultural and human diversity. While respecting the past, current and relevant knowledge is integrated into developing respectful and effective relationships, communication, and developmental practice methods that incorporate culture and diversity. When we work through the continuum of understanding the diversity and culture competency, client services develop organizational cultures that help recruit and retain a more diverse and highly motivated staff better able to deliver high-quality services to the children and families in care (Delano, 2004). Culture and human diversity are woven into the tapestry of all of our relationships with children, youth, families, and communities.

A. FOUNDATIONAL KNOWLEDGE

The professional practitioner is well versed in current research and theory related to cultural and human diversity, including the nine major factors that set groups apart from one another and give individuals and groups elements of identity. These are age, class, race, ethnicity, levels of ability, language, spiritual belief systems, educational achievement, and gender differences.

- Cultural structures, theories of change, and values within culture variations
- Cross-cultural communication
- History of political, social, and economic factors that contribute to racism, stereotyping, bias, and discrimination
- Variations among families and communities of diverse backgrounds (Child and Youth Care Certification Board [CYCCB], 2016)

B. PROFESSIONAL COMPETENCIES

1. Cultural and Human Diversity Awareness and Inquiry

a. Describe own biases

Before you begin, it's important to acknowledge that this activity can bring up lots of feelings. As you read, experience, and discuss, be aware of how you are feeling. How comfortable are you with having this discussion? Has safety been created in the classroom and/or your group? If it doesn't yet feel safe enough to have this discussion, talk to your professor/instructor/facilitator, mentor, and supervisor directly or send them a message. They need to know that you need to feel safe enough to participate. The inclusion of all individuals enriches the tapestry of conversation and learning, which is why instructors should strive to create a safe sharing environment for everyone.

Once safety is created, you can continue with the activity. Each of the items identified below is a belief, value, or thought that separates, judges, or marginalizes a person or group of people. Remember that we can have a **bias**, even if we never act on it. Spend some time looking at how each of these types of bias is defined. Do you share any of these? (This is an internal question; you do not need to answer this in a group unless you feel that you're in an environment where it is safe to do so.)

Please provide an example of how one can recognize this bias in behaviour. What is an example of a demonstrated bias you might see directed to a child/youth/family or community? You can use online resources to help complete this chart. Do you have some local examples that have been shared in the media?

As you move through the exercise, remember that it might precipitate feelings that are upsetting to you or others, even if the environment is safe and you initially felt very comfortable. You can reach out to your professor, instructor, or group facilitator, mentor, and supervisor at any time to discuss your feelings. He/she/ze/they may also want to refer you for additional support.

Bias	Define It		
	What is this type of bias? You may research information online/at your library or via discussion with other learners.	What does it look like in behaviour toward children/youth/families/communities?	What can the CYCP do about it?
Ableism			
Anti-Black Racism			
Anti-Semitism			
Biphobia			
Classism			
Discrimination			
Hate Crime			

Bias	Define It		
	What is this type of bias? You may research information online/at your library or via discussion with other learners.	What does it look like in behaviour toward children/youth/families/communities?	What can the CYCP do about it?
Heterosexism			
Homophobia			
Implicit Bias			
Islamophobia			
Microaggression			
Oppression			
Prejudice			

Bias	Define It		
	What is this type of bias? You may research information online/at your library or via discussion with other learners.	What does it look like in behaviour toward children/youth/families/ communities?	What can the CYCP do about it?
Racism			
Racism against Indigenous Persons			
Sexism			
Stereotyping			
Systemic Oppression			
Transphobia			
Xenophobia			

Students and CYCPs have individual biases that can impact their judgment and ability to utilize professional values when interacting with marginalized groups in practices (Wahler, 2011).

Supporting one group over another, such as believing that women can do a job better than men, or that a white youth worker can only work with white youth and a black youth worker can only work with black youth, can also be a bias. The question is who the youth needs to meet their needs, not what *we* think is needed. We need to ask the youth.

We all have biases that are based on our own experiences or what we have learned from the experiences of others. Biases may represent what we believe is our truth even though it might not be the truth of others. It is important that child and youth care practitioners know what their biases are (Moore, 2001). Unfortunately, we often do not know what our biases are until we mindfully reflect on them and/or someone else brings them to our awareness. Biases may benefit some groups of people and risk oppressing others.

Will a South Asian youth be more comfortable with a South Asian CYCP, the same as a woman may be more comfortable with a female physician? Are you able to support parents in their parenting development when you have never been a parent? These are the questions and discussions that "bring our bias to the forefront" and instigate worthy discussions that may lead to differences, but also can lead to greater awareness, acceptance, and celebration of diversity. Working inclusively is a process, not an event. We always need to be evaluating, reflecting on, and consistently conscious to become aware of biases so we are not oppressing others and are instead celebrating inclusivity.

Describe the interaction between your own cultural values and the cultural values of others.

We each are brought up exposed to certain cultural values. Children are socialized from birth in the way that they are dressed, the colours they wear, the toys they play with, the friends they associate with, the style of their play, and how they engage with others (Moore, 2001). It is up to the CYCP to investigate, attempt to learn more about these values, and help the children and youth learn more about the cultural values of others. In some instances, the CYCP will encounter children and youth who are not in touch with their own cultural values. As CYCPs, it is our responsibility to involve culture and the values we have received from our culture. Culture may include our ancestry, youth culture, social media culture, education culture, spiritual culture, art culture, child protection culture, CYC culture, and more. When the CYCP attends to how meaning is construed, then they can begin to understand the young person and their behaviour (Garfat, 2004).

Discussion Opportunity 3:1

Johnna is adopted and joined her family at two years of age. She is adopted by a white family but is the biological child of a First Nations teenager and an older white man. At 13 years of age, she is described as being "defiant" and "rejecting." Her parents verbalize that they cannot care for her and surrender her to the local child protection agency. She is placed in a residential treatment centre after gaining the reputation of being a "runner."

She refuses to talk with centre staff for the first three days post-admission. Johnna does not communicate with the other residents. She does try to sit near another girl who identifies as Indigenous. The older resident talks to Johnna about smudging. With staff support (due to the girls using a lighter), the two girls begin to smudge daily. Soon, other youth want to join in, as do some staff members. The staff then contact the closest friendship centre and invite an Elder (who is from Johnna's band) to have dinner with the girls and staff. This Elder invites the resident girls and staff to attend a Pow Wow. Johnna is initially not interested in going, but with staff and peer encouragement, she becomes more invested in learning more about her culture and her band's history.

One of the staff, Monica, is not interested in attending the Pow Wow. She voices her discomfort with smudging in the residence and identifies that these practices are in conflict with her own religious practices. She feels that the girls should be encouraged to pray as a way to feel more at peace. She cites fire safety as being in conflict with smudging practices.

1. How do you think the supervisor can respond to these concerns? How could Johnna be supported? How can Monica be supported? How can both the youth and the staff member be supported to learn more about their treasured cultures?
2. What are some of the biases that you think you have about various religious or spiritual practices? Identify any privileges that you have in practising your religion or spirituality.
3. What is an example of a bias that you have observed by other members of your family?
4. How could you ask a co-worker about a bias you wonder about? Have you ever received feedback about a bias you may have? How did you handle it?
5. What do you need in a relationship to feel safe receiving feedback about a bias you may have? (We know that this is a tough reflective question.)

In some instances, our values will come into conflict with the values of others. This happened in Canada for seven generations in the Residential School system that Indigenous children were forced to attend. The school management forced their values on the children, who were taken from their families and communities. Families were disrupted to prevent the transmission of cultural values and identity from one generation to the next (Truth and Reconciliation Commission of Canada, 2015), and cultural genocide occurred.

b. Describe own limitations in understanding and responding to cultural and human differences and seeks assistance when needed

We all have our own limitations when responding to cultural and human differences. CYCPs need to make safe space to explore our bias and limitations to reduce the risk of harm or judgment. We make constant decisions that are impacted by culture. Garfat (1993) states that, when deciding what to do, I base my decision on what I know, and at times I know I need to know more. We have blind spots and blank spots (Garfat, 1993). We need to make space with children, youth, families, colleagues, and supervisors that promotes being aware of what we may or may not know: without judgment but with curiosity, exploration, and engagement.

c. Recognize and prevent stereotyping while accessing and using cultural information

Cultural **stereotyping** is embedded in North American culture: Halloween costumes that represent ethnic groups, sports teams that use slurs against or stereotyped imagery of specific cultures or peoples, insults that are used to describe a faith community or sexual identity or gender identity.

It's important that Child and Youth Care Practitioners avoid stereotyping, but we must also discourage stereotyping among the children/youth/families that we have the privilege to work with. We can begin modelling when describing the children or youth that we work with. Are we working with a nine-year-old child or a nine-year-old racialized boy? Is it relevant that the child is nine or a boy or African Canadian/African American? Sometimes it might be relevant, but sometimes it is not relevant to the communication being shared. We always need to be cognizant of what information we are sharing and the purpose of sharing it. What information are we party to listening to and why? *"Do not assume. When in doubt, check it out"* (Ventrella, personal communication, 2017).

When cultural information is being judged, generalized, or stereotyped within any of the life spaces that we are working in, CYCs have a responsibility to label this, address the bias, and support the use of a different lens. The children/youth and families we walk alongside are always watching, if not taking direction from our modelling.

Discussion Opportunity 3:2

1. How would the practitioner feel, think, or react if the child/youth/family read the file that is being written about them?
2. How would practitioners feel if the files were subpoenaed to court? Do the notes only contain relevant and respectful information?

d. Access, and critically evaluate, resources that advance cultural understandings and appreciation of human diversity

CYCPs can seek out current research or information published about diversity, **inclusion**, and oppression so they can not only access but also critically evaluate resources that advance cultural understanding and appreciation of human diversity. Current research and narratives are opportunities for learning. Evaluating the information and the context of this information is critical to understanding their practice and the field. Seeking wise counsel from stakeholders who understand the cultural experience CYCPSs are seeking makes good sense and will enhance the practice of CYCPs.

e. Support children, youth, families, and programs in developing cultural competence and appreciation of human diversity

Cultural competence and the appreciation of human diversity is an ongoing process. It may be a challenging process when the CYCP is working with individuals who struggle with overcoming bias or prejudice. Face-to-face, online, and written resources can be solicited locally, provincially, and nationally that will help the CYCP understand the cultural communities around them, so they can also share these with the children, youth, and families they interact with.

> I first heard the expression, "nothing about us, without us" in South Africa in 1983. Michael Masutha and William Rowland, two leaders of disabled people in South Africa, separately invoked the slogan which they had heard used by someone from Eastern Europe at an International Disability Rights conference. The slogan's power derives from its location of the source of many types (disability) oppression in the context of control and voice. . . . As Ed Roberts, one of the leading figures of the disability rights movement has said, if we have learned anything from the civil rights movement in the U.S. is that when others speak for you, you lose. (Charlton, 2000)

If we are building cultural competence, this is a process that includes challenging how we define culture and our understanding of the impact and role of culture in our life spaces (Gharabaghi & Anderson-Nathe, 2012).

f. Support children, youth, families, and programs in overcoming culturally and diversity based barriers to services

Even in the twenty-first century, there are resources and barriers that impede accessible services. Barriers need to be eliminated, and accessibility needs to serve everyone. For example, a newly built child protection office is located in an isolated geographical area not easily accessed by public transportation. Additionally, they do not have service hours that permit people who work various shifts to access services. These are examples of barriers that impact people who may not have access to private transportation or jobs that have time flexibility. Other examples of barriers include schools that schedule tests on religious holidays or community program flyers that are only printed in English.

2. Relationship and Communication Sensitive to Cultural and Human Diversity

a. Adjust for the effects of age, cultural and human diversity, background, experience, and development on verbal and nonverbal communication

At times, CYCPs assume that they know much about a specific culture because they have worked with someone or know someone from that culture. However, just like in our own cultures, age, generational norms, and experiences impact cultural practice.

Assuming to know someone's story is an ignorant response to relationship building. Culture experienced by a grandparent may be different than the culture experienced by the grandchildren, especially if other cultural experiences have been interwoven into the familial or individual life spaces between generations. Culture is fluid and ever-evolving and needs to be reflective of many different kinds of lived experiences (Gharabaghi & Anderson-Nathe, 2012).

Discussion Opportunity 3:3

1. Share an example about a time you have made an assumption about someone's culture based on their presentation/name/voice.
2. Share an example of when someone made an assumption about your culture that is not true for you.

b. Describe the non-verbal and verbal communication between self and others (including supervisors, clients, or peer professionals)

Verbal communication includes the sounds we make when sharing messages, and nonverbal communication is how we look to others (we sometimes call this "body language"). We may think we are communicating one message with our body or voice, but the message is received very differently than we intended. Having a dialogue with others can help clarify our communication. CYCPs often invite those they are communicating with to share what they have heard.

Our communication patterns will vary based on who we are communicating with and the type of relationship we share with that person(s).

We can also communicate our biases to others using specific types of communication called microaggressions. **Microaggressions** are forms of communication that reflect oppression, lack of cultural awareness, lack of cultural competency, and even bias. Microaggressions are both nonverbal and verbal. Microaggressive communication can also be present in the milieu or policy. Microaggressions can be purposeful or unintentionally insulting but nonetheless communicate derogatory messages that target persons only because of their social location (Sue, Capodilupo, Torino, Bucceri, Holder, Nadal, & Esquilin, 2007; Sue, 2010).

For example:

*   Asking a female co-worker what her husband's name is because she stated she is married
*   Assuming a racialized student is on scholarship or an international student
*   Making comments about retirement to a colleague that you assume is close to retirement

Ensuring that you are seen as someone who is open to feedback will create opportunities for learning and dialogue when we unintentionally communicate messages verbally or nonverbally toward others.

Discussion Opportunity 3:4

Tanya states in a team meeting that she and her partner are going to take vacation in the winter this year due to her partner's new work schedule. Another team member asks where Tanya's husband works. The co-worker has made an assumption based on heterosexual norms. Tanya then shares that her wife works at a construction company.

Look around the classroom and get curious about the assumptions you have made about your colleagues or your professor/instructor. For example, I meet someone who has a different skin colour than my own, is 5'10", with piercings and tattoos, and doesn't smile at me. As I have never met this person before, my mind fills the space with the following thoughts: *This person is independent, is streetwise, doesn't trust easily, and questions authority.* I may be completely wrong about this person, but that's what I tell myself based on other people I have met who present in a similar way. Note how my beliefs, values, and attitudes have created this picture based on my past experiences.

Take a moment and assess if your assumption is accurate. Is the other person streetwise? Do they question authority? What beliefs/values or attitudes have led you to your assumptions?

Our assumptions can lead to microaggressions such as assuming Tanya's partner is male. Please share an example when you have used or observed a microaggression. Please also share how this was labelled by yourself or others. How did it impact or appear to impact the relationship between the persons involved?

Discussion Opportunity 3:5

Penny is transitioning to Patrick. Child and youth care staff from his residence continue to use feminine pronouns when Patrick has asked to be referred to using "they/theirs" or the name Patrick. Other residents refuse to use the name Patrick, and some staff do not intercede because they do not feel that Patrick's transition plan is well thought out or even appropriate.

These are examples of microaggressions that can occur in the life space.

1.   Pick one milieu and identify how adults in the milieu can ensure that there is safety in the milieu for a gender non-conforming youth.

c. Describe the role of cultural and human diversity in the development of healthy and productive relationships

Culture and human diversity impact healthy and productive relationships. How we even define "healthy and productive" can be different from one person to the next.

Spend a moment in your group or class discussing what makes a relationship healthy and productive.

Is there a difference between what makes a personal or professional relationship healthy? Does your developmental or chronological age make a difference or impact the healthy status of the relationship?

Cultural and human diversity is part of our relationships because it is part of our individual and often intersectional identities. It is part of our familial identities. It is part of our community identities. Some refer to this as our **social location**. How do we see ourselves in relation to another person that we view as similar or different than ourselves? What can others teach us because they have different experiences than our own?

CYCPs strive to engage with the whole person when we engage with others. This includes understanding the intersectionality of their culture in relation to our own. This means we need to understand each of our social locations and the **we-space** between us (Lundy, 2008). This is not just skin colour or who we identify with. Our social location includes gender, faith, sexuality, where we grew up, and everything that contributes to our own identity.

Walking alongside the whole person contributes to really seeing, hearing, and growing with each other honestly and authentically so we are sharing/contributing in the development of healthy and productive relationships.

Discussion Opportunity 3:6

Julien lives in a foster home with four other teens and one younger child. Two of the teens are the children of the foster parents, and one teen is Julien's younger biological brother. They have all lived together since Julien was about six years of age. For the most part, everyone gets along really well. Sometimes, Julien's brother is super annoying, but Julien knows this is just who Thomas is. Thomas has a hard time getting along with other kids; he interrupts, argues, and is always trying to be the centre of attention.

Julien has known from an early age that he is gay. He is pretty sure that other people know he is gay too, but no one talks about it at home or school or anywhere else. During dinner one night, Julien decides to tell the family that he is gay because he wants to invite his boyfriend over for dinner. He is happy to finally share the news. His brother, Thomas, becomes very quiet and then very animated. He starts yelling, stating that he does not believe it. He does not understand how anyone can decide that they are gay. One of the other children tells Thomas that Julien was already gay, and he didn't just wake up gay today.

Julien is surprised that others know, and he appreciates that the rest of the family (except for Thomas) congratulates him for telling them how he felt. His foster parents also ask him to ask his boyfriend what his favourite dinner is.

Julien's boyfriend comes over for dinner. He seems to enjoy the dinner conversation and admits that he is a little nervous about meeting everyone, especially because they know he is Julien's boyfriend and not white like Julien. Tyrone is also surprised that there is another teen of colour in the house. His family is not accepting of his sexuality or that he is spending time with a white kid. He has heard Julien talk about his foster family before, and he imagined that they were like foster families you hear about in the news or television—essentially not very nice. This family is different. The kids laugh; they clearly are not related but are nice to each other (except for Thomas). Thomas keeps giving him dirty looks, but aside from Thomas, nothing makes Tyrone feel uncomfortable in this loud, busy house except when he is driven home. The foster mom tells both him and Julien that she and her husband are glad that they have found each other. Both foster parents want to make sure that Julien and Tyrone are practising sexual safety and not rushing into a sexual relationship too quickly.

1. How can you initiate a safe sex conversation with Julien and Thomas? What resources do you want to obtain in order to proceed with this conversation?

Relationships cannot feel safe or healthy if the people that are *in* relationship do not respect each other. Julien's foster parents are kind to all the children in their home (however they identify) and also expect the children to be respectful each other. Child and Youth Care Practitioners need to underscore the importance of safe life spaces for all children/youth/families they work with (Burns, 2006).

d. Employ displays of affection and physical contact that reflect sensitivity for individuality, age, development, cultural, and human diversity, as well as consideration of laws, regulations, policies, and risk

CYCPs display affection and physical contact intentionally by considering the stage of relationship and the milieu setting that they are working in. They need to ask: what impact will physical contact (affection) have on the child/youth developmentally and relationally? In order to answer this very complex question, the CYCP needs to consider the child's chronological and developmental age, culture, previous life experiences, and human diversity.

Some milieus (such as educational settings) dictate that there can be no physical contact between adults and children/youth. Therefore, if allowed and approved by the children's treatment team, physical contact needs to be intentional action on the part of the clinician or CYCP while being aware of what the policies, agency regulations, laws, and/or risks are for child/youth and/or practitioner. This is especially important when we may work with children who are "wards of the state" during their childhood. If no one hugs them, how do they learn about appropriate contact or consent?

CYCPs know that physical touch is a base-level brain wiring activity (Ludy-Dobson & Perry, 2003). This means that if infants and children are not touched, their development is interrupted. This is well documented in children who have been raised in orphanages, as well as children who have had multiple early caregivers.

Another example is when working with children who have been sexually violated. They may misinterpret pleasantly intended interactions with grooming behaviour and therefore feel the abuse is likely to begin again (Rimer & Prager, 2016). Teams need to be cognizant that every touch and every display of affection can be experienced positively or negatively both consciously and unconsciously for both child/youth and CYCP. Touch is reciprocal. In all milieus, CYCPs need to find the correct balance between engaging and modelling developmentally appropriate physical contact and identifying and helping children/youth and families to practise healthy physical interaction.

Discussion Opportunity 3:7

Boris is a slim eight-year-old who has been adopted from an orphanage in Russia by a couple who try hard to parent him. After two years, they were reported by the school for locking him in his room at night because he would go downstairs and try to light fires by using paper with the stove element. He has already spent six months in an Alberta treatment centre with five other children, and when staff attempt to put sunscreen on him, help him wash his hair, or essentially touch him in any way, he will tantrum and self-harm while screaming loudly. When he is agitated, he will often rub his penis against a particular chair armrest. Michael, a new CYCP practicum student, plays cards with Boris. Boris gets frustrated about losing the game and throws his cards up into the air and then runs to his favourite chair.

Michael comes to supervision and asks how to handle this situation if it occurs again. What are some ideas you have to help Michael and ultimately Boris figure out a way to self-soothe and self-regulate when he is frustrated? Is there any activity that involves healthy and age-appropriate touch?

e. Include consideration of cultural and human diversity in providing for the participation of families in the planning, implementation, and evaluation of services impacting them

It is important for CYCPs to include families in the planning, implementation, and evaluations of services impacting them. This may be challenging for some families depending on their social location and the social location of the CYCP.

Marjory met with a family at their temple. She went to shake the hand of the father, who withdrew his hand immediately. He explained that his faith did not permit him to touch other women. The consultation continued, and Marjory was careful to be respectful of the physical boundaries established by the father.

f. Give information in a manner sensitive to cultural and human diversity

In order to understand the importance of sharing information sensitively, one needs to have an understanding of the impact of **colonization**, power/privilege, the culture of the child, the culture of their parents, the culture of their family, and the culture of their community (Burns, 2006). All CYCPs know that although communication cannot replace human interaction or special therapy, it can support children to understand that they are not alone. Communication can also provide examples of how they and others can cope and be comforted (UNICEF, 2011).

Discussion Opportunity 3:8

When Shamar enters the home of a little boy he is going to work with, he sits down without being invited to and furthermore sits in the father's chair. Out of respect for his power and privilege as an "expert" hired by the local family and children's services agency, the family does not correct Shamar, but they verbalize later that having someone understand their customs is more important to them than having a male CYCP. They are adamant that their son needs to learn respect of cultural norms and they need a CYCP who also understands the importance of these versus someone who just "plays" with their child.

Although the child learns much about taking turns, positive affirmations, and teamwork by playing with Shamar, the family states that they have a very difficult time recognizing this due to their first impressions and early experiences with Shamar.

1. If you were a CYCP meeting a family for the first time, how would you enter into their space in a culturally respectful manner, being aware of your role, power, and privilege?

g. Contribute to the maintenance of a professional environment sensitive to cultural and human diversity

When we decorate staff offices and common spaces, we need to try to be aware of who might use the space: boys/girls, gender-neutral kids, gay families, straight families, short kids, tall kids, large kids, thin kids, and people of various cultures. Additionally, CYCPs who want to post a symbol that indicates the environment is safe need to recognize that it is not as easy as posting a symbol. The safe space symbol indicates that this is a place where people can find allies, so a symbol alone cannot create a safe space. The people present must work to be allies.

A **safe space** is a place where anyone can relax and fully express themselves, without fear of being made to feel uncomfortable, unwelcome, or unsafe on account of biological sex, race/ethnicity, sexual orientation, gender identity or expression, cultural background, religious affiliation, age, or physical or mental ability. It is a place where the rules guard each person's self-respect and dignity and strongly encourage everyone to respect others (Safe Space Network, n.d.).

h. Establish and maintain effective relationships within a team environment by:

1. Promoting and maintaining professional conduct.

Novice to seasoned Child and Youth Care Practitioners need to establish effective relationships within their teams. All team members need to acknowledge and respect the culture, diversity, and stages of development of each individual CYCP. Professional conduct means that we build individual strengths to meet their full potential and respectfully challenge further development. It is inevitable that relationships and team members may experience deregulation. Therefore, it is vital that the team agrees in advance how to problem solve such events so communication can be open and honest within the safety of the individual and the relationship/culture. When teams are able to model diversity resolution and safe relationships, these skills can be transferred to the residence, day-treatment classrooms, community programs, shelters, summer camps.

If you contribute to creating a safe environment, you are committed to work in the best interests of children/youth/families by following the Child and Youth Care Code of Ethics.

2. Negotiating and resolving conflict.

Negotiating and resolving conflict are important team skills that occur on teams, boards, and committees. Negotiation allows for all parties to have a voice to practise flexibility and resolve conflict in a way that meets some of the needs of the relationships. Children and youth also have the right to voice their feelings, beliefs, and needs. Practising these skills supports not only long-term growth but also quality service (Snow, 2009). Staff who model the same among each other are supporting this growth.

The risk of not negotiating and resolving conflict is that team members themselves experience fight/flight/freeze, split teams, gossip, mental unwellness, stress, and burnout. All these conditions get in the way of the interactions that CYCPs want to share with children/youth/families and communities.

For example, students in CYCP programs often verbalize that they disdain and find group work challenging. They would rather complete assignments on their own because they are not happy to have "their marks impacted because of the work of others." CYCP program professors/instructors need to be cognizant about how we model conflict resolution and provide the tools of negotiation with our students. We all need to "walk the walk and talk the talk." Often when students say they disdain group work, what they might be saying is that they are uncomfortable with conflict.

Here are some great questions to ask your practicum supervisor or supervisee:

- Is there confidentiality, and how does each person define confidentiality?
- What are our expectations of each other in regards to communication?
- What process will be followed when conflict arises?
- How can team members support each other to work through conflict?
- Is it acceptable to email each other, or will we agree to meet face to face?
- How will the team hold each other accountable?

3. Acknowledging and respecting cultural and human diversity.

CYCPs must respect cultural and human diversity. We demonstrate in our relationships that we are mindful of inclusion and diversity. We recognize that everyone we meet has an intersectionality of identities, and with curiosity we seek to learn more about cultures, subcultures, values, and beliefs and hopes and dreams. It is important not to assume culture; instead we seek opportunities to discuss and join with others.

3. Developmental Practice Methods Sensitive to Cultural and Human Diversity

a. Integrate cultural and human diversity understandings and sensitivities in a broad range of circumstances

Cultural and human diversity understandings and sensitivities are big concepts. They include practices such as inclusivity, equality, and equity. Some CYCPs will talk about employing an **anti-oppressive lens** in their work as well. As practitioners, our own social location in relation to the social locations of others will impact how we integrate cultural and human diversity.

Social location can be considered by looking at the groups that an individual belongs to. Think of the individual as carrying a knapsack with something that represents each of these groups or statuses. Then consider the tasks, jobs, or roles that the person takes on as a result of this bag of statuses (Atal, 2015). They carry these items (locations) and tasks with them wherever they go. Sometimes we can see them, and sometimes they are hidden in their bag.

One way to identify your intersectional social location is to complete the power flower exercise (Arnold, Burke, James, Martin, & Thomas, 1991). Use the following resources to complete the activity:

- http://www.msvu.ca/site/media/msvu/Documents/POWER_flower.pdf
- http://lgbtq2stoolkit.learningcommunity.ca/wp/wp-content/uploads/2014/12/flower-power-exercise.pdf

Discussion Opportunity 3:9

A child protection agency has a spot open on their community advisory committee. The agency provides service to peoples from various cultures, yet existing advisory members do not represent this diverse population. When it was identified that the board should have diverse members, an existing member wondered if perhaps the bylaws could be changed so that more than one new board member could be engaged. She was able to raise the concern that it is difficult to have a voice when one feels like the only informed voice or representative comes from a specific population. Given the bylaws could not be changed in a timely manner, another board member agreed to step down so that at least two board seats were open.

1. Why is it important to be aware of the construction and representativeness of a board, committee, or team when establishing these?

b. Design and implement programs and planned environments, which integrate developmental, preventive, and/or therapeutic objectives into the life space, through the use of methodologies and techniques sensitive to cultural and human diversity

1. Provide materials sensitive to multicultural and human diversity.

Providing materials that allow for people to read, write, and hear in ways that respect their multiculturalism and diversity is important for programs to integrate developmental and relationship techniques. Pamphlets and flyers that are only printed in English in a community that speaks Urdu, Spanish, or Hindi may help some residents but makes it challenging for people who may speak English as their second language or not at all. CYCPs need to be aware of the communication needs of those they work with to ensure that information is received with equity. In the Peel Region of Ontario, Canada, the local child protection agency has added multi-language brochures on their website, using the local census population results to determine which languages their community speaks. There are also flyers that explain legislated parenting practices that may be new to someone who learned to parent in a different culture. Photographs and graphics also need to represent the diversity of the community.

For example, a teen who is hard of hearing or deaf and unable to access resources is at a disadvantage that can result in a large conceptual and background knowledge gap, lack of sexuality awareness and education, communication frustration, social isolation, academic difficulties, and relationship problems. These then may manifest in pursuant feelings of depression, antisocial behaviours, drug and alcohol abuse, and criminal behaviour (Andrews, Shaw, & Lomas, 2011; Sebald, 2008). If we believe that part of our role is to empower, then it is our responsibility to provide the usable tools for all.

2. Provide an environment that celebrates the array of human diversity in the world through the arts, diversity of personnel, program materials, etc.

Celebrating and honouring different cultures using art and the expertise of all involved in the program, in addition to culturally relevant program materials, enriches the experience of all who live or spend time in the milieu.

CYC programs benefit from having staff/volunteers/consultants who can share their unique expertise. This could also include administrative and cleaning staff. Programs also benefit from creating opportunities for program consumers to share their unique cultural experiences and wisdom. For example, a CYCP trained foster parent engaged a resident mother to come and teach all staff how to make Jamaican meals with cooking steps that could not have been accurately reflected by reading the recipe alone. Special holidays can be observed by learning how to make traditional foods, such as latkes at Chanukah or pancakes on Shrove Tuesday.

A program that successfully shares diverse cultural experiences has processes in place to plan, implement, and evaluate diverse programming. It is important that consultation occurs with cultural "experts." These experts can be family members, community systems, or the children and youth themselves. This consultation can help to determine how programming funds are used to ensure that materials reflect diversity and inclusion. Increasing diversity and experiencing cultures that are new or different increase the creativity of all participants in the milieu (Maddux, Adam, & Galinsky, 2010).

Discussion Opportunity 3:10

Craig begins working in a community centre that is primarily staffed by Caucasian CYCPs who are all from Anglo-Saxon backgrounds. Although the community centre users appear to be all Caucasian, there is a large population of Slavic immigrants. Craig encourages his staff team to post calendars that identify various cultural holidays. He also assigns summer students to investigate games and activities that may be familiar to children for the upcoming day camp programming. In subsequent team meetings, his staff discuss how easy it is to assume that all people of one visible skin colour identify in the same way culturally. By doing so, we rob those we work with (as well as ourselves) of the opportunities to learn how to celebrate each other's differences. Additionally, Canadian and American CYCPs may have insight about their own geographical communities that can be acknowledged.

3. Recognize and celebrate particular calendar events which are culturally specific.

It is important that meetings, special events, and training sessions are not scheduled on religious holidays. This is the most minimal action that can be taken to recognize and respect particular calendar events that are culturally specific. Learning what culturally specific events are and celebrating these can be expected in all settings where children/ youth visit. We all benefit from learning about others, travelling, trying foods and games, and playing with toys from and learning about other geographical areas or cultural groups (Tirrell-Corbin, 2015).

4. Encourage the sharing of such culture-specific events among members of the various cultural groups.

Cultural opportunities are all around us. We sometimes take for granted that others understand our cultural practices, experiences, and stories. The children, youth, and families we work with may also assume that others understand their cultural perspective, or they may know that they are isolated in their ways of knowing. Either way, there is opportunity to attend cultural events, share cultural foods, and share stories of customs and traditions. After July 2017, the City of Halifax now has four safe zones. Nova Scotians are proud that they have created spaces that will help others understand the impact of Residential Schools on First Nations peoples. Vegreville, Alberta, has a large sculpture of a *pysanka*, a Ukrainian-style Easter egg, that is a tourism spot. In the United States, an example of a cultural symbol is the pagoda that can be found in Reading, Pennsylvania, or a Dutch windmill that can be found in Holland, Michigan.

Luckily, the CYCPs of today can access cultural information using the Internet, where information can be not only obtained but also shared, helping those we work with learn more about their culture and perhaps their own identity or providing them with the resources to share this expertise and knowledge with us.

Discussion Opportunity 3:11

Ruth works in a community where many of the youth come from a Caribbean background. In the rural group home where Ruth works, the girls request hair grease that cannot be purchased at the local grocery store. Ruth is able to go online with the girls so they can choose the hair products they need for their hair.

Have you heard of the Ontario Provincial Advocate Hair Story Program? It provides an excellent example of sharing cultures within CYCP programs. Check it out by visiting https://provincialadvocate.on.ca/storyofmyhair/index.html. This program stresses that it is important for children and youth to experience a sense of belonging in the service provision they receive. Mentors and role models who also share similar cultural experiences can help to create a sense of safety for children/youth/families and communities while helping other CYCPs become informed allies.

c. Design and implement group work, counselling, and behavioural guidance with sensitivity to the client's individuality, age, development, and culture and human diversity

Group work, counselling, and behaviour guidance require CYCPs to take into consideration the individuality, age, development, and cultural and human diversity of children/youth/families and their communities (Burns, 2006). Designing and implementing programming for and with those we work alongside can ensure that we are both consulting and engaging. The adage "nothing about us, without us" is also applicable here (Charlton, 2000).

There are many sub-skills CYCPs need to develop for successfully facilitating groups. Groups are a common vehicle for the CYCP to interact with children and youth; therefore the CYCP needs to have, at a minimum, a foundational understanding of **group intervention**, for example, building relationships in groups, group stages (forming, storming, norming, performing [Tuckman, 1965] and adjourning [Tuckman & Jenson, 1977]), and group interventions such as in-the-moment skill development.

BUILDING RELATIONSHIPS IN GROUPS

The Child and Youth Care Practitioner often works with children/youth and families within groups. The skills we use to facilitate groups are not always the same skills we use when we work with individuals.

GROUP STAGES

The following chart is meant to provide a few examples of group and individual group member behaviours that can be observed in each stage of group development. There is space for the reader to add to these.

Group Stage	Activity Examples	Signs of Achievement
	What activities can be used to facilitate growth used in this stage?	What behaviour do you see in group members that will tell you this stage of group development has been achieved?
Forming	Invite group members to create a team name. Invite group members to think about group rules. Invite group members to create a contract. Ask the group to identify what the group's purpose is. Invite group members to identify group roles and be curious about who can take on these roles, such as chairperson or leader/recorder/time keeper.	Members call each other by names. Group members are spending time meeting.
Your Ideas		
Storming	Invite group members to reflect on their group contract and personal actions/their patterns of communication.	Group members appear to be struggling with group process or individual group members.
Your Ideas		
Norming	Invite group members to reflect on group contract and if individual group members are adhering to the contract.	Group members are adhering to their pre-established contract. Group members are contributing to group process by adhering to pre-determined roles.

Group Stage	Activity Examples	Signs of Achievement
Your Ideas		
Performing	Invite group members to identify how they will know that they are getting the job done.	The group purpose is being achieved.
Your Ideas		
Adjourning	Invite the group to determine post-group communication. Engage group members in activities that honour the efforts of the whole group and individual members.	The group can identify highlights of group functioning. They engage in group reflection and debrief functioning.
Your Ideas		

GROUP SKILLS

CYCPs often co-facilitate groups with other CYCPs. This requires CYCPs to respect each other as individuals and professionals and to create safety with each other and the group. There needs to be a balance of power, and roles and duties need to be clearly determined and adhered to.

Proficiency in counselling skill development requires not only an understanding of theory to practice but the opportunity to practise skills and be supported by the supervisor and other CYCP mentors.

Behaviour guidance is an opportunity within the relationship to teach new skills, gain new knowledge, and have a reciprocal experience. This relationship teaches us about ourselves and provides opportunities for us to be both authentic and genuine. Reflection follows for all parties.

As practitioners, we have to practise making nonverbal messages match verbal messages (Crisis Prevention Institute [CPI], 2016). Behaviour guidance is different than behaviour management. Instead of controlling (managing) the behaviour of those we work with, behaviour guidance means being a translator of behaviour, such as:

- Identifying and labelling concerning behaviours without shaming
- Explaining how behaviour impacts those around us (Tanis & Warger, 1999)
- Helping children/youth and families understand what precipitates their behaviour (Pudney & Whitehouse, 2012)
- Helping children and youth understand what precipitates the behaviour of self and others (Kuypers, 2016)
- Helping children/youth and families experience the joy of interacting with those that we are in relationship with (Booth, 2015)

Discussion Opportunity 3:12

Adriana works with a nine-year-old boy who needs lots of vestibular input. He often moves his body back and forth so much that chairs become unglued. Instead of having to remind him regularly to try and sit still, she engages him in a conversation to ask what he thinks he needs. He uses a yoga ball at home; hence she requests that the school purchase a yoga ball for him. The yoga ball provides the opportunity for him to sway and bounce so that he can focus enough to complete academic tasks.

Some team members identify that the child is being rewarded for what they see as "problematic" behaviour. Adriana explains (with the help of the school's occupational therapist) that his body movements serve a need and prevent him from making impulsive choices.

How is the CYC demonstrating sensitivity to the nine-year-old boy's individuality? Do you believe that staff are rewarding the boy's behaviour?

d. Demonstrate an understanding of sensitive cultural and human diversity practice in setting appropriate boundaries and limits on behaviour, including risk-management decisions

SENSITIVITY TO CULTURE AND HUMAN DIVERSITY

It is important to understand a child/youth/family/community by being sensitive to their culture and human diversity. It is difficult to be sensitive to culture and human diversity if you do not know what you do not know. Instead, CYCPs should become curious when working with any individual/family or community that does things differently than how they have experienced the world. Seek to learn what you do not know and then work toward understanding it.

SETTING APPROPRIATE BOUNDARIES/LIMITS ON BEHAVIOUR

When setting boundaries and limits, it is important for CYCPs to be sensitive to the culture of the children/youth/families/communities they work with. For example, some families may have practices around mealtimes that differ from the experiences of the CYCP. The CYCP needs to be curious about these practices in order to understand the purposes they serve. Some cultures may expect children to be quiet—children are seen and not heard—while others invite children to voice their ideas, concerns, and feelings. Navigating these variances requires a curious Child and Youth Care Practitioner who can look at the needs of the child/youth/family/community as well as the practice setting where contact is occurring.

RISK-MANAGEMENT DECISIONS

CYCPs need to be comfortable with having clear boundaries to ensure that a sense of safety is provided. This means that when the rule in the group home is that there is no rough play, the CYCP should recognize the need for physical activity while also ensuring that program rules are adhered to. CYCPs need to gain confidence in their role of setting limits. For examples, CYCPs working with children who have had multiple previous caregivers may need to be very clear about expectations in order to prevent the child from feeling that they need to control the environment and all those in it. The first step to intervening in a crisis or preventing a crisis is to know that the CYCP is responsible for creating and maintaining safety and reducing risk factors. **Risk factors** can be anything that can increase the chances for harm for any member in the relationship. Risk-management decisions can only be made when all aspects of the situation are clear. Policy and protocols are also sourced and utilized.

Discussion Opportunity 3:13

Suppose a seven-year-old child (who is the oldest of three children) has lots of experience helping his parents empty and fill his siblings' lunchboxes. He climbs up and down from stools to access juice boxes and requires little direction to safely maneuver around the hostel kitchen.

Another seven-year-old has had little experience in household chores. One day, when his mom was folding laundry, he tried to make his lunch for school tomorrow. The CYCP suggested to him that he should wait for his mom to make lunch (as this is a hostel rule anyway), and the child became rude.

The CYCP is worried that, without prior experience navigating around the kitchen, he could get hurt opening and closing cupboards and using the kitchen stool. This is an in-the-moment risk-management decision the CYCP needed to make, taking into consideration all that he/she/ze/they knew about the child and the milieu.

What can you say to a child who appears to be trying something that he has not had experience doing before, which could mean that he could build resiliency but also carries a risk he could get hurt? How can you balance risk-management decisions with limits on boundaries or behaviour?

Chapter 3 Learning Outcomes Evaluation

- Please provide two examples of competencies noted under the cultural and human diversity domain of CYC practice that are areas of strength.
- Please provide a field example that demonstrates the application of a competency in this domain.
- Please provide an example of a competency that you observed being demonstrated by a colleague.
- How would you use the language of these competencies in discussions in the classroom or workshops with colleagues? Provide two examples.
- Do you have artifacts (e.g., a journal entry, drawing, certificates) that provide evidence of competency strengths?
- What are competencies that you can develop in the cultural and human diversity domain of practice? (You can use Appendix A as a resource.) Develop a SMART goal in relation to one competency.

REFERENCES

Atal, Y. (2015). *Sociology study of the social sphere* (2nd edition). New Delhi: Pearson Education.

Andrews, J., Shaw, P., & Lomas, G. (2011). Deafness and hearing loss. In D. P. Hallahan & P. Pullen (Eds.), *Handbook of special education* (pp. 233–246). Upper Saddle River, NJ: Pearson Higher Education.

Arnold, R., Burke, B., James, C., Martin, D., & Thomas. B. (1991). *Educating for a change.* Toronto, ON: Doris Marshall Institute for Education and Action and Between the Lines Press.

Booth, P. (2015). In K. J. O'Connor, C. E. Schaefer, L. D. Braverman (Eds.), *Handbook of play therapy.* Hoboken, NJ: John Wiley & Sons.

Burns, M. (2006). *Healing spaces: The therapeutic milieu in child and youth work.* Kingston, ON: Child Care Press.

Charlton, J. I. (2000). *Nothing about us without us: Disability oppression and empowerment.* Los Angeles, CA: University of California Press.

Child and Youth Care Certification Board (CYCCB). (2016). Cultural & human diversity. College Station, TX: Author. Retrieved from https://www.cyccb.org/competencies/cultural-human-diversity

Crisis Prevention Institute (CPI). (2016). *CPI's top 10 de-escalation tips.* Milwaukee, WI: Author.

Delano, F. (2004). Beyond cultural diversity: Moving along the road to delivering culturally competent services to children and families. *Journal of Child and Youth Care Work, 19,* 26–30.

Garfat, T. (1993). On blind spots and blank spots. *Journal of Child and Youth Care, 8*(4), v–vii.

Garfat, T. (1998). The effective child and youth care intervention. *Journal of Child and Youth Care, 12*(1–2), 1–168.

Garfat, T. (2004). Meaning making and intervention in child and youth care practice. *Scottish Journal of Residential Child Care, 3*(1), 9–16.

Gharabaghi, K., & Anderson-Nathe, B. (2012). The problems and prospects of culture. *Child & Youth Services, 33*, 89–91.

Kuypers, L. (2016, November). All the zones are OK!: Tips for managing the zones you're in. *Social Thinking.* Retrieved from https://www.socialthinking.com/Articles?name=all-the-zones-are-ok

Ludy-Dobson, C. R., & Perry, B. D. (2010). The role of healthy relational interactions in buffering the impact of childhood trauma. In E. Gil (Ed.), *Working with children to heal interpersonal trauma: The power of play* (pp. 26–43). New York, NY: Guildford Press.

Lundy, T. (2008). Presence and participation: Being at the heart of change. In G. Bellefeuille & F. Ricks (Eds.), *Standing on the precipice: Inquiry into the creative potential of child and youth care practice* (pp. 207–230). Edmonton, AB: MacEwan Press.

Maddux, W. W., Adam, H., & Galinsky, A. D. (2010). When in Rome . . . Learn why the Romans do what they do: How multicultural learning experiences facilitate creativity. *Personality and Social Psychology Bulletin, 36*(6), 731–741. doi: 10.1177/0146167210367786.

Moore, P. (2001). Critical components of an anti-oppressive framework. *Journal of Child and Youth Care, 14*(3), 25–32.

National Association for the Deaf. (n.d.). *Position statement on quality foster care services continuum for deaf children.* Retrieved from https://www.nad.org/about-us/position-statements/position-statement-on-quality-foster-care-services-continuum-for-deaf-children/

Ontario Government. (2016). *Child and youth care program standard.* Retrieved May 1, 2017, from http://www.tcu.gov.on.ca/pepg/audiences/colleges/progstan/humserv/60701e.pdf

Pudney, W., & Whitehouse, E. (2012). *Little volcanoes: Helping young children and their parents to deal with anger.* London, UK: Jessica Kingsley Publishers.

Rimer, P., & Prager, B. (2016). *Reaching out: Working together to identify and respond to child victims of abuse.* Scarborough, ON: Nelson College Indigenous.

Safe Space Network. (n.d.). *What is a safe space.* Retrieved from http://safespacenetwork.tumblr.com/Safespace

Sebald, A. M. (2008). Child abuse and deafness: An overview. *American Annals of the Deaf, 153*(4), 376–383.

Snow, K. (2009). Vulnerable citizens. *CYC-Online: E-journal of International Child and Youth Care Network,* (130). Retrieved from http://www.cyc-net.org/cyc-online/cyconline-dec2009-snow.html

Sue, D. W. (2010). *Microaggressions and marginality: Manifestation, dynamics and impact.* Hoboken, NJ: Wiley.

Sue, D. W., Capodilupo, C. M., Torino, G. C., Bucceri, J. M., Holder, A. M. B., Nadal, K. L., & Esquilin, M. (2007). Racial microaggressions in everyday life: Implications for clinical practice. *American Psychologist, 62*(4), 271–286. doi: 10.1037/0003-066X.62.4.271

Tanis, B., & Warger, C. (1999). The amazing discoverers' club: Helping youngsters understand human behavior. *Reclaiming Children and Youth, 8*(1), 20.

Tirrell-Corbin, C. (2015, August). How to teach children about cultural awareness and diversity. *PBS Parents Online.*

Tuckman, B. W. (1965). Developmental sequence in small groups. *Psychological Bulletin, 63*(6), 384–399.

Tuckman, B. W., & Jensen, M. A. (1977). Stages in small group development revisited. *Group and Organizational Studies, 2*(4), 419–427. doi: 10.1177/105960117700200404

Truth and Reconciliation Commission of Canada. (2015). *Honouring the truth, reconciling for the future: Summary of the final report of the Truth and Reconciliation Commission of Canada.* Ottawa, ON: Author.

University of Victoria. (n.d.) *Cultural safety: Module two: People's experiences of oppression glossary.* Retrieved May 27, 2018, from https://web2.uvcs.uvic.ca/courses/csafety/mod2/glossary.htm

UNICEF. (2011). *Communicating with children: Principles and practice to nurture, inspire, excite, educate and heal.* New York, NY: Author.

VanderVen, K. (1991). How is child and youth care work unique—and different—from other fields? *Journal of Child and Youth* Care, *5*(1), 15–19.

Wahler, E. A. (2011). Identifying and challenging social work students' biases. *Social Work Education, 31*(8), 1058–1070. doi:10.1080/02615479.2011.616585

Wallace, L., Debicki, A., Vander Vennen, M. V., & de Visch Eybergen, E. (2015). Canadian WrapAround: A case study of a volunteer-driven, community-based approach for families, children, and youth with complex needs in Hamilton, Ontario. *Relational Child and Youth Care Practice, 27*(4), 53–66.

CHAPTER 4

Applied Human Development

Learning Outcomes

This chapter will help you to meet the following objectives:

- Review the applied human development domain of CYC practice.
- Apply the domain and competencies to field examples.
- Engage in discussion with colleagues about the domain and competencies.
- Identify areas of strength and development.

Professional CYC practitioners promote the optimal development of children, youth, and their families in a variety of settings. The developmental-ecological perspective (Bronfenbrenner, 1979; Bronfenbrenner & Ceci, 1994; Bronfenbrenner & Morris, 2006) emphasizes the interaction between persons and their physical and social environments, including cultural and political settings. Special attention is given to the everyday lives of children and youth, including those at risk and with special needs, within the family, neighbourhood, school, and larger sociocultural context. Professional CYCPs integrate current knowledge of human development with the skills, expertise, objectivity, and self-awareness essential for developing, implementing, and evaluating effective programs and services (Child and Youth Care Certification Board [CYCCB], 2017).

A. FOUNDATIONAL KNOWLEDGE

The professional practitioner is well versed in current research and theory in human development, with an emphasis on a developmental-ecological perspective.

- Lifespan human development
- Child and adolescent development as appropriate for the arena of practice (including domains of cognitive, socio-emotional, physiological, psychosexual, and spiritual development)
- Exceptionality in development (including at-risk and special needs circumstances such as trauma, child abuse/neglect, developmental psychopathology, and developmental disorders)
- Family development, systems, and dynamics

B. PROFESSIONAL COMPETENCIES

1. Contextual-Developmental Assessment

a. Assess different domains of development across various contexts

CYCPs strive to look at a child's functioning from a holistic perspective. Many Aboriginal peoples believe wellness is achieved through the balance of body, mind, emotion, and spirit. Holistic health incorporates the physical, mental, emotional, and spiritual needs of the individual, family, and community (Fearn, 2006). Child and Youth Care Practitioners assess relational functioning; mental wellness; strengths; psychosocial and cognitive, spiritual, and ethical functioning; motor skills; and the behavioural domains of development across different contexts. In order to better understand the effects of multiple environmental factors on children's cognitive and socio-emotional development, a holistic, multidisciplinary, and multilevel approach that encompasses the complex interactions between biological, physical, and psychosocial factors impacting children's developmental outcomes is needed (Ferguson, Cassells, MacAllister, & Evans, 2013).

INDIVIDUAL ASPECTS OF HOLISTIC YOUTH DEVELOPMENT

- Personal health
- Educational learning
- Communication
- Self-confidence
- Personal and social responsibility
- Self-independence
- Family and friends
- Community aspects of holistic youth development

- Everyday care and help
- Personal safety
- Community relationships
- Play and fun
- Guidance and support
- Right responsibilities
- Understanding family background

WORLD ASPECTS OF HOLISTIC YOUTH DEVELOPMENT

- Support from friends and the larger community
- School and learning opportunities
- Access to local resources of all sorts, including educational, recreational, social, spiritual, cultural, and economic
- Opportunities to generate, contribute, and consolidate resources for the community, family, and self
- Safe, comfortable housing
- Belonging (Fletcher, 2014)

CYCPs need to have a foundational understanding of expected development of individuals in order to have a *baseline* to compare developmental versus cognitive functioning. For example, it is important to understand how early speech develops or when a child engages in magical thinking (Piaget, 1969) to understand how to plan and intervene for this individual.

Discussion Opportunity 4:1

Andreas attends a community camp. He is 14 years of age and has a diagnosis of autism. He enjoys drawing, birdwatching, and swimming. The community camp has planned for Andreas to be placed in a group with other teens who are his age, but like soccer and track and field. The CYCP (who was hired as a camp coordinator for youth with special needs) states that she wants to meet with Andreas before placing him in any groups to ensure he is placed in a group that matches his needs, abilities, strengths, and interests. After meeting Andreas, she places him in a group with younger children who share his interest with birdwatching and drawing. The youth plan to create a book of birds that are often seen in Whitehorse, Yukon, that will be published as a fundraiser for the community centre.

How did the CYCP ensure that Andreas's developmental needs were met?

Different contexts can have significant influence on child and youth development. It is not uncommon for a teacher to have a different perspective on a child's development versus the parent's perspective. For example, a parent has shared that their child's behaviour at home is destructive, and people from the community provided feedback that the child responds well with direction. Each person and setting provides valuable information about the relationships to different people, given we know that children can perform differently depending on the relationships they share in the life space.

b. Evaluate the developmental appropriateness of environments with regard to the individual needs of clients

CYCPs need to consistently evaluate if the environment is developmentally appropriate to meet the needs of children, youth, and families. If the fit is not an effective match, it will be more challenging for needs to be met successfully. Prior to exposing children and youth to an environment, CYCPs need to assess if the environment will support the development of the child, youth, and family. Assessing "fit" is an important step to ensuring that children and youth will successfully have their needs met. Goodness of fit is supported, in that having a good fit between teacher–child relationship and temperament is predictive of increased prosocial behaviour (Hipson & Séguin, 2016).

For example, Khasan is academically struggling in his mainstream classroom while displaying aggressive behaviours at school. The recommended program has a suspension policy for any demonstrated aggression. This program may match Khasan's educational needs but not psychosocial needs. The CYCP takes into consideration all needs when assessing and implementing interventions.

c. Assess client and family needs in relation to community opportunities, resources, and supports

According to the **ecological model**, we never assess children and youth in isolation from their environment (Bronfenbrenner, 1979). Communities are extensions of families. CYCPs need to assess how the needs of children, youth, and families are being met in relationship to their community. What opportunities does their community provide that support the child's, youth's, and family's needs?

CYCPs assess needs before implementing approaches, strategies, and interventions. CYCPs also assess these needs thinking holistically and systemically with children/youth/families and the life spaces and communities that they function in (VanderVen, 1991).

Discussion Opportunity 4:2

Angelo lives in a small community, and he is an exceptional artist. Neither his local school nor his community provides him with opportunities to develop his artistic skills. Angelo struggles academically, and he all but stops practising his art. As his art is impacted, so is his willingness to attend school. If Angelo were living in a different community, his artistic, cognitive, and social development might receive total support.

If you were a CYCP working in Angelo's school, what ideas might you have to support his interests?

Who would you talk to if Angelo lived in your community and attended a local school?

Discussion Opportunity 4:3

Terry frequently has to use the food bank to feed her five children. Child protection is involved with the family to ensure basic needs are being met. Initially, Terry is allowed to use the food bank twice a week, but given that resources have become limited, the food bank's policy has changed to reduce food sharing to once a week per family. For a year, Terry takes the bus 40 kilometres to go to another food bank in another community. After a year, all community food banks develop a general database that records how often families use various food banks. Families then become restricted to any food bank use once weekly. This new change in the community had great impacts on Terry being able to meet her family's basic food security needs.

If you were the community CYCP, what could you do to decrease Terry's family's experience with food insecurity?

Discussion Opportunity 4:4

Tyler identifies as a trans male. Tyler is new to his community and wants to connect with LGBTQ2+ resources. The CYCP's assessment needs to include the opportunities, resources, and supports Tyler can use during his F2M (female-to-male) transition. More opportunities, resources, and support available to Tyler will ensure his optimal development.

If you had a magic wand, what resources, opportunities, and supports would you like the community to offer to Tyler? How can these systems impact the holistic development of this individual?

2. Sensitivity to Contextual Development in Relationships and Communication

a. Adjust for the effects of age, culture, background, experience, and developmental status on verbal and nonverbal communication

"Communication that balances and gives complementary attention to all their developmental needs best serves all children, from infants to adolescents" (UNICEF, 2011, p. 32). Children are not just their physical or developmental functioning, and they cannot be communicated to in isolation of their cognitive functioning. CYCPs respond to children holistically, taking into consideration all aspects of their functioning and potential.

CYCPs need to adjust their verbal and nonverbal communication according to the child's, youth's, and parent's age, culture, background, experience, and development status. It is imperative that CYCPs have an understanding of developmentally matched expectations to developmental stages (UNICEF, 2011, pp. 18–23). According to Battersby (2009), **nonverbal communication** is "the process of communication through sending and receiving wordless messages." This type of communication relies on your senses: sight, smell, touch, or even taste. You'll speak very differently to a 4-year-old in school versus an 18-year-old considering higher-level education. Culture has significant perspective on nonverbal and verbal communication. It is important that you do not generalize culture; instead have the child, youth, or family share with you their values and beliefs. One culture may interpret giving a hug as safety, while another culture may perceive a hug as intrusive. Experiences can have great impact on the developmental status of verbal and nonverbal communication.

Discussion Opportunity 4:5

Leroy lives primarily on the street and has had experiences that have shaped his development in communication. Leroy says, "You learn to observe signs to know if people are safe." He is sensitive to nonverbal communication when he is with others who also live on the street.

If you communicate the same way with Leroy versus someone who may not have the same experiences, your relationship with Leroy will be impacted. You could represent someone to be feared instead of someone who will provide support.

What nonverbal communication patterns will you intentionally share with Leroy?

Discussion Opportunity 4:6

Julianna is working the weekend shift at a closed custody residential centre. The staff decide to take the kids swimming. Given the pool acoustics, it is important not to talk loudly, so staff use sign language with youth to ensure they walk on the pool deck instead of running.

Explore different ways we communicate nonverbally with children and youth when we are not close enough to them to be heard.

b. Communicate with the client in a manner which is developmentally sensitive and that reflects the client's developmental strengths and needs

A core concept of the child and youth care field is to build on each child, youth, and family's strengths at each stage of development (Brendtro & Ness, 1995; Greene, 1998; Hewitt, 2005). Adjust communication according to the child, youth, and family's developmental capacity, then build on their strengths in order to meet needs. Communication comes in many forms. Children and youth will only communicate effectively if the other person receives the communication in a way that they can hear and understand. As CYCPs, it is our responsibility to match communication abilities respectfully and inclusively.

Discussion Opportunity 4:7

Leo stayed in school for every recess for a week. The CYCP from his group home takes him to the skateboard park. She walks beside Leo and listens to his story as he grinds the rails. After 30 minutes, Leo and the CYCP stop for a water break under a tree and chat about the difficult week Leo has experienced.

Reflect on your own life and identify how adults join with you to discuss strengths and needs.

Discussion Opportunity 4:8

The agency is planning a family camp. Families came in for a barbecue prior to camp to fill out forms and meet the other families. The CYCP hands out forms and notices that two parents do not fill out the camp forms. After everyone leaves, the couple shares that they struggle with reading and writing. The CYCP needs to be more sensitive to the parents' needs and not make assumptions. This CYCP assumed participants could fill forms out without needing additional supports or explanation. The last family in the room models the importance of being respectful to different needs of everyone and not making assumptions.

What other assumptions can a CYCP make about families and parents when planning events?

1. Recognize the influence of the child/youth's relationship history on the development of current relationships.

All our history influences who we are today and how we relate to others. For example, a history of many different factors can influence Aboriginal child development: "Social maladjustment, abuse of self and others and family breakdown are some of the symptoms prevalent among First Nation baby boomers. The 'Graduates' of the 'Ste Anne's Residential School' era are now trying and often failing to come to grips with life as adults after being raised as children in an atmosphere of fear, loneliness and loathing" (Royal Commission on Aboriginal Peoples, 1996, cited in Fearn, 2006). Our history influences our values, beliefs, and the ethics we live by. Embracing our history teaches where we have come from, where we are today, and what is important for our future. Our ancestors, who had the courage to speak for equality and diversity, paved the way for choices they may not have had. Embrace the children, youth, and families to share their history, particularly so you have an understanding of how the past impacts the present of who they are today.

Discussion Opportunity 4:9

Rosie shared that her parents were raised in Residential Schools, and she still experiences the pain and suffering her parents endured. It continues to impact Rosie's sense of safety in the world. Rosie's lack of safety has created anxiety and loneliness. She feels guilty and, to numb the loneliness, she will consume excessive amounts of alcohol.

Summer was raised in care and lived in multiple group homes before she found a foster family that did not give up on her. Even after 15 years of stable parents and love, she anticipates another move and continues to struggle in intimate relationships. She worries that everyone she cares for will leave her. Summer's history has impacted her social and emotional development.

Embrace your history and examine how it has continued to benefit/hinder your development. How could your parents respond to their history and how it impacted their development and parenting?

2. Employ displays of affection and physical contact that reflect sensitivity for individuality, age, development, cultural and human diversity, as well as consideration of laws, regulations, policies, and risks.

Affection and physical contact are vital for secure attachment. Physical contact with an attachment figure is the ultimate signal to the infant that he/she/ze/they are safe and secure (Weiss, Wilson, Hertenstein, & Campos, 2000). Physical contact is a central requirement of proximity and felt security (Bowlby, 1969). CYCPs need to be creative in how we offer affection and physical contact to children, youth, and families. It is important to ask the individual what feels safe for them, so we model and practise the respect of interpersonal boundaries, especially because we may not know the person's previous experience with touch.

A 12-year-old may feel more comfortable greeting someone with a "fist bump" over a hug, or perhaps a special handshake or just a simple "hi." Different cultures may display affection and physical contact in different ways. Be open to learning about how cultures greet. How do they say goodbye? Is it okay to touch your elbow or hand?

Respecting someone's request to say no to touch or physical contact is very important in order to build safety and honour the other person's intention to set limits (consent). All affection and physical contact must follow the law, agency regulations, the Code of Ethics, policies, and the child, youth, or family's request.

Discussion Opportunity 4:10

What are some expressions of affection that CYCPs can demonstrate with or without physical contact with colleagues and the children/youth and families you work with?

3. Respond to behaviour while encouraging and promoting several alternatives for the healthy expression of needs and feelings.

Behaviours are a great indicator that the child and youth are communicating with others. Anglin (2018) shared the concept of "pain-based behaviour," which indicates that behaviour is a way for a person to share their pain (Anglin, 2014; Glover, 2018). We look deeper into the behaviour and gain a greater understanding of the person's experience, thoughts, and feelings. We do not always understand the needs or feelings or thoughts that the behaviour is conveying. CYCPs teach clients the skill of expressing what they need, feel, and think to ensure they can communicate with them, rather than engaging in acting out behaviour that is not optimal for their development. CYCPs need to create space, educate, and allow opportunities to practise healthy methods of expression. Changing patterns of expression can take time and many lessons. We need to remember the behaviour is intended to meet a need. Allow opportunities for children and youth to learn to express any thoughts, feelings, and reactions in ways that convey respect, so that the recipient can get the message. This also includes in digital communication where possible and appropriate:

> The use of smartphones and apps has changed the way we communicate with one another and the methods by which we connect. When I think about a young person . . . potentially there is a sense of safety and security in sending the message (not having to be face-to-face), however, a written message is actually quite permanent (if kept, it can be read over at any time). Upon further reflection, perhaps it is purposeful—our text message

stream may read like a trail of appreciation and belonging, noting strengths and accomplishments; supporting a different way of being in the world. Maybe this new-ish method of communication has benefits for our practice. (De Monte, 2016)

c. Give accurate developmental information in a manner that facilitates growth

Many children and youth will ask, "Is it normal for . . . ?" CYCPs must give accurate developmental information in a way that facilitates growth in mental wellness, strengths, psychosocial and cognitive functioning, motor skills, and the behavioural domains of development across different contexts. Cognitive, social, and psychological well-being are also strength-based. Information must be shared in an effective way, which means it can be understood and presented accurately. If your own values or religious or spiritual beliefs conflict, supervision can support you until you have the knowledge and skills to share accurate information.

Margarita is pregnant at the age of 17. She asks the CYCP where she can get an abortion. The CYCP struggles with sharing this information because she has strong beliefs against abortion; however, with support, she is able to provide accurate information about where a nearby sexual health clinic is located.

Seven-year-old Blaine's mother is diagnosed with cancer. Blaine asks, "Is there is a heaven?" The CYCP answers, "What do you think?" Blaine tells her that her mother told her that heaven has beautiful gardens, bright colours, and fluffy clouds from where she watches over her. The CYCP supports Blaine's description of heaven and how a child understands loss and grief.

d. Partner with family in goal setting and designing developmental supports and interventions

Providing a sense of partnership with families, youth, and children is an important skill, because it empowers them to have a voice in the direction and goals they want to develop. Families, youth, and children must be actively engaged in developing supports and interventions that promote optimal development and change. Change requires a respectful process that engages everyone's commitment to the goals. When goal setting and designing a plan for change, families, youth, and children need to be included and empowered to use their voice to share what is best for them. They will teach us what they need.

e. Assist clients (to a level consistent with their development, abilities, and receptiveness) to access relevant information about legislation/regulations, policies/standards, and additional supports and services

Children, youth, and families need to be informed of their rights, regulations, policies, and standards. One such way is to share rights, such as the rights noted under the UN Convention on the Rights of the Child (1989); all countries have recognized the rights in the Convention, except the United States (Rothschild, 2017).

Rights information must be conveyed in ways that can be comprehended at the client's stage of development. In the case of child protection agencies in Ontario, Canada, children have their rights and responsibilities reviewed every 90 days during plan-of-care meetings.

Those we walk alongside benefit from learning about services and supports that assist children, youth, and families and support their rights. These services and supports can ultimately replace the need for the CYCP! CYCPs can provide advocacy, office contact information, and information on community resources that can support children/youth and families.

3. Practice Methods That Are Sensitive to Development and Context

a. Support development in a broad range of circumstances in different domains and contexts

CYCPs need to consider development from a range of circumstances and different contexts. For example, how does joining a hockey team help develop motor and social skills? How can the social skills learned in that environment be transferred to school and academic working groups? How can belonging to a place of faith affect moral, emotional, and psychological development? How can working on relational skills with a child support the child's development with family members and friends, at future jobs, and in education? We need to build on the strengths of children, youth, and families in order to develop in various contexts. The relationship with the CYCP is a safe place to practise development and reflect on the learning, and discover how to transfer the learning to other relationships and systems.

Discussion Opportunity 4:11

What skills have you learned from your family that are transferred to your social, educational, and employment skills? What areas of development do you want to enhance that will support your CYC development?

b. Design and implement programs and planned environments, including activities of daily living, which integrate developmental, preventive, and/or therapeutic objectives into the life space through the use of developmentally sensitive methodologies and techniques

CYCPs design and implement programs that include skills for daily living and support future development. Miranda lived in care from age 8 to 18, and when she no longer could live in residential care, her transition to independent living (for the first time in her life) was very stressful. Transitional support assists her in organizing her home and learning how to shop, budget, take public transit, open a bank account, and look for employment. After three months, Miranda feels more comfortable living on her own, but struggles with budgeting and setting limits with peers. The focus needs to be on learning how to make better choices that will continue to support her independent living.

Discussion Opportunity 4:12

Tatianna is a single mom and works long hours. Morning routines are a challenge. The school has noticed that the children either come in late or miss school altogether. The children are 4, 10, and 15 years of age. The community CYCP supports Tatianna at 7:00 a.m. to model morning routines that are important for everyone. Once the children are off to school, the CYCP helps structure Tatianna's evening routines.

Brainstorm creative ways the CYCP can support Tatianna in developing a bedtime routine for each of her children. What activities can be implemented to support the whole family and each child as an individual?

CYCPs design programs that build relationships and communicate respect without judgment. The goal is to set up systems that support the well-being of a family and opportunities for the children in education and community. What are daily living skills that are important for relationship building and child development? CYCPs make meaning of daily life events within the life space (Garfat, 1998; Krueger, 1998; Wilder, 2007).

Prevention: Developmentally Sensitive Methodologies

CYCPs develop and facilitate preventative programs in various milieus. School CYCPs may run lunchtime mindfulness, social skills, friendship, and anti-bullying programs. These are especially valuable as interventions directed to children who may need opportunities to learn and practise **self-regulation**. Community CYCPs may provide healthy sexuality or needle exchange programs. Suicide prevention programs may be initiated in communities that have high suicide rates. Each of these preventative programs is planned intentionally and sensitively with the children/youth/families' and community's needs in mind in order to build resilience and reduce crisis. Each type of intervention has to be carefully and intentionally provided in accordance with the developmental (not chronological) needs of those the CYCP is walking alongside (Oles, 1991).

c. Individualize plans to reflect differences in culture/human diversity, background, temperament, personality, and differential rates of development across the domains of human development

Each individual child, youth, and family deserves a strengths-based plan that meets their cultural, diversity, temperament, and personal needs across the domains of human development. Students deserve individual academic plans that support their learning and social development in a nurturing environment. It is important to consider the temperament of the CYCP along with the child/youth/family and community with which they are developing a therapeutic alliance.

Discussion Opportunity 4:13

When you were a child, what individual consideration could have supported your development? If you could have had an accommodation at school, what would it have been and how would it have benefited your learning? How do you think your temperament aligned with that of adults with whom you developed relationships?

d. Design and implement group work, counselling, and behavioural guidance, with sensitivity to the client's individuality, age, development, and culture

CYCPs design many different groups, for example, social skills programs, camps, life skills programs, employment groups, activity-based groups, and so on. The relational practice of groups supports development by using guided interactions and modelling to create a safe environment for taking risks and learning. Many children and youth express themselves through behaviours, which can be understood as symptoms of communicating a need. Guiding children and youth to develop communication skills and more effective behaviours meets their needs.

What are some examples of behaviour guidance that supports children and youth?

What type of group do you hope to design and for what population?

e. Employ developmentally sensitive expectations in setting appropriate boundaries and limits

When CYCPS set appropriate limits and boundaries, they connect these with the development of group members. Each milieu has different boundaries and limits. Boundaries and limits allow children to have clear expectations that offer predictability and safety (Fraser, 2011; Mann-Feder, 1999). CYCPs need to clearly highlight boundaries in the relationship right from the beginning, just as boundaries (Mahler, Pine, & Bergman, 1975) and connections are developed for the infant with their primary caregiver (Bowlby, 1969; Schore, 2000).

It is important to support the child or youth developmentally by teaching and modelling how to respect boundary and limits in relationships. In-the-moment interventions are effective in relationships with children and youth who need to learn about boundaries. Children and youth then can transfer this knowledge to other relationships in different settings. Boundaries and limits will change in keeping with the development of the child and youth, for whom developmental transitions can be confusing until new boundaries are established.

Discussion Opportunity 4:14

What boundaries and limits did you have as part of your childhood? Which were difficult for you to accept? Which made you feel safe? How will your practice maintain boundaries and limits, yet accommodate different developmental stages?

f. Create and maintain a safe and growth-promoting environment

A safe and nurturing environment encourages children and youth to take risks in relationships and supports their learning (Perry, 2009). Promoting acceptance and a sense of belonging while creating an environment that empowers children and youth toward exploration leads to development growth.

g. Make risk-management decisions that reflect sensitivity for individuality, age, development, culture, and human diversity, while also ensuring a safe and growth-promoting environment

Risk-management decisions reflect sensitivity to individuality, age, development, culture, and human diversity while contributing to environments that are growth promoting. Programs and agencies in today's world also need to provide support while taking into consideration factors such as technology and emergency response systems (Lu, Jain, & Zhang, 2016). It is a challenge, however, to have these decisions reflect the needs of all persons in the milieu. For example, self-reported peanut allergy doubled among children between 1997 and 2002, and peanut allergies, tree nut allergies, or both continue to be reported by more than three million Americans (Sicherer, Muñoz-Furlong, & Sampson, 2003, p. 1206). Considering the seriousness of this allergy, it is an increasing health concern.

Many schools around North America ban peanut butter products. They do not, however, instruct students to wash their hands first thing in the morning. Any child that has peanut butter on their hands (from breakfast) could touch a doorknob or common space, and a child with a nut injury could be impacted. The other side of the argument is about the impact of banning an affordable protein on other community members. In 2015, the Canada Daily Bread Food Bank in Toronto, Ontario, distributed an estimated 141,000 pounds of peanut butter because it is an inexpensive protein for families facing food insecurity (Sharma, 2016). The risk-management decision of banning nuts to prevent fatal allergic reactions has a negative impact on students who will lack a balanced lunch due to affordability.

Safety is always the main priority in any relationship we develop. Risk-management plans need to take into consideration the individual's age development, culture, and diversity. If the child and youth have the cognitive capacity to help develop the risk-management plan, it is important to include them. Each individualized plan can ensure the person's dignity is respected and also continue to ensure that person feels safe while balancing the needs of the many.

Discussion Opportunity 4:15

Giordano attends a treatment class that has seven other students. He frequently becomes aggressive in class and at times destroys other students' things. The team create a risk-management plan without Giordano, which means he is withdrawn from class and put in the quiet room whenever he acts out. Instead of helping him, the isolation causes his behaviour to escalate, and he is very vocal. Staff do not understand that Giordano is communicating a sense of abandonment that causes him great fear. Reviewing the plan with him results in staff learning the source of his anxiety. They also become aware of his history, including that his parents experienced substance dependence and, as a result of their challenges, he has been raised in multiple care settings. Creating a plan that works for him can both allow him to stay in class and also decrease his acts of aggression.

Brainstorm other activities Giordano can engage in that will create safety, decrease aggression, and regulate his emotions.

4. Access Resources That Support Healthy Development

a. Locate and critically evaluate resources which support healthy development

CYCPs locate and evaluate resources that support healthy development for the children/youth and families that they engage with. Parents can be excellent sources for connections and information about what is available in the community, in addition to the resources CYCPs already know. For example, a mother knew which churches in her community provided free dinners and clothing. The more connections, the greater the depth of support and opportunity for children, youth, and families.

Discussion Opportunity 4:16

Imagine that your team will be given $1,000 to create a resource in the community for teenagers. You can identify the community (big/small, rural/urban) and the unmet development needs of youth. Then design a resource that will be available. Be creative! What is your team going to do?

b. Empower clients and programs in gaining resources which support healthy development

A very important role for CYCPs is to advocate for the maintenance of ongoing services and for the development of additional services to meet the needs of children, youth, and families. The CYCP will then direct others to utilize these services but also to consult on their effectiveness to service providers. A strengths-based approach to learning and self-teaching puts children, youth, and families in a position of self-reliance and capacity building. Best practice for a CYCP is to provide opportunities for children, youth, and families to grow, and for communities and individuals in their milieu to benefit from their experience. One example of youth empowerment is discussed in Jeary (2001), where a school community involves students in the creation of a resource manual for safe and caring schools. The manual is subsequently used throughout the province of Alberta elementary and secondary schools.

Chapter 4 Learning Outcomes Evaluation

- Please provide a field example that demonstrates the application of a competency in this applied human development.
- Please provide an example of a competency that you observed being demonstrated by a colleague.
- How would you use the language of these competencies in discussions in the classroom or workshops with colleagues? Provide two examples.
- Do you have artifacts (e.g., a journal entry, drawing, certificate) that provide evidence of competency strengths?
- What are competencies that you can develop in the cultural and human diversity domain of practice? (You can use Appendix A as a resource.) Develop a SMART goal in relation to one competency.

REFERENCES

Anglin, J. P. (2014). Pain-based behaviour with children and adolescents in conflict. *Reclaiming Children and Youth, 22*(4), 53–55.

Anglin, J. P. (2018, May). From pain and survival to effective action and flourishing. Paper session presented at Child and Youth Care Association of British Columbia, Richmond, BC.

Battersby, S. L. (2009). Nonverbal communication: Increasing awareness in the general music classroom. *General Music Today, 22*(3), 14–18. doi:10.1177/1048371309331498

Bowlby, J. (1969). *Attachment and loss* (vol. 1): *Attachment.* New York, NY: Basic Books.

Brendtro, L., & Ness, A. (1995). Fixing flaws or building strengths? *Reclaiming Children and Youth, 4*(2), 2–7.

Bronfenbrenner, U. (1979). *The ecology of human development: Experiments by nature and design.* Cambridge, MA: Harvard University Press.

Bronfenbrenner, U. (1994). Ecological models of human development. *Readings on the Development of Children, 2*(1), 37–43.

Bronfenbrenner, U., & Ceci, S. J. (1994). Nature-nurture reconceptualized in developmental perspective: A bioecological model. *Psychological Review, 101*(4), 568–586.

Bronfenbrenner, U., & Morris, P. A. (2006). The bioecological model of human development. In R. M. Lerner & W. Damon (Eds.), *Handbook of child psychology: Theoretical models of human development* (pp. 793–828). Hoboken, NJ: John Wiley & Sons.

Child and Youth Care Certification Board (CYCCB). (2017). III. Applied human development. Retrieved January 25, 2018, from https://www.cyccb.org/competencies/applied-human-development

De Monte, A. (2016). The internet of relationships. *CYC-Online: E-journal of the International Child and Youth Care Network (CYC-Net),* (206), 36–38. Retrieved May 20, 2018, from https://www.cyc-net.org/cyc-online/apr2016.pdf

Fearn, T. (2006). *A sense of belonging: Supporting healthy child development in Aboriginal families.* Best Start: Ontario's Maternal, Newborn and Early Child Development Resource Center.

Ferguson, K. T., Cassells, R. C., MacAllister, J. W., & Evans, G. W. (2013). The physical environment and child development: An international review. *International Journal of Psychology /Journal International de Psychologie, 48*(4), 437–468. doi:10.1080/00207594.2013.804190

Fletcher, A. (2014). *A short guide to holistic youth development.* Olympia, WA: The Freechild Project.

Fraser, T. (2011). *Adopting a child with a trauma and attachment disruption history: A practical guide.* Ann Arbor, MI: Loving Healing Press.

Garfat, T. (1998). The effective child and youth care intervention. *Journal of Child and Youth Care, 12*(1–2), 1–168.

Glover, L. (2018). Exploring early adolescents' experiences of their challenging behaviour in a child and youth care centre. Retrieved September 2018 from https://repository.nwu.ac.za/bitstream/handle/10394/31136/GloverL.pdf?sequence=1&isAllowed=y

Greene, R. (1998). *The explosive child.* New York, NY: Harper Collins.

Hewitt, M. B. (2005). The importance of taking a strength-based perspective. *Reclaiming Children and Youth, 14*(1), 23–26.

Hill, A., Watson, J., Rivers, D., & Joyce, M. (2007). *Key themes in interpersonal communication: Culture, identities and performance.* Maidenhead, UK: McGraw-Hill Education.

Hipson, E. W., & Séguin, G. D. (2016). Is good fit related to good behaviour? Goodness of fit between daycare teacher–child relationships, temperament and prosocial behaviour. *Journal Early Child Development and Care, 186*(5), 785–798. doi:10.1080/03004430.2015.1061518

Jeary, J. (2001). Students and teachers develop a resource manual for safe and caring schools. *Reclaiming Children and Youth, 9*(4), 207–209.

Krueger, M. (1998). *Interactive youth work practice.* Washington, DC: CWLA.

Lu, J., Jain, L. C., & Zhang, G. (Eds.). (2016). *Handbook on decision making* (vol. 2). New York, NY: Springer.

Mahler, M., Pine, F., & Bergman, A. (1975). *The psychological birth of the human infant: Symbiosis and individuation.* New York, NY: Basic Books.

Mann-Feder, V. R. (1999). You/me/us: Thoughts on boundary management in child and youth care. *Journal of Child and Youth Care, 13*(2), 93–98.

Oles, T. P. (1991). Matching therapeutic style with developmental level: A guide for child care workers. *Journal of Child and Youth Care, 6*(3), 63–72.

Piaget, J. (1969). *The child's conception of the world.* Totowa, NJ: Littlefield, Adams & Co.

Perry, B. D. (2009). Examining child maltreatment through a neurodevelopmental lens: Clinical applications of the neurosequential model of therapeutics. *Journal of Loss and Trauma, 14*(4), 240–255. doi: 10.1080/15325020903004350

Rothschild, A. (2017). Is America holding out on protecting children's rights? *The Atlantic.* Retrieved April 19, 2019, from https://www.theatlantic.com/education.archive/2017-05/holding-out-on-childrens-rights/524652

Sharma, N. (2016). Peanut free spaces have dire consequences for food bank users. *Torontoist.* https://torontoist.com/2016/09/peanut-free-public-spaces-food-bank-users/

Schore, A. (2001). Attachment and regulation of the right brain. *Attachment & Human Development, 2*(1), 23–47. doi:10.1080/146167300361309

Sicherer, S. H., Muñoz-Furlong, A., & Sampson, H. A. (2003). Prevalence of peanut and tree nut allergy in the United States determined by means of random digit dial telephone survey: A five-year follow-up study. *Allergy and Clinical Immunology, 112*(6), 1203–1207. https://www.jacionline.org/article/S0091-6749(03)02026-8/abstract

UNICEF. (2011). *Communicating with children: Principles and practice to nurture, inspire, excite, educate and heal.* New York, NY: Author.

VanderVen, K. (1991). How is child and youth care work unique—and different—from other fields? *Journal of Child and Youth Care, 5*(1), 15–19.

Weiss, S. J., Wilson, P., Hertenstein, M. J., & Campos, R. (2000). The tactile context of a mother's caregiving: Implications for attachment of low birth weight infants. *Infant Behaviour and Development, (23),* 91–111.

Wilder, Q. (2007). Owning the job: How three youth workers make meaning of their work. *CYC-Online: E-journal of the International Child and Youth Care Network (CYC-Net), (107).* Retrieved from https://www.cyc-net.org/cyc-online/cycol-0712-wilder.html

CHAPTER 5

Relationship and Communication

Learning Outcomes

This chapter will help you to meet the following objectives:

- Review the relationship and communication domain of CYC practice.
- Apply the domain and competencies to field examples.
- Engage in discussion with colleagues about the domain and competencies.
- Identify areas of strength and development.

The Child and Youth Care Certification Board (2016) states that:

> Practitioners recognize the critical importance of relationships and communication in the practice of quality child and youth care. Ideally, the service provider and client work in a collaborative manner to achieve growth and change. "Quality first" practitioners develop genuine relationships based on empathy and positive regard. They are skilled at clear communication, both with clients and with other professionals. Observations and records are objective and respectful of their clients. Relationship and communication are considered in the context of the immediate environment and its conditions; the policy and legislative environment; and the historical and cultural environment of the child, youth or family with which the practitioner interacts.

A. FOUNDATIONAL KNOWLEDGE

- Characteristics of helping relationships
- Characteristics of healthy interpersonal relationships
- Cultural differences in communication styles
- Developmental differences in communication
- Communication theory (verbal and nonverbal)
- Group dynamics and teamwork theory
- Family dynamics and communication patterns (including attachment theory as it relates to communication style)

B. PROFESSIONAL COMPETENCIES

1. Interpersonal Communication

a. Adjust for the effects of age, cultural and human diversity, background, experience, and development of verbal and nonverbal communication

Both verbal and nonverbal communication between people are complex and challenging in relationships. The nature and quality of our interactions are impacted by our age, culture, human diversity, background, and experience. Understanding each of these factors and their underlying concepts is key to the quality of relationship a CYCP will have with clients and peers and, in fact, with just about anyone. Foremost must be the recognition that every one of us brings our unique individuality to our relationships. It need not be only our similarities that bind us together. If we acknowledge and respect our differences, and even see them as complementary and full of possibilities, our interactions can be even more meaningful and enriching. The great diversity of background and experiences among us can be a source of intrigue and fascination, and an object of exploration, reflection, acceptance, supportiveness, and celebration.

Society has come a long way in improving how we communicate. In the past, children did not have a voice—they were meant to be seen and not heard. Until recently, it was still common practice to develop goals and recommend resources without the child present or participating. Now we understand how vital it is that children and youth add their voices to any discussion of their past, present, and future. Children and youth require adults that can hear, communicate, and connect with them. They are impacted when adults are unable to do so (Freeman, 2013).

Discussion Opportunity 5:1

1. If members of your family are silent, what does it mean for the relationship?
2. Do you think that your nonverbal communication matches your verbal communication? If so, what is an example of this? If not, what can you improve on?

3. Can you provide an example of a time where you could hear what an authority figure was saying but you felt that a different message was being communicated? If you can, also share how you felt in this interaction and/or this relationship?

4. How can you adjust the way you communicate for greater inclusivity?

We have also renewed and increased our recognition of the contribution of grandparents as storytellers and keepers of the family's culture and history, as well as significant caregivers. While many still believe that teenaged or single parents could never be able to provide a stable family environment, today we strive to redefine what a family is and expand the boundaries of its definition. We are beginning to grow in our consideration of historical facts with respect to acknowledging that some cultures have been oppressed by others; others have benefited from such exploitation.

There is an increased understanding that some cultures parent collectively, which acknowledges that parenting is a role that develops with time and experience while parenting skills mature (Capoferri, 2014), while others see the identified parent as being responsible for the child's optimal growth (Ontario Ministry of Training, Colleges and Universities, 2014). Committed CYCPs are highly engaged in learning about their client's culture, background, outlook, and experiences because these are sources and resources from which the most intelligent plans and compassionate relationships can be developed for the children, youth, and families in their care. A child cannot live without models that allow him/her/hir/them to mirror and keep the memory of himself/herself/hirself/themselves (Capoferri, 2014). CYCPs are professionals, but we are first and foremost people, with our own sets of beliefs, values, and ethics, as well as our biases regarding age, diversity, culture, experiences, and communication styles.

Here are some sample biases; have you ever held any of these beliefs?

*   Same-sex partners lack the ability to parent properly
*   Immigrant children from violent countries will default to aggressive behaviour when in conflict
*   All children who are sexually abused will perpetrate sexual abuse toward others
*   Racialized children can only have racialized CYCPs support them, and Caucasian children can only have Caucasian CYCPs support them

Some customs can be viewed in entirely different ways from culture to culture. For example, handshaking might be seen as respectful to one person and invasive to another. Making eye contact might be supportive or insulting. While the offer of food might be a way of welcoming someone, accepting it might be considered impolite. It is a constant study to self-reflect and understand your own beliefs, values, and ethics and to educate yourself on those of the children, youth, and families you serve. Keeping the lines of communication open with colleagues, mentors, and supervisors will provide a CYCP with essential support and encouragement.

Discussion Opportunity 5:2

The Chu family (whom I visit weekly in their home) immigrated to the United States from Vietnam. Dad and son contribute most of the conversation. Assuming that this is normal in Vietnamese culture, I did not interfere. After the fifth session, it appears that the mother wants to speak, but when I invite her to share her thoughts, she just looks at the floor and tells me "no." I can feel my body tensing up from my reaction of frustration and conflicting values. It takes me 40 minutes to ask her why she is holding back. I also request that the other family members allow her to speak. She gives me an earful and a lesson in culture: "Why do you wear shoes in my home? You bring bad luck into my house. I like you and am grateful that you are helping us, but you must take off your shoes when you enter my home." I realize that I am confused thinking that she does not feel safe speaking in front of her husband and children! There is a part of me that wants to react by giggling at the culture clash. My "holding training and defusing techniques" workshop has taught me to keep my shoes on for safety reasons. Mrs. Chu and I ended up having a good laugh, and I adjust by bringing along my indoor shoes from then on.

Have you ever learned that your perception of a situation, specifically in the area of cultural traditions, is inaccurate? Can you share an example of this with your colleagues?

b. Demonstrate a variety of effective verbal and nonverbal communications skills, including

1. The use of silence.

Silence is a powerful intervention when practised with intention (Maier, cited in Garfat, 1993); even the silence has something important to say. CYCPs need to learn the skill of using silence and learning to listen within the space of silence.

The discipline of silence and refraining from reaction leaves space for, and encourages, discovery and provides an opening for possibilities without words, such as reflection. Silence helps people become more closely attuned to their senses and experience the moment. Pausing becomes an opportunity for awareness of being in relationship with another and to reflect on its meaning. Silence can be the space from which mindful interactions begin.

During silence, the brain is able to regulate. We now know from the research of Dr. Bruce Perry that when the limbic system is in full swing, the frontal cortex shuts down (Ludy-Dobson & Perry, 2010). Stress and trauma experiences or re-experiences precipitate this. Given the frontal cortex is responsible for language, it makes sense that people have trouble talking when upset. Not speaking is an opportunity to connect not only with others but with a deeper, inner self. Perry and others talk about using this time to engage in "patterned, repetitive, rhythmic somatosensory activity"—literally, bodily sensing exercises (Ludy-Dobson & Perry, 2010; Perry, 2009a, 2009b).

Discussion Opportunity 5:3

A mother whose daughter has just attempted suicide asks the CYCP to sit and pray with her. It is exactly the connection she needs, and the CYCP is glad to have recognized her need in that moment. Doing something and not talking is what supports the mom then and there.

"You are the first worker who does not force me to speak," Michael, a young client, tells his CYCP. The CYCP agrees with the Ojibwa grandmother who tells her that "helpers" sometimes spend too much time talking and not enough time connecting with the earth. Another time, a CYC professor is happy to let a student leave class early in order to meditate. "It relaxes me and lets me connect to myself and a higher being," she said. The professor recognizes this need because she works with many youth who communicate, "You can't force me to talk!"

Juliano, who is a soccer player, shares that when I show up to watch his game, I make him feel cared for. Actions speak louder than words. When CYCPs model, integrate, and teach the skill of making space through silence, they build mindful relationships where a pause in emotional reactivity leads to reflection and gives rise to intention in the very next interaction.

2. Appropriate nonverbal communication.

Some of the children and youth we work with read nonverbal communication very well, while others do not. Some children, youth, and their parents may struggle with specific challenges where their lack of understanding of nonverbal communication is symptomatic of a larger issue, such as a learning or developmental disability. However, a CYCP needs to be aware of the child's ability to read and process nonverbal communication and be mindful of this when smiling, gesturing with their hands, creating eye contact, and using other forms of body language.

3. Active listening.

Active listening means that the CYCP is intellectually and emotionally present when a client is communicating (Rogers & Farson, 1957/2015). Communication is more than words and visual stimuli; it is the ability to connect the various forms of communication and to demonstrate commitment to retaining the information that the sender has shared. Active listening means we are not simply waiting for the other to finish before we jump in, we do not multitask while someone is speaking, we are *present*, and we convey our understanding of the meaning of what has been communicated from the perspective of the child, youth, parent, or guardian. Active listening is an important skill for building trust in relationships, as well as a safe space in which to suspend our own story in order to experience the other's story without judgment.

Discussion Opportunity 5:4

Mantish tries to share with zer teacher that ze could not participate in the assembly that morning. The teacher explains that everyone is expected to attend and continues with programming. Mantish resists attending, which leads to a verbal confrontation with staff and eventually the principal. Following a one-day suspension, Mantish returns to school and shares with the CYCP that ze had been sexually assaulted at a party the night before the assembly and had been afraid to see the perpetrator in the auditorium.

If the teacher had used the skill of active listening, how could this have made a difference in Mantish's life?

4. Empathy and reflection of feelings.

One definition of **empathy** says, "The state of empathy, or being empathic, is to perceive the internal frame of reference of another with accuracy and with the emotional components and meanings which pertain thereto as if one are the person" (Rogers, 1980).

A common saying is that to practise empathy, we need to walk in another person's shoes. This saying actually comes from an 1895 poem written by Mary T. Lathrap:

> Pray, don't find fault with the man that limps,
> Or stumbles along the road.
> Unless you have worn the moccasins he wears,
> Or stumbled beneath the same load.
> There may be tears in his soles that hurt
> Though hidden away from view.
> The burden he bears placed on your back
> May cause you to stumble and fall, too.
>
> Don't sneer at the man who is down today
> Unless you have felt the same blow
> That caused his fall or felt the shame
> That only the fallen know.
>
> You may be strong, but still the blows
> That are his, unknown to you in the same way,
> May cause you to stagger and fall, too.
>
> Don't be too harsh with the man that sins.
> Or pelt him with words, or stone, or disdain.
> Unless you are sure you have no sins of your own,
> And it's only wisdom and love that your heart contains.
>
> For you know if the tempter's voice
> Can whisper as soft to you,
> As it did to him when he went astray,
> It might cause you to falter, too.
>
> Just walk a mile in his moccasins
> Before you abuse, criticize and accuse.

If just for one hour, you could find a way
To see through his eyes, instead of your own muse.

I believe you'd be surprised to see
That you've been blind and narrow minded, even unkind
There are people on reservations and in the ghettos
Who have so little hope, and too much worry on their minds.

Brother, there but for the grace of God go you and I.
Just for a moment, slip into his mind and traditions
And see the world through his spirit and eyes
Before you cast a stone or falsely judge his conditions.

Remember to walk a mile in his moccasins
And remember the lessons of humanity taught to you by your elders.
We will be known forever by the tracks we leave
In other people's lives, our kindnesses and generosity.

Take the time to walk a mile in his moccasins.

You can read more at: AAA Native Arts, "Walk a mile in his moccasins—Native American poetry" (http://www.aaanativearts.com/native-american-poetry/walk-a-mile-in-his-moccasins#ixzz4n0CemuAo).

Discussion Opportunity 5:5

Think of a time when you were in conflict with someone that you share a closer relationship with. How did you practise empathy with that person? Were you able to accurately understand the situation from the other person's perspective?

When we practise empathy, we need to include mindful reflection practices. Reflection involves an experience upon which one reflects and then has a new experience, and this is considered a circular process. There is reflection, followed by consequential action, more reflection, and more action (Cornish & Jenkins, 2012). Reflection is a learning opportunity wherein time and space grant possibilities for discovery of novel ideas, insight, and experiences.

Discussion Opportunity 5:6

Xavier attends a day-treatment classroom. He is very bright academically and is very creative building structures. His family owns a very successful business, which means that his parents both travel the world for several days at a time and often several times a month. Xavier says that when they leave, "it feels like an eternity," even though he stays with a caring relative. He struggles with making friends. For example, when other children ask him to participate in team games, he refuses in an aggressive way. After several discussions, Xavier reflects on how his reactions make it difficult for him to make friends. He begins to see how his actions are contradictory to his goals. On reflection, he realizes that it had been the fear of losing any friends he has made or being left alone, just as he has been experiencing with his parents, that makes him push people away. When he shares his new awareness with his parents, they in turn realize how their actions have been impacting their son. The family adapts by agreeing that only one parent will travel at a time. Within a few months, Xavier is making new friends at school.

Let's take a moment to reflect on an interaction that you have shared with someone significant in your life where you have pushed others away emotionally. Are you conscious of why you pushed the person away in the moment? Let's reflect on what this means for you in your current relationships. You do not need to share what you have reflected on with colleagues; however, remember this reflection as you may want to use it in a future counselling session or perhaps even a supervision session.

5. Questioning skills.

If it leads to understanding the other person's story better and more fully, questioning is a very important skill that can build a trusting and safe relationship between a CYCP and a child, youth, or family. The kinds of questions that have the intention of exploration through dialogue are open-ended and investigate the meaning of the discussion. The purpose of close-ended questions is to provide a clear answer to a direct question (Ivey, Ivey, & Zalaquett, 2015). Some examples of close-ended questions include "Are you going to school?" and "Did you listen to the teacher today?" **Open-ended questions** support the direction of a person's story and experiences and lead to further development. Knowing what questions to ask and when to ask these are highly developed skills for a CYCP. When these are fine-tuned, they can keep the process of relationship building on track because they perpetuate meaningful discussions.

6. Use of door openers to invite communication, and paraphrasing and summarization to promote clear communication.

Language incorporates endless ways of making meaning. Words, phrases, and discourses reflect the meaning-making activity of multiple generations of people (McLeod & McLeod, 2011). The search for common understanding spans many alternative ways to talk about issues and concerns between CYCPs and the people they are with. To paraphrase is to say the same thing in a different way, and it can take the form of renaming a thing, differentiating between things, or finding novel ways to say the same thing with the intention of finding common ground between talker and listener. Hearing one's thoughts paraphrased can be affirming to the speaker if the listener has understood; it also gives the speaker a chance to rephrase their point to make their meaning better understood by the CYCP. Paraphrasing also helps the listener understand the meaning that the speaker experienced when hearing the words (Garfat, 1998; Irmsher, 2000; Jung, Howard, Emory, & Pino, 1973;

Krueger, 1994; VanderVen, 1992). Searching for new words also makes it possible for the speaker to reflect and observe the impact of their words on the listener.

7. Awareness and avoidance of communication roadblocks.

Awareness of communication is the foundation of the relationships between the CYCP and children, youth, and families; therefore, it is essential to understand what **roadblocks**, if any, stand in the way of effective communication. By identifying the source of misunderstandings and blocks, we can develop creative solutions. Social location can become a roadblock. Power imbalances can also lead to roadblocks.

Discussion Opportunity 5:7

Think of a time when you were communicating with someone, and the conversation was ineffective. What were some of the "roadblocks" that got in the way?

Let's brainstorm communication roadblocks. Sue and colleagues (2007) provide us with an example of how our own beliefs and biases can prevent effective communication:

> When we are not ready to appreciate the differences among human characteristics, values and practices, our communication will reflect our biases and our mistaken beliefs or lack of knowledge regarding the experiences of others and what is meaningful to them. For example, when you hear that grandparents are raising their grandchildren, what assumptions do you make? And what if those same grandparents are also of a same-sex couple *and* identify with Indigenous culture? Are your assumptions the same or different? One factor alone requires careful consideration and sensitive communication, but when several factors intersect, it can be challenging to work with our own perhaps limited perceptions against the perceptions of themselves the people we are trying to support have. These assumptions can also be communicated as micro-aggressions.

PASSING JUDGMENT

Passing judgment is making assumptions about others based on your own experiences, values, beliefs, and culture. Judgments are subjective and also evaluative, packed with meaning both emotional and conceptual in moment-by-moment interactions (Apter, 2018). Consider the following examples of judgmental statements: *You should know better. When has that ever worked for you? What would happen if you were kinder? Your faith is not important. Why are you making bad choices? You are old and can never understand!* Reflecting on your own value system and beliefs can uncover judgments you are likely to impose on yourself and others.

TALKING OVER EACH OTHER

There are many examples in society of no one listening, and everyone trying to talk over each other; this happens even in government debate processes. When people believe they are right, they are not willing to hear the other person's side of the story and will not honour their values or rights. Such communication between two people or groups represents adversarial rather than cooperative intentions. The reciprocity of communication is lost for all parties when we do not listen to the other's message.

Discussion Opportunity 5:8

Reflect on a conflict you had in your life. Were you able to listen, or did you prefer to speak? How effective was the interaction?

> A wise old owl lived in an oak,
> The more he saw, the less he spoke
> The more he spoke, the less he heard
> Why can't we be like the wise old bird?
> (Opie & Opie, 1997, p. 403).

This saying is especially helpful for practitioners who are new to the field and beginning their first placement or internship. Watching how seasoned CYC elders interact with children/youth/families and colleagues can provide valuable learning opportunities. Even better can be to log these interactions and review them with the elder or CYCP supervisor.

Discussion Opportunity 5:9

A CYCP and Matia, a 14-year-old male, are having a conversation about his suspension from school. The CYCP is focused on the consequences and informing Matia of school rules and expectations. Matia is discussing his frustrations about being bullied and how he wants to stand up to the students who have been teasing him for months. He agrees that aggression is breaking school rules, but he believes that no one is protecting him. The CYCP is only focusing on the message the principal had asked her to pass on to the student.

Reflect on a conversation that moved in the same direction and one that went in many different directions. Which was more effective? What contributes to the effectiveness of the interaction?

LABELLING

Labelling is a form of identification based on assumptions of future behaviours (Carroll, 1956/1997; Darley & Gross, 1983; Eberhardt, Dasgupta, & Banaszynski, 2003; Rosenthal & Jacobson, 1992). For example, you might think of a grandparent who labels his grandchild a "troubled child," or the community that labels a family as "problematic." Even "perfect child" or "accomplished child" are labels, as much as a "slow child" or "unorganized child," and all can find it a struggle to live up to or overcome expectations associated with the label. Explore labels that are imposed on you, or labels you impose on yourself, and those you perhaps impose on others.

AGGRESSION

Aggression in any form, whether verbal or physical, has a negative effect on a sense of personal safety and undermines trust in relationships (Straus, Gelles, & Steinmetz, 2017). If a parent yells at a child and slams their hand on the table, the emotional level of communication has escalated the conversation, with the result of both being negatively impacted from the interaction. Reflect on a time when someone spoke to you in an aggressive manner. What was your response, and how did the interaction affect the relationship?

INABILITY TO SIT IN SILENCE

"All of humanity's problems stem from man's inability to sit quietly in a room alone" (Pascal, 1958). Silence allows people to reflect on, process, and regulate the interaction, and it is particularly essential to provide silence in the relationship process and learning. People need quiet time without external stimuli to gather themselves in the moment and to reflect on their awareness. Children, youth, and families will benefit and need to learn the skills to sit in silence because meditation develops greater control of their mental processes, culminating in regulatory abilities that lead to well-being and emotional balance (Menezes, Pereira, & Bizarro, 2012). Reflect on how comfortable you are with sitting in silence. What does silence mean to you? How does silence promote communication and awareness?

CREATING POWER STRUGGLES

"You are expected to be in programming, right now! If you do not go, you will miss the community outing and lose your allowance." This is an example of interpersonal behaviour that sets up a power struggle. The CYCP is focused on the consequence and does not use "in-the-moment" interaction, which would allow the person to consider what it means to not attend the program. Controlling and ordering a child, youth, or parent is an ineffective way to intervene in a situation (Sikorski & Vittone, 2016), because it does not use a strength-based, in-the-moment, life space approach. It creates power struggles. Reflect on a time when someone ordered you to do something. What was your reaction, and how did it impact the relationship?

DECREASED WINDOWS OF TOLERANCE OR DISTRESS TOLERANCE

When a CYCP working in a juvenile detention centre offered support to Matthew, he responded with "F--- you! Leave me alone, b*tch," and then went back to his room.

Matthew's emotions indicate he has a smaller **window of tolerance** (Schore, 2012). This is a roadblock to receiving support and engaging in effective relational skills.

DISTRUST

Distrust can be hard to overcome, even when the CYCP's intentions are to be support-ive. An example occurred with a homeless youth who was offered food and coupons for clothing and responded with "What do I have to give in return? No one gives anything without expecting any favours." It is clear that the relationship has not yet achieved a feel-ing of safety for that youth. Effective communication requires that both people feel safe in the relationship. Creating and maintaining safety means both individuals can shift their focus of *me* (self-protection) to *we* so their energy is collaboratively focused on connection (Phelan, 2003). How can you communicate with someone you did not feel safe with? What are the risks?

TRANSFERENCE/COUNTERTRANSFERENCE

Transference and **countertransference** occur in helping relationships (Fox, n.d.). A stu-dent studying to become a CYCP is participating in a role play. About halfway through the experience, the student walks out of class. The student who has been in the role of the client shared a story about how lonely she feels in the world. The CYCP student was surprised by how powerful the transferred feelings of loneliness, depression, and difficult family times were in the moment.

The CYC student is able to return to class and share how powerful this transfer of feelings was for her. She was surprised by how strongly she feels the emotions that she had previously worked through in her own counselling. Transference and countertransference can also have positive effects on relationships with children, youth, and families. For ex-ample, when we take families to winter camp, parents recognize the positive relationship with the staff team make them feel safe and accepted. These are the feelings staff want to transfer to their own families.

NOT "GETTING" THE OTHER PERSON'S EXPERIENCE

Nigel is a 10-year-old from an African immigrant family. Nigel roams through the com-munity after school. Child protection receives several calls from the community concerned with his safety. The community reports that Nigel eats many meals at the homes of neigh-bours. It is also common for Nigel's family to feed his friends during the weekend. When we visit the family, we find caring, loving people who share with us that in their communi-ty it is common to eat "wherever you land" and that it considered rude to eat and run. Nigel is clearly not at risk.

Have you ever interacted when you did not "get" the other person's experience? Have you been in a situation where the other person did not understand your experience? In order to get to know each other and problem solve conflict, we need to understand someone else's experience and see things from their perspective (Chan, 2016).

ATTACHMENT STYLES

Attachment is an emotional relationship where,

> the infant and young child can experience a warm, intimate, and continuous relationship with the mother (or permanent mother substitute) in which both find satisfaction and enjoyment given in this relationship emotions such as anxiety and guilt (which in access characterize mental ill health) will organize in a moderate and organized way. (Bowlby, 1951)

Not to do so may have significant and irreversible mental health consequences.

If CYCPs work from an attachment perspective, they believe that **attachment style** can impact lifelong relationships. It is therefore important that we understand our emotional attachment to our caregivers. How our caregivers connected with us impacts how we relate and communicate with others. In secure attachment, when a parent leaves the child, the child is upset that the parent has left them but trusts that the parent will return. In ambivalent attachment, the child gets very upset when a parent goes away and is anxious and perhaps cannot self-sooth or calm themselves because they do not believe that the caregiver will return, nor can they trust that a caregiver will meet their needs. In avoidant attachment, a neglected child learns to avoid interactions with the caregiver and is uninterested in joining emotionally. Disorganized attachment describes the lack of clarity the child experiences in relating to the caregiver, with confusion between feeling reassured and feeling anxious (Ainsworth & Bell, 1970).

Attachment styles affect the communication skills you experience and learn from your primary caregiver (Ainsworth & Bell, 1970; Bowlby, 1951). Reflect on what form of attachment you had with your primary caregiver. How does your form of attachment impact your relationships with children, youth, families, and teammates and supervisors? What skills or lack of communication skills did you experience as a child? How will these skills affect your communication with the children, youth, and families you interact with?

LACK OF SKILLS

CYCPs use relationships and **in-the-moment interactions** as opportunities to teach skills. Skills need to be broken down step by step, as opportunities to practise in different settings and with different people. Practice provides opportunity to praise, provide feedback, and continue building skills. For example, effective communication is a skill that can be taught and learned. As CYCPs, it is our responsibility to practise and teach the skills of effective communication and, equally important, the skills of listening. Once we listen, we need to make meaning of the conversation. Students practise the skill of "empathy" and quickly learn that they want to solve the problem. How effective are you communicating, listening, and making meaning? Do you communicate the same way or differently depending on the relationship? We also can model and teach the skills of distress tolerance to those we walk beside so they and we can communicate how we feel versus reacting to emotional/relational or environmental **triggers** (Linehan, 2014).

Discussion Opportunity 5:10

Now that you are aware of some communication roadblocks, provide an example of a roadblock that has impacted one of your current relationships.

c. Recognizing when a person may be experiencing problems in communication due to individual or cultural and human diversity and history. Helping clarify communication. Resolving misunderstandings

People's culture, diversity, and history impact their communication and perception and the meaning of what they are trying to convey and to hear. The CYCP is responsible for embracing, if not celebrating, diversity. CYCPs ensure that they clarify what they hear and make meaning from the conversation for themselves, other team members, and the community they are working within.

Discussion Opportunity 5:11

Two CYCPs visit the home of an Italian family, which includes the maternal grandparents. The grandfather begins by addressing one worker, who is heavier set, by saying she looks beautiful and strong. He then looks over at the other worker, who is thinner. He calls her skinny and tells her she can come over for meals. The rest of the family reacts with embarrassment and cannot wait for the grandfather to leave the room. A few months later, the grandfather explains his comment: "When you are raised in times of war, you do not want to be thin. Heavier means that you have money to eat." He had only wanted to take care of the thinner worker because she is helping his children and grandchildren. How would you have perceived the grandfather's remarks?

d. Assist clients (to a level consistent with their development, abilities, and receptiveness) to receive relevant information about legislation/regulations, policies/standards, and supports pertinent to the focus of service

CYCPs value the process of child/youth/family/community involvement in goal setting, treatment planning, and service evaluation. In many Canadian provinces, it is mandated that children over the age of 12 who are "in care" attend plan-of-care meetings and engage in the conversations about them. The voices of the children, youth, and families are an essential part of the conversation.

It is also mandated that children sign a form affirming they have had their "rights" explained. The UN Convention on the Rights of the Child has 54 articles in all. Articles 43–54 are about how adults and governments can work together to make sure that all children can exercise all their rights. Go to www.unicef.org/crc to read the Convention, with particular attention to these articles.

Discussion Opportunity 5:12

CYCP and foster parent Theresa tries very hard to help her foster children experience life, as do their peers who are not "in care." For example, instead of having conversations about what child rights are, there is dinner-time discussion about what all kids in the world deserve. This includes the basics: food, education, housing, and so on, but also input in decisions that impact them. Privacy visits with child welfare workers can occur to ensure safety, but Theresa advocates strongly that these take place in common areas of the house, and the family can leave the child with their legal guardian in the commons space (living-room/kitchen). She maintains that in non-foster homes it is not common that children take adults (that they have only just met) to their bedroom for a private chat (Fraser, personal communication, 2017).

Another example of child rights is that in educational settings, children and youth receive report cards but are not often made aware that they and their caregivers can access the school record that is stored in the school board to which they belong. This file includes report cards, assessments, anecdotal reports, suspension reports, and so on. Policies vary from board to board, country to country, but it is important for the CYCP to become informed and advocate and, even more importantly, help the child, youth, family, and community develop the capacity to self-advocate for their rights.

For example, in some school districts or boards, the principal of the school can "pull" a suspension report at the end of a school year when a child/youth has "turned their behaviour around." This fresh start (the absence of suspensions reports) can help students feel less ashamed. They may then experience school staff as being motivated to establish relationships based on currently interactions rather than past suspension errors. Sharing this information with youth so they can learn their rights and make such a request could be one way of modelling how to self-advocate.

e. Provide for the participation of children, youth, and families in the planning, implementation, and evaluation of services impacting them

Children, youth, and families need to be active in planning, implementation, and evaluation of the services impacting them. We need to provide opportunities for them to understand that they are experts on themselves. Having a voice and taking an active part in the developmental process empowers children, youth, and families (Snow, 2006). Throughout their relationship, it is important to reflect on and evaluate the process.

Here are some things to consider in planning:

- Who would the child like to invite to the discussion (such as an Indigenous Elder, a school crossing guard, etc.)?
- The topics to be discussed need to be respectful (in other words, not shaming the child when the subject of errors arise)
- It is important to consider Elders, cultural representatives, extended family, spiritual or faith supporters

f. Set appropriate boundaries and limits on the behaviour using clear and respectful communication

Boundaries and limits are important for children, so they can have clear expectations and predictability and safety in relationships. Giving children boundaries and limits is an opportunity to teach them skills in relating respectfully within those limits; however, boundaries need to be open, flexible, and maintained by respecting the dignity, values, beliefs, and culture of children, youth, and families. Not implementing boundaries and limits sends confusing messages within the relationship. CYCPs also need to be cognizant that boundaries can be created due to their own social locations. "Social interactions between young people and practitioners, boundaries are put in place through three dimensions (value judgments, social distance and knowledge)" (Snow, 2006). As practitioners, we do not want to oppress or undermine the voice of those we work with; we must be aware of the impact of these dimensions on our relationship-building interactions.

Discussion Opportunity 5:13

A newly hired CYCP at an agency is excited about his first job in the field. Bruce arrives at the day treatment program and recognizes a youth. Later that night, the youth knocks on Bruce's door. It turns out that he lives down the street. Bruce has to tell the youth that he will see him at the program tomorrow, because seeing the youth outside of the program is a staff/youth boundary issue.

Here's another boundary example.

New forms of communication, like text messaging and video chat, have made it easy to get in touch with people almost instantly. The majority of people in Canada and the United States have a cellphone, so they're never very far from contact. A second-year CYCP student provides a family with his cellphone number and sets a boundary to only call him if they need to cancel an appointment. Two weeks later, the 15-year-old child video-calls his cellphone 10 times a day because he is feeling anxious and negative thoughts are perseverating. He also sends dozens of text messages, which the CYCP student doesn't answer.

What boundaries should be considered with newer forms of communication, like text messaging and social media, for children/youth and families? How can we use these new technological tools to benefit the relationship and development of children, youth, and families?

What boundaries and limits are important to clearly outline at the beginning of your relationship with a child and youth? What are some boundaries and limits that you need to implement about using social media in your professional relationships?

g. Verbally and nonverbally de-escalate crisis situations in a manner that protects dignity and integrity

The dignity and integrity of children/youth and families must be kept intact when de-escalating conflicts. This is hard sometimes. CYCPs are people too. Just like others around us, we have feelings and we get frustrated. Our verbal and nonverbal skills need to match and provide congruent messages. Being aware of how we present and what we say during a crisis influences whether the crisis will de-escalate or escalate (Crisis Prevention Institute [CPI], 2011). Asking a child/youth or adult what is bothering them while having your arms crossed may send a mixed message; the person you're talking to may read this as "you're in trouble!" or "we are about to restrain you!" The message then has a negative impact on how the person will respond. It may also prompt an aggressive response. We also need to ensure that the verbal and nonverbal messages we are providing show empathy for the person. An example of good practice is to ask, "What do you really want me to hear? Did I get it right?" It is important that we hear what is important for children, youth, and families in a crisis and allow them to tell us. De-escalating is an opportunity to use relational practices to bring messages of safety, respect, and caring.

Discussion Opportunity 5:14

Jacob, an 11-year-old, attends a day-treatment education classroom. Jacob tells his CYCP that he is not feeling well that day. He wonders if he is feeling sick because he has new medication. When he asks to stay in for recess, his CYCP allows him to sit and read on a couch. By lunchtime, Jacob is further withdrawn, staying at his desk. The teacher begins the lesson and asks everyone to take out their spelling workbooks. When Jacob does not respond, his CYCP approaches him to invite him to engage in the learning lesson. Jacob suddenly stands up and up-turns his desk. He begins physically attacking staff, pulling down shelves, and throwing the computers out of the windows. The rest of the children are evacuated as Jacob continues his destructive rampage. The school principal becomes involved and immediately summons the police and ambulance. Jacob is taken away in handcuffs, feeling alone, shamed, and scared.

Jacob's crisis was the result of his new medication, but he didn't attend school for two years and he rarely leaves home because he has been labelled the "crazy kid." Perhaps giving Jacob more time to process his thoughts and feelings before making demands on him might have prevented the incident escalating to a level of violence. This event is traumatic for everyone and especially damaging for Jacob.

What skills could have been useful to de-escalate the situation? How do we balance dignity with integrity when trying to de-escalate a crisis?

2. Relationship Development

a. Assess the quality of relationships in an ongoing process of self-reflection regarding your impact in relationship, in order to maintain a full presence and an involved, strong, and healthy relationship

Relationships are connections in constant flux, requiring continuous assessment and reflection on the moment and the behaviours that are influencing the relationship (Ruch, 2005). Assessment and reflection can be done individually with colleagues and supervisors, within safe relationships (i.e., where confidentiality is being respected and dignity is honoured). When CYCPs are in an emotionally secure environment, it is possible to take risks and make confident use of their knowledge and skills. Mindfully assessing the flow of the relationships with oneself and others supports the personal and professional development of a CYCP.

Discussion Opportunity 5:15

How do you demonstrate being mindfully present in the moment with a child, youth, or family? What skills or knowledge do you have that promote strong, healthy relationships?

b. Form relationships through contact, communication, appreciation, shared interests, attentiveness, mutual respect, and empathy

Consistent and predictable contact provides safety in any relationship. Nonverbal and verbal communication needs to be congruent and respectful (Pickhardt, 2013). (Have you heard this before?) Building on the strengths and interests of children, youth, and families and appreciating what they bring to the relationship recognizes their importance to the relationship. Being attentive in the moment to the messages conveyed by one's body language and verbal expressions builds trust and secure connections. Mutual respect and empathy show commitment and reliability. Without these new behavioural templates, children will interact with others based on prior experiences, sometimes anticipating that prior treatment and interactions will be repeated (Fraser, 2014).

Discussion Opportunity 5:16

Twelve-year-old Michael is very vocal about not wanting to participate in individual sessions, but he agrees to allow the CYCP to visit his home. When she visits, he does not want to engage in dialogue about his challenges. The CYCP handles his ambivalence by continuing to visit and engage Michael in a fun way, listening to his stories about school and essentially listening to anything Michael wants to share stories about. The CYCP does this with attention, respect, and empathy. In formal therapy, this is called a **child-centred approach** (Landreth, 2002). For the seventh session, the CYCP arrives late to the session and finds that Michael is not engaging nor interacting with the CYCP. It takes 20 minutes of mindful waiting before Michael is able to share that the CYCP's lateness has made Michael feel unimportant and that he has lost trust that she is coming. He also has lost trust in their relationship. The CYCP allows Michael to set his own pace and listens with empathy until he is able to share his feelings of invisibility and rejection. Michael then is able to reinvest in the relationship because he recognizes the CYCP is an adult that does not make excuses for behaviour and still wants to "stick it out" with him.

Reflect on a positive relationship in your life and explore how you both demonstrated communication, attentiveness, mutual respect, and empathy.

c. Demonstrate the personal characteristics that foster and support relationship development

Personal characteristics can exemplify the strengths that make a CYCP unique.

Discussion Opportunity 5:17

When Ms. Carol wants to start a knitting program with Grade 7 and 8 students in the day-treatment program, many think that the students will resist. Then, all of a sudden, math and language studies are being completed quickly so that everyone can knit. The students made iPad holders, socks, gifts, and scarves for shelters.

In another example, children request Mr. C to attend camp because he is a skilled guitar player. The staff request Mr. J to attend camp because he wakes up early and brings coffee to your tent. Emily brings flexibility and creative problem solving. John makes the best Sunday morning brunch with fresh whipped cream. Carol brings canvas and paints to every session. Deirdre loves telling wonderful Irish folktales. Puneet has travelled and shares her stories about fascinating places. Nax, the agency nurse, has a knack for settling a rambunctious room of children whenever he walks in. Paul knows how to advocate for the needs of the team and promote the development of each CYCP. Jose's jokes make children embrace laughter and humour. Telling jokes is quite a skill!

What personal characteristics do you bring to your relationships?

d. Ensure that, from the beginning of the relationship, applicable procedures regarding confidentiality, consent for release of information, and record keeping are explained and clearly understood by the parent/caregiver and by the child, as appropriate to developmental age. Follow those procedures in a caring and respectful manner

Every agency needs to have a policy on confidentiality, consent for release of information, and record keeping (Administration for Children and Families, 2014). When CYCPs become aware of policy and how to implement these, they are putting policies into action. Every geographic area might have slight differences in policy, and it is the CYCP's responsibility to be informed of these details. Parents, children, and youth also need to be aware of the policy and the purpose for procedures so they can self-advocate and feel secure within the system.

CYCPs need to be aware that there is a difference between **absolute confidentiality** and **relative confidentiality**. Absolute confidentiality means that client disclosures are not shared with anyone. A priest retains absolute confidentiality. Relative confidentiality means that information is shared within the agency, outside the program agency with the client's permission, or in a court of laws when information is subpoenaed. Usually, children/youth and families can be assured of relative confidentiality, as there is a legislated "duty to report" for CYCPs. Child and Youth Care Practitioners need to discuss (in advance of service provision) what information is to be shared with other members of the team in the child's circle of care and what information is not to be shared—unless the child may cause harm to themselves or others (Solomon, 2017).

Discussion Opportunity 5:18

What are some challenges in respecting confidentiality and report writing? Provide some examples of explaining procedures to parents and children in a respectful manner.

e. Develop relationships with children, youth, and families that are caring, purposeful, goal-directed, and rehabilitative in nature; limiting these relationships to the delivery of specific services

Any relationship needs to not only be caring for children, youth, and families but also serve a practical purpose regarding their needs and development. CYCP interventions are intentional and purposeful (Freeman & Garfat, 2014). Both CYCPs and their clients need to be active in developing their goals, which need to be holistic and measurable in order to meet the emotional, physical, psychological, cognitive, and spiritual well-being of children, youth, and families. Having an understanding of what you can provide and what is outside your scope of practice is important to know and respect.

Discussion Opportunity 5:19

A CYCP, Dolores, has been employed at a school board for four years before finding a new position. Dolores is excited but knows she is going to miss the students in the old program, who put on a farewell celebration for her. At this celebration she promises to visit them weekly and email them as well.

Reflect on how realistic the very specific promises are. What effect will it have on Dolores's former students if she doesn't follow through on these promises? Whose needs were being met when she made that promise?

f. Set, maintain, and communicate appropriate personal and professional boundaries

Setting personal and professional boundaries and maintaining them outlines how clear expectations and limits build mutual trust and respect in relationships. Personal boundaries are a part of CYCP's self-care, designed to protect their well-being (Davidson, 2000).

Discussion Opportunity 5:20

A CYCP working in a residential treatment has just finished a challenging 3:00 to 11:00 p.m. shift when the house supervisor asks him to stay until 3:00 a.m. He is tired and feeling overwhelmed by an extra shift.

Can this CYCP set and maintain his personal boundary? Why or why not? What are the CYCP's options?

Discussion Opportunity 5:21

A CYCP is on a school trip to the local science centre when a student named Edvin becomes frustrated with the large crowds and long line-ups and begins to pace. Edvin asks the CYCP to lend him her phone to play games, which she does. He then begins to go through her personal pictures and show them to others. How can the CYCP respond in a supportive way to Edvin? Are the consequences appropriate and/or applicable, or can she tell Edvin how she feels about her privacy being disrespected? Could she have given Edvin different limits when he begins to use her phone?

What professional boundaries are not maintained? How could boundaries make this relationship develop in a positive way?

g. Assist clients to identify personal issues and make choices about the delivery of service

In the process of development, children, youth, and families may need help identifying the personal issues on which they want to focus. CYC practice is grounded in the strong belief that children, youth, and families need to have choice about the delivery of service. There is no greater expert on their own lives than the child sitting in front of you, and when they know that you genuinely believe that, they'll join with you in a trusting relationship (Bell, 2014).

Discussion Opportunity 5:22

Alfi has been diagnosed with depression and anxiety and has not left his home for three months. During these three months, he enjoys playing his guitar and plays video games with Internet friends. His parents are very concerned for their son because he is not interested in face-to-face peer contact. When Alfi tells his mother that he does not want to live anymore, she contacts the community CYCP, who agrees that he needs to go to a hospital. The attending doctor, nurse, social worker, and CYCP all take part in Alfi's assessment during his two-week stay and are instrumental in developing a safety plan for him. Together with his parents and the CYCP, Alfi is able to identify what he needs, and a strategy is implemented that will best serve his needs to get him back home.

Brainstorm service options that could keep Alfi out of the hospital and assist him in leaving his room. How can Alfi be supported to make decisions about what services he needs?

h. Model appropriate interpersonal interactions while handling the activities and situation of the life space

CYCPs have both the privilege and challenge to be in relationship with the children, youth, and families with whom they engage. They need to model both healthy relationships and interactions in many life spaces. There seem to be endless opportunities to practise interpersonal role modelling between CYCP staff and to carry the examples forward in the presence of children, youth, families, and other systems.

Discussion Opportunity 5:23

Charmaine, a CYC professor, always tells her students that who she is in the classroom is who she is at home, as well as who she is when she is working with children, youth, and families. Do you believe her? Are you the same person in your many life spaces, or do you have a professional persona that you wear at work? Do you think that CYCPs need to develop such a persona? Why or why not?

i. Use structure, routines, and activities to promote effective relationships

Structure and **routine** promotes safe and predictable relationships (Snow, 2013). CYCPs are responsible for developing and implementing activities that contribute to creating and maintaining effective relationships. Foster parents have reported that structure and routines are also important in building trust with children. Some of the children we work with depend on structure and routines to get through their days. Some children are highly observant of structure and routine changes, because, in their lives, such changes mean that a problem, conflict, or crisis is pending (Perry & Szalavitz, 2017).

CYCPs need to be aware of how our individual window of tolerance (Siegel, 2011, 2012) impacts our ability to manage moments. Also, our window of tolerance can change moment to moment. Our window of tolerance is developed based on what we are able to handle, manage, and incorporate in our lives. Schore (2012) states that we use the therapeutic relationship to support our clients to re-experience dysregulation effects in tolerable doses within the context of a safe environment, so that overwhelming traumatic feelings can be regulated and incorporated as part of the person's emotional life.

The unknown can be scary based on the child, youth, or family's worldview (unintegrated experiences of the past). Therefore, we apply meaning to the unknown. This often becomes dedicated to the space we define as "unknown." CYCPs prepare children/youth for the unknown when they talk about and plan for transition time activities or when they assist an individual in registering for a new school. Helping others and ourselves navigate the unknown is important to self-regulation.

> Transitions permeate our lives. The capacity to successfully transition from one place to another, one activity to another, one internal state to another is fundamentally related to the capacity to self-regulate. And this, of course, is one of the main areas of difficulty with children and youth who have been exposed to developmental chaos, threat and trauma. And, as you might expect me to say, self-regulation is a brain-mediated function. (Perry, 2009)

Discussion Opportunity 5:24

Dan attends a day-treatment educational classroom due to his experiences with anxiety. When the principal asks all of the Grade 1 to 4 students to attend an assembly in the gym for 9:20 a.m., Dan throws his chair and knocks all his books to the floor. He is given the choice to spend some time alone in the "calm room" or sit quietly at his desk while his peers are all at the assembly. Later, Dan is able to share that he has difficulty with the changes of routine and did not feel safe attending the assembly.

Children like Dan need transitions to prepare them for changes. What structures and routines are in your life that promote effective relationships and safety? How do you handle changes and help those you work with handle changes that will increase their windows of tolerance (Siegel, 2011, 2012)?

j. Encourage children, youth, and families to contribute to programs, services, and support movements that affect their lives by sharing authority and responsibility

Child, youth, and families come with strengths that they can contribute to community programming and services. Strength-based CYCPs know that their strengths, once harnessed, can significantly support an organization or community.

Discussion Opportunity 5:25

Edwardo is living at a residential treatment centre. He tells everyone that his mother is an amazing cook. She agrees to come to the residence and share her cooking skills and cook a meal for everyone. Edwardo and his mother are very much appreciated by everyone in the home. During winter camp, Singh, a CYCP, is allotted a few hours to develop entertainment for the evening program, along with children, youth, and parents. The collective creative results bring laughter and joy to the camp experience.

In a day-treatment classroom, it is a common practice for children to work in pairs or groups that support each of them to promote their strengths and contribute to the learning of everyone. Brainstorm ways that CYCPs can encourage children, youth, and families to contribute to programs in different ways. What are some barriers that stand in the way of children, youth, and families contributing to programs and services? Do you have any belief systems that can be obstacles to progress?

k. Develop and communicate an informed understanding of social trends, social change, and social institutions. Demonstrate an understanding of how social issues affect relationships between individuals, groups, and societies

Social trends are constantly changing; it is the responsibility of CYCPs to be aware of these changes and to understand how they impact relationships and social institutions. Perhaps the most impactful, expansive, and even disturbing trends are happening in social media (Martin, 2013; Martin & Alaggia, 2013). Pornography is easily available, with images downloaded to phones with one click. It is also evident that children and youth communicate and relate to one another differently than generations that have come before them. For example, many young people post on multimedia forums and share information with large numbers of people. They receive feedback very quickly, but not always with beneficial outcomes. Many express a preference for communicating electronically or online versus real-time, face-to-face encounters within their communities.

Discussion Opportunity 5:26

An online friend of Maddy's teaches her how to cut her body to release pain. She interacts less with her face-to-face friends and cuts with her online friend.

Pietro is a very good soccer player and has been considered for a scholarship. Once he becomes addicted to online gaming, his education and performance are negatively impacted. Sadly, in addition to losing the scholarship, Pietro is no longer able to play on the soccer team.

Discuss ways that social media has impacted children and youth in both positive and challenging ways.

Discussion Opportunity 5:27

What social trends impacted your development as a child or youth? What are some current trends that are impacting children, youth, and families and how they relate to each other?

l. Identify community standards and expectations for behaviour that enable children, youth, and families to maintain existing relationships in the community

Communities impact children, youth, and families directly and indirectly, at best involving them in activities that make them feel connected and provide them with a strong a sense of belonging. Part of a CYCP's mandate is to impart standards that support children and youth in having healthy relationships with their community. Lack of contact with community has impacted many First Nations youth in Canada and the United States because they do not have their **"safe base"** to return to during the treatment process.

Where youth are safe, we also need to be building and reinforcing connections to family as much and as often as possible. Blum and Rinehart (1997) reported that when youth are strongly connected to family, they are less likely to engage in risky behaviour. So if supports reinforce healthy family connections, we are also addressing potential vulnerabilities or risk factors.

Discussion Opportunity 5:28

Thirteen-year-old Justin enjoys going to his local coffee house with his dad on Sunday mornings; he particularly enjoys their one-on-one conversation. However, if there are more than six people in the space at one time, he is uncomfortable and refuses to order his food. Justin and his family reach out for support for the anxiety that Justin experiences with large groups and talking to strangers. His relationship with the CYCP gradually exposes Justin to going out into the community and practising the skills of being in the moment in that environment. One goal is that he orders his own meal. Three sessions later, Justin orders coffee and hot chocolate with a double-dipped donut. Teaching relational skills continue to benefit Justin's relationships with his family, friends, and community.

Provide an example of a skill that you expect children to be able to demonstrate when they are in the community when they are developmentally 12, 15, and 17. Share these skills with a classroom neighbour.

Do they share the same expectations as you? Then discuss with your neighbour examples of community experiences that help children/youth and families to learn these skills.

3. Family Communication

a. Identify relevant systems/components and describe the relationships, rules, and roles in the child/youth's social systems and develop connections among the people in various social systems

As well as working with children, youth, and families, CYCPs also must explore the relationships between systems and how a system relates to the development of a child.

Discussion Opportunity 5:29

Mattia is driven to school, which takes one hour each way, to ensure safety for himself and others. When asked whom he wants to attend his treatment plan review, he requests the taxi driver who drives him to school. The staff are all surprised by his request, but he describes his time with the cab driver as supportive all the way to school and back. This dynamic is often also true with volunteer drivers who may drive children (placed in child welfare settings) to and from court-ordered access visits or medical appointments.

Samantha's husband dies on the way to pick up his children from school. The devastating loss is very difficult for the family. Samantha is a practising Catholic but has not attended church in several years. After her loss, she and the children begin to attend church regularly, where members of the congregation become a support system to the whole family in many different ways. Their renewed faith also contributes to the healing process.

When children, youth, and families are actively connected to systems, the rules and their roles within integrate in forming the development of sometimes healing and supportive relationships.

Discussion Opportunity 5:30

What systems in your family life have had great impact on who you are today? What rules and roles are part of the relationship to these systems?

b. Recognize the influence of the child's relationship history and help the child develop productive ways of relating to family and peers

Each child's history is part of the present and continues to be part of their future. Celebrating our history connects us to our ancestors, who have contributed to our identity, and in large part the values, beliefs, and ethics that are part of our present suite of attributes. Some First Nations communities talk about how decisions can be made taking into account our future generations—the next seven to be exact, according to the **seven-generation principle** referenced in the Great Binding Law of the Iroquois Nation. This philosophy can be applied to our work with all children.

> Oren Lyons, a Seneca Faithkeeper of the Onondaga Nation, shared, "the Peacemaker taught us about the Seven Generations. He said, when you sit in council for the welfare of the people, you must not think of yourself or of your family, not even of your generation. He said, make your decisions on behalf of the seven generations coming, so that they may enjoy what you have today." (Lyons, n.d.)

Discussion Opportunity 5:31

Alkia's history is connected to Indigenous people who were put into Residential Schools. Her grandparents and parents are directly impacted, which impacts their ability at times to relate and trust each other and others. Alkia indicates that her parents' ability to care for her is impaired by their self-medication with alcohol and drugs, which they use as a way to escape their pain. For many years, she blames her parents for her own pain and suffering. Alkia now knows that her parents love her and support her as best they can, when they can. She appreciates her culture and the community that her family is a part of, and in time, she is able to better understand how the intergenerational trauma history impacts her family's ability to relate to each other. This understanding has shifted her perspective from blaming them to accepting what cannot be changed. She realizes that she has the power to change her patterns of relating to others.

Ed is the first of his family to attend college. Education is not needed or promoted in his family's history. His father discourages Ed from engaging in higher-level education. He wants his son to work where he works, like his father before him, which creates ongoing conflict in their father/son relationship. Eventually, Ed's father accepts his son's goals as they communicate, explore new patterns of relating, and are able to agree that they can have different personal goals and still be loyal to their family and their family's way of being.

c. Encourage children and families to share folklore and traditions related to family and cultural background. Employ strategies to connect children to their life history and relationships

Notwithstanding the need for change when change is needed, **folklore** and traditions remain of great value in keeping people connected more intimately to their history and as a unifying force in multigenerational relationships. CYCPs can encourage the expression and sharing of folklore and traditions that all cultures carry forward and from place to place in many intriguing and imaginative forms.

How are we to form relationships with young people if we are only marginally present in terms of who we are and how we live (Skott-Myhre, 2018)? We also can consider sharing our own folklore and our stories.

Discussion Opportunity 5:32

What folklore and traditions are part of your culture? How do your parents tell you stories about your culture, traditions, and folklore? Do you know how their parents met, fell in love, decided to live, and so on? Have you ever asked your parents what was going on in their lives when they heard that you were joining the family through birth/adoption/foster care? The children/youth we work with need to hear these stories as well. It helps them recognize they are part of a larger group. They belong, and when we hear the stories, we are included in the circle of belonging.

d. Support parents to develop skills and attitudes which will help them to experience positive and healthy relationships with their children/youth

Parents exert great influence on children; therefore, how children experience their relationship with their parents influences every relationship that follows. When CYCPs support and encourage parents to develop strong relationship skills and constructive attitudes, they are also indirectly promoting positive and healthy relationships for the children and youth as well. Parents might need to be taught how to be in the moment, which a CYCP can model in relating to them and with their children.

Discussion Opportunity 5:33

During a family camp, parents are given "in-the-moment" feedback and opportunities to practise positive teaching moments. Tamara is a mother of three children, aged 6, 9, and 11, who starts out at camp by spending most of her time with the adults and not her children. During a family craft project, the CYCP notices Tamara go out for a cigarette and takes the opportunity to speak with her about the importance of participating with her children. Tamara's belief is that her children needed to be more independent. It becomes apparent that she is trying to teach them a skill that was important for her when she was a child. When they return to the activity, the CYCP models praise and encourage the family to work together and share a laugh, and in the end, the family shares what a positive time they are having together.

CYCPs need to ensure that they are not imposing their own value system and judgments on parents. Instead, we need to embrace that parents are doing the best they can with the skills, knowledge, self-awareness, and resources they have. We can assist them to add to their skill sets, knowledge, and resources so they can experience positive and healthy relationships with their children/youth.

Discussion Opportunity 5:34

What skills and attitudes do you think are important when guiding parents toward more mindful relationships with their children? What did you seek from your parent/child relationships that you may or may not have received? Did the children you work with receive what they needed from their parents? How do you think we learn to be strength-based parents? Can this skill be taught?

4. Teamwork and Professional Communication Skills

a. Establish and maintain effective relationships within a team environment by promoting and maintaining professional conduct, negotiating and resolving conflict, acknowledging individual differences, and supporting team members

Team members' relationships are important for the functioning of the team environment and the ability to provide effective relational practices. The CYCP Code of Ethics addresses the importance of maintaining professional relationships. Team cohesion is essential for CYCPs to provide effective and relational practice to children, youth, and families. Teams need the skill of negotiating and resolving conflict in ways that are respectful to the differences of beliefs, values, thoughts, reactions, and feelings. CYCPs are responsible for maintaining professional relationships with team members and supporting other team members. Having a sense of safety in teams and relationships allows the development of a CYCP; therefore, a team needs to be a safe place to take risks without fear of judgment or repercussions to any member. In the CYC field, you will not likely work alone, and frequently, you will not get to choose who is on your team. It is important that you figure out how to collaborate, appreciate, and navigate differences (Jamieson, 2017).

Discussion Opportunity 5:35

Paul, a supervisor of a home support team, allots time during team meetings to build the relationship among team members. He states, "If the team is functioning well, then the children, youth and families will be fine." When we work together, it is with self-respect and respect for others. The team culture allows for differences, and we support each other. At winter family camp, parents are asked to say what contributes to them coming and having a great time with their family. One parent responds by saying, "The staff team. They have a sense of humour. And it is clear that you all respect each other."

Reflect on a team that you work with and identify what functions well in this team. What characteristics support the relationships on the team? Reflect on a team that does not have supportive relationships. How does this lack of support impact your effectiveness on the team? You can also ask yourself what you need from the teams that you work with. Lastly, what do you do to contribute to these team relationships and overall functioning?

b. Explain and maintain appropriate boundaries with professional colleagues

Communicating clear boundaries and providing an explanation for those boundaries support professional relationships. There needs to be space on teams for each member to discuss personal and professional boundaries so that each member feels supported and respected as an individual as well as a contributor to the team's values and boundaries (Davidson, 2000, 2009).

Discussion Opportunity 5:36

During a team meeting, a CYCP staff member, Jacob, refers to the team as a family. Sonny, another team member, responds by asking team members not to refer to him as family. This is a very important boundary for Sonny, who explained his need, and the team makes the commitment to respect his request.

Emma works on a home support team as a CYCP. She indicates that she will not check emails and phone messages after her shift. Some staff share that Emma's boundary challenges their personal values. Emma explains that maintaining her boundaries is important for her self-care and respecting her family time.

Some examples of team boundaries are: contact expectations, sharing personal information, variances in communication styles, and problem-solving strategies and conflict resolution. What personal and professional boundaries do you need respected in your relationships with colleagues and team?

Discussion Opportunity 5:37

What are the risks of not explaining and maintaining boundaries?

c. Assume responsibility for collective duties and decisions, including responding to team member feedback

As a CYCP, it is important that each member on the team take responsibility for the collective duties of the team. With the privilege of working with children, youth, and families in their life space comes the responsibility and duty to promote and model caring relationships, something that requires every team member working together with other team members to achieve. Teams work in milieus that encompass a variety of duties, which may even include helping a youth clean their room.

We also each benefit when we are able to accept feedback from other team members. We cannot always see and recognize things from other perspectives. Sometimes the feedback is not easy to hear for the CYCP, student, or supervisor. We may be embarrassed that we make errors, or we may worry that our mistake impacts the view that others have of us. Receiving feedback means we engage in the conversation, then make thoughtful choices about when, if, and how to implement the feedback. We can then go back to the team member to find out if he/she/ze/they feel he/she/ze/they were heard (Stone & Heen, 2015).

d. Use appropriate professional language in communication with other team members, consult with other team members to reach consensus on major decisions regarding services for children and youth and families

The use of **professional language** when communicating with team members builds respectful relationships on teams. Professional language includes language that is respectful to yourself and the people with whom you are communicating, and it allows for diverse ways to communicate. Always remember why you are using the words you are using.

Professional language can bring people together because the content is clear. Professional language can also be divisive (if not oppressive) when we walk alongside children, youth, families, and communities. For example, ask yourself: do we work with clients or walk alongside youth? Who is the audience, and what words need to make sense to all parties that do not alienate or divide?

CYCPs never work in isolation. It is important to reach out to team members and reach a consensus on major decisions regarding services. Working together with inclusivity allows the team to function effectively and decisively. The feeling of having played an important part in decision making validates each team member and lends authenticity to the team. High-functioning teams stand out to those we work with.

Discussion Opportunity 5:38

In residence, a house head makes a decision to change the evening programming without communicating with the staff on shift. The staff tell the children what the evening programming is going to be and later communicate the plan needs to change. The children react with disappointment and frustration. The house head goes home, and the staff are left to debrief with the children.

Day-treatment staff cancel gym class because the majority of the children have not finished their homework. CYCP staff disagree with the decision, believing that gym class (body breaks) are important to the children's well-being and focus during afternoon classes.

The preceding examples illustrate the importance of interaction and communication between teams and staff members for the sake of consistency and follow through, because children, youth, and families need clear and consistent messages.

Discussion Opportunity 5:39

What are strategies to make effective team decisions? Have you had the chance to practise some of these when in school or practicum or work? Please provide some examples that you've participated in or witnessed. If you cannot identify any, share an example of an ineffective team decision-making process you have witnessed. Who did the decision benefit?

e. Build cohesion among team members through active participation in team-building initiatives

Each member is responsible for cohesion in the team. Building relationships and taking initiative is the mandate of each CYCP; supervisors and CYCPs alike need to explore initiatives that support the team.

Discussion Opportunity 5:40

A supervisor encourages yearly retreats, a space in which to be in the moment and build relationships and cohesion within the team. Cohesion makes working together a safer environment in which to take creative initiatives. A new supervisor joins a team and schedules a yearly retreat, but when the staff arrive, they are tasked with reviewing the Policy and Practices Manual in preparation for a yearly government audit.

Both process and content are important for healthy team functioning.

Discussion Opportunity 5:41

Reflect on some initiatives you know that promoted cohesion and relationship on a team. What behaviours or characteristics hinder cohesion and negatively affect team relationships?

f. Collect, analyze, and present information in written and oral form by selecting and recording information according to identified needs, agency policies, and guidelines. Accurately record relevant interactions and issues in the relationship

Team members are responsible for knowing and understanding their agency's recording policies and guidelines. Collecting and analyzing information needs to be done in a professional way and according to the expectations of the funding source or government. Recording must be documented and presented in a respectful manner, with the intention of meeting the needs of children, youth, and families. Documents can be subpoenaed to court; therefore, they need to be completed in professional manner. The following is an example of the risk of not recording accurately.

Discussion Opportunity 5:42

The parents of Jules are engaged in a custody dispute over visitation rights. The CYCP records some assumptions about the father, which are used in court as an alienation tactic. Fortunately for the children, the lawyers dispute the credibility of the CYCP reports, but the situation reflects badly on the CYCP. Accurate recording best serves and protects children, youth, families, and the CYCP. When writing any reports, consider how you would feel if the children/youth or family were reading them now or within seven years. (Many records are required to be kept for seven years, and you may not be present if the youth comes back to read them.)

g. Plan, organize, and evaluate interpersonal communications according to the identified need, context, goal of communication, laws/regulations, and ethics involved. Choose an appropriate format, material, language, and style suitable to the audience

CYCPs provide accurate and timely written documentation of both routine and special situations regarding residents, staff, and program activities through the use of observation and recording skills (Roush, 2001). Daily shift logs, medical or dental forms, quarterly plan-of-care reports, and family functioning assessments are all very different forms of writing. The CYCP needs to consider:

- Who the audience is for the writing they are preparing
- Where the report is to be utilized

- How the child/youth/family can contribute
- How to first share reports with the children/youth/families we are working with

Recommendations in a plan-of-care report should never be a surprise to the child/youth/family. In fact, they should always have advance opportunity to read reports and provide input and feedback if reports will be updated based on progress. Reports also need to reflect the voice of the child.

It is always paramount that if, in a CYCP report, a diagnosis is noted, the CYCP identifies who made the diagnosis and when it was made. *It is important that the CYCPs operate within their* **scope of practice** *and do not diagnose.*

h. Acknowledge and respect other disciplines in program planning, communication, and report writing using multidisciplinary and interdisciplinary perspectives. Communicate the expertise of the profession to the team

Children, youth, and families benefit from the expertise of many different disciplines. Many CYCP teams consist of multidisciplinary members. Different disciplines bring their own perspectives, which together form a holistic perspective. For example, one development assessment team is comprised of a psychiatrist, psychologist, speech pathologist, a social worker, a CYCP worker, and placement students; in addition, a few case nurses and medical doctors are also consulted. The CYCP assesses the child in the child's home, at school, and during the intervals of assessment. The rest of the team capitalizes on the supportive relationship the CYCP has built with the child. The CYCP shares her reports with the assessment team, and the assessment results are shared with the child and family. This child truly benefits from a **holistic assessment** and recommendations because each team member brings their expertise and lens to the discussion. Sometimes, these teams need to discuss how they will problem solve and formulate conflict when common ground or common team values are not immediately shared (Frost & Robinson, 2007; Robinson & Cottrell, 2005).

Discussion Opportunity 5:43

What unique ability do you think that you can contribute to a **multidisciplinary team**? What are the benefits of working in multidisciplinary teams?

i. Establish and maintain a connection, alliance, or association with other service providers for the exchange of information and to enhance the quality of service

CYCPs work with multidisciplinary professionals both within and outside of their organizations. We need to make sure we are transparent with children, youth, and families by advising them of whom we share information with, particularly at the informed consent phase of intervention. There are forms that must be completed in order to exchange information between systems. The sharing of information must be in the best interest of the children, youth, and families, with the goal of providing quality of service. CYCPs must be sure they are sharing only that information that needs to be shared.

Discussion Opportunity 5:44

Juan receives a development and educational assessment from a multidisciplinary team. The results indicated that Juan has dyslexia and comprehension challenges. The information benefits Juan when the report is shared with his teacher and system, because the school is able to accommodate his learning style so that he can learn more effectively.

Aruba is living in residential care after she is apprehended from her family due to concerns of neglect and abuse. Her parents continue to work with the child protection agency, receiving education and developing more effective parenting skills. The residential treatment staff and child protection agency develop a connection to best meet the needs of the whole family. In the past, such alliances had very rigid boundaries, and systems worked in isolation.

Jolene, a school CYCP, has a youth ask to be taken to the sexual assault centre. With the youth's permission, Jolene shares this appointment with high school administration instead of just letting the team know that there is a community appointment, while letting her supervisor know where they will be in the community. This precipitates a meeting where school staff develop a plan to support Jolene if additional issues arise.

What are the risks of not building connections, alliances, or associations with other providers? How can you promote flexible alliances with other professionals and systems?

j. Deliver effective oral and written presentations to a professional audience

Education and experience (praxis) in the field are sources of a CYCP's knowledge.

It is vital to share what we know with others. Oral and written presentations enrich the learning community. Some opportunities for presenting are: local agencies, your placement/practicum, and community organizations, school systems, and CYCP and other associations, as well as speaking up at case conferences and more. Contributing and experiencing a CYCP community of practice builds capacity in our relationships as a community. Learning through group interaction and conversation may lead to higher-order thinking skills and the creation of new knowledge or artifacts (Bond & Lockee, 2018).

Discussion Opportunity 5:45

If you are to give a presentation to an audience, what topic would you present, and who would your audience be? What actions would you take to belong to a CYCP learning community?

k. Demonstrate proficiency in using information technology for communication, information access, and decision making

Technology is very much part of our world today. CYCPs need to be proficient in using technology for communication and accessing information, and as a way of making decisions. Social media and other web-based technologies that mediate human communication have transformed the way people communicate, collaborate, and consume (Aral, Dellarocas, & Godes, 2013). It is extremely important that confidentiality be respected and policy on technologies be followed. Clear boundaries around technology must be developed to ensure everyone understands exactly how the technology is being used.

Discussion Opportunity 5:46

A CYCP student gives a 16-year-old male client his personal mobile number. At 3:00 a.m., the student gets a text from the boy, indicating that he is going to kill himself. Not knowing how to respond and not wanting to contact his supervisor at that hour, the student decides to call in the police, who find the boy at home, quiet and safe, but feeling sad and sleepless.

Discussion Opportunity 5:47

What are the drawbacks and advantages of using technology? What boundaries and safeguards need to be put in place in order to use this for a vehicle in communication? What questions can CYCP students bring to supervision about the use of technology with children/youth and families?

Chapter 5 Learning Outcomes Evaluation

- Do you have a greater understanding of the competencies noted under the relationship and communication domain of CYC practice?
- Are you able to apply the domain and competencies to field examples?
- Are you able to use the language of the competencies in discussion you share in and outside of the classroom/workshop with colleagues? Which ones?
- What are some areas of strength (competencies) that you have in this domain?
- Do you have artifacts that provide evidence of this strength?
- What are competencies that you can develop in the relationship and communication domain of practice? (You can use Appendix A as a resource.) Develop a SMART goal in relation to one competency.

REFERENCES

Administration for Children and Families. (2014). *Confidentiality toolkit. A resource tool from the ACF Interoperability Initiative*. Washington, DC: Author.

Ainsworth, M. D. S., & Bell, S. M. (1970). Attachment, exploration, and separation: Illustrated by the behavior of one-year-olds in a strange situation. *Child Development, 41*(1), 49–67. doi: 10.2307/1127388

Apter, T. (2018). *Passing judgement: Praise and blame in everyday life.* New York, NY: W. W. Norton and Company.

Aral, S., Dellarocas, C., & Godes, D. (2013). Introduction to the Special Issue—Social media and business transformation: A framework for research. *Information Systems Research, 24*(1), 3–13. doi: 10.1287/isre.1120.0470

Bell, D. (2014). Recognizing youth as the experts in their own lives is more than humble or respectful, it is a good strategy for engagement and promoting positive behavioral change. [Film]. USA: American Academy of Pediatrics.

Blum, R. W., & Rinehart, P. M. (1997). *Reducing the risk: Connections that make a difference in the lives of youth.* [Monograph]. Bethesda, MD: Add Health.

Bond, M. A., & Lockee, B. B. (2018). Evaluating the effectiveness for faculty inquiry groups in communities of practice for faculty professional development. *Journal of Formative Design in Learning, 2*(1), 1–7. doi:10.1007/s41686-018-0015-7

Bowlby, J. (1951). *Maternal care and children's mental health.* Geneva, Switzerland: World Health Organization.

Capoferri, C. (2014). The collective parent: Theory and process. *Transactional Analysis Journal, 44*(2), 175–185. doi:10.1177/0362153714545313

Carroll, J. B. (Ed.). (1997). *Language, thought, and reality: Selected writings of Benjamin Lee Whorf.* Cambridge, MA: Technology Press of Massachusetts Institute of Technology. (Original work published 1956)

Chan, D. (2016). Learning to see things from another's perspective. *The Straits Times.* Retrieved from https://www.straitstimes.com/opinion/learning-to-see-things-from-anothers-perspective

Child and Youth Care Certification Board (CYCCB). (2016). Relationship & communication. College Station, TX: Author. Retrieved from https://www.cyccb.org/competencies/relationship-communication

Cornish, L., & Jenkins, K. A., (2012). Encouraging teacher development through embedding reflective practice in assessment. *Asia-Pacific Journal of Teacher Education, 40*(2), 159–170. doi: 10.1080/1359866X.2012.669825

Crisis Prevention Institute (CPI). (2011). De-escalation tips. Retrieved June 17, 2018, from https://www.crisisprevention.com/Blog/June-2011/De-escalation-Tips

Darley, J. M., & Gross, P. H. (1983). A hypothesis-confirming bias in labeling effects. *Journal of Personality and Social Psychology, 44*(1), 20–33. doi: 10.1037/0022-3514.44.1.20

Davidson, J. C. (2000). Knowing where to draw the lines: Professional boundaries with clients. [Training manuscript]. Houston, TX: Protective Services Training Institute of Texas, University of Houston.

Davidson, J. C. (2009). Knowing where to draw the lines: Professional relationships boundaries and child and youth workers. *CYC-Online: E-journal of the International Child and Youth Care Network (CYC-Net),* (128). Retrieved from http://www.cyc-net.org/cyc-online/cyconline-oct2009-davidson.html

Eberhardt, J. L., Dasgupta, N., & Banaszynski, T. L. (2003). Believing is seeing: The effects of racial labels and implicit beliefs on face perception. *Personality and Social Psychology Bulletin, 29*(3), 360–370.

Fraser, T. (2014). Home can be where your story begins. *Relational Child and Youth Care Practice, 27*(1), 27–34.

Freeman, J. (2013). The field of child and youth care: Are we there yet? *Child and Youth Services, 34*(2), 100–111. doi:10.1080/0145935X.2013.785875

Freeman, J., & Garfat, T. (2014). Being, interpreting, doing: A framework for organizing the characteristics of a relational child and youth care approach. *CYC-Online: E-journal of the International Child and Youth Care Network (CYC-Net)*, (179), 23–27. Retrieved from http://www.cyc-net.org/cyc-online/jan2014.pdf#page=23

Frost, N., & Robinson, M. (2007). Joining up children's services: Safeguarding children in multidisciplinary teams. *Child Abuse Review, 16*(3), 184–199. doi:10.1002/car.967

Fox, L. (n.d.). Understanding and reducing power struggles: Transference and countertransference in treatment relationships. Retrieved from http://www.cyc-net.org/Documents/powercontrolhandouts.pdf

Garfat, T. (1993). Listen to the silence: The multigenerational influence of the work of Henry Maier. *Journal of Child & Youth Care, 8*(2), 105–110.

Garfat, T. (1998). The effective child and youth care intervention. *Journal of Child and Youth Care, 12*(1–2), 1–168.

Irmsher, K. (2000). Communication skills for leaders. *CYC-Online: E-journal of the International Child and Youth Care Network (CYC-Net)*, (15). Retrieved from http://www.cyc-net.org/cyc-online/cycol-0400-skills.html

Ivey, A., Ivey, M., & Zalaquett, C. (2015). Essentials of intentional interviewing: Counseling in a multicultural world (3rd ed.). Pacific Grove, CA: Brooks Cole.

Jamieson, D. (2017). Vintage baby boomer: Other care. *Relational Child and Youth Care Practice, 30*(3), 103–107.

Jung, C., Howard, R., Emory, R., & Pino, R. (1973). *Interpersonal communications: Participant materials and leader's manual*. Portland, OR: Northwest Regional Educational Laboratory.

Krueger, M. (1994). Rhythm and presence: Connecting with children on the edge. *Journal of Emotional and Behavioral Problems, 3*(1), 49–51.

Landreth, G. L. (2002). *Play therapy: The art of the relationship*. New York, NY: Brunner-Routledge.

Lathrap, M. T. (1895). *The poems and written addresses of Mary T. Lathrap with a short sketch of her life*. Bay City, MI: Woman's Christian Temperance Union of Michigan.

Linehan, M. (2014). *DBT skills training manual*. New York, NY: Guilford Press.

Ludy-Dobson, C. R., & Perry, B. D. (2010). The role of healthy relational interactions in buffering the impact of childhood trauma. In E. Gil (Ed.), *Working with children to heal interpersonal trauma: The power of play* (pp. 26–43). New York, NY: Guilford Press.

Lyons, O. (n.d.). Seven generations—The role of the chief. Retrieved from http://www.pbs.org/warrior/content/timeline/opendoor/roleOfChief.html

Martin, J. J. (2013). Out of focus: Exploring practitioners' understanding of child sexual abuse images on the Internet. *Tspace*. Retrieved from https://tspace.library.utoronto.ca/bitstream/1807/68955/7/Martin_Jennifer_J_201306_PhD_thesis.pdf

Martin, J., & Alaggia, R. (2013). Sexual abuse images in cyberspace: Expanding the ecology of the child. *Journal of Child Sexual Abuse, 22*(4), 398–415. doi:10.1080/10538712.2013.781091

Menezes, C. B., Pereira, M. G., & Bizarro. L. (2012). Sitting and silence mediation as a strategy to study emotional regulation. *Journal of Psychology and Neuroscience, 5*(1), 27–36. doi:10.3922/j.psns.2012.1.05

McLeod, J., & McLeod, J. (2011). *Counselling skills: A practical guide for counsellors and helping professionals.* Maidenhead, UK: McGraw-Hill Education.

Ontario Ministry of Training, Colleges and Universities. (2014). *Child and youth worker program standard.* Ottawa, ON: Queen's Printer for Ontario.

Opie, I., & Opie, P. (1997). *The Oxford dictionary of nursery rhymes* (2nd ed.). Oxford, UK: Oxford University Press.

Pascal, B. (1958). *Pascal's pensees.* New York, NY: E. P. Dutton and Co.

Phelan, J. (2003). Creating safe relationships. *CYC-Online: E-journal of the International Child and Youth Care Network (CYC-Net),* (54). Retrieved from http://www.cyc-net.org/cyc-online/cycol-0703-relationships.html

Pickhardt, C. (2013). Surviving your child's adolescence: How to understand, and even enjoy, the rocky road to independence. Hoboken, NJ: John Wiley and Sons.

Perry, B. D. (2009a). Examining child maltreatment through a neurodevelopmental lens: Clinical applications of the neurosequential model of therapeutics. *Journal of Loss and Trauma, 14*(4), 240–255. doi:10.1080/15325020903004350

Perry, B. (2009b). On the brain: Transitions. *CYC-Online: E-journal of the International Child and Youth Care Network (CYC-Net),* (121). Retrieved January 1, 2018, from http://www.cyc-net.org/cyc-online/cyconline-mar2009-perry.html

Perry, B. D., & Szalavitz, M. (2017). *The boy who was raised as a dog and other stories from a child psychiatrist's notebook: What traumatized children can teach us about loss, love, and healing.* New York, NY: Basic Books.

Robinson, M., & Cottrell, D. (2005). Health professionals in multi-disciplinary and multi-agency teams: Changing professional practice. *Journal of Interprofessional Care, 19*(6), 547–560. doi: 10.1080/13561820500396960

Rogers, C. (1980). *A way of being.* Boston, MA: Houghton Mifflin.

Rogers, C., & Farson, R. E. (2015). *Active listening.* Eastford, CT: Martino Publishing. (Original work published 1957)

Rosenthal, R., & Jacobson, L. (1992). *Pygmalion in the classroom: Expanded edition.* New York, NY: Irvington.

Roush, D. (2001). The juvenile careworker. *CYC-Online: E-journal of the International Child and Youth Care Network (CYC-Net),* (24). Retrieved June 2, 2018, from http://www.cyc-net.org/cyc-online/cycol-0101-detention.html

Ruch, G. (2005). Relationship-based practice and reflective practice: Holistic approaches to contemporary child care social work. *Journal of Child and Family Social Work, 10*(2), 111–123. doi:10.1111/j.1365-2206.2005.00359.x

Schore, A. N. (2012). *The science of the art of psychotherapy.* New York, NY: W. W. Norton & Company.

Skott-Myhre, H. (2018). No perfections, no purity. *CYC-Online: E-journal of the International Child and Youth Care Network (CYC-Net),* (232), 7–12. Retrieved from https://www.cyc-net.org/cyc-online/june2018.pdf

Siegel, D. J. (2011). *Mindsight: The new science of personal transformation.* New York, NY: Bantam Books.

Siegel, D. J. (2012). *Pocket guide to interpersonal neurobiology: An integrative handbook of the mind.* New York, NY: W. W. Norton & Company.

Sikorski, P., & Vittone, T. (2016). How to avoid power struggles. [Blog post]. Crisis Prevention Institute. Retrieved from https://www.crisisprevention.com/Blog/April-2016/How-to-Avoid-Power-Struggles.

Solomon, R. (2017). *Consent, documentation, confidentiality and disclosure in an era of privacy concerns.* PHIPA in Practice. Retrieved from http://www.excellenceforchildandyouth.ca/sites/default/files/docs/phipa_presentation.pdf

Snow, K. (2006). Bilingualism: The two languages of young people in care. *Scottish Journal of Residential Child Care, 5*(2), 45–55.

Snow, K. (2013). Habits for life: Routines as fundamental to CYC practice. *Relational Child and Youth Care Practice, 26*(2), 53–56.

Straus, M. A., Gelles, R. J., & Steinmetz, S. K. (2017). *Behind closed doors.* New York, NY: Routledge.

Stone, D., & Heen, S. (2015). *Thanks for the feedback.* New York, NY: Penguin Books.

Sue, D. W., Capodilupo, C. M., Torino, G. C., Bucceri, J. M., Holder, A. M. B., Nadal, K. L., & Esquilin, M. (2007). Racial microaggressions in everyday life: Implications for clinical practice. *American Psychologist, 62*(4), 271–286.

VanderVen, K. (1992). From the side of the swimming pool and the evolving story of child and youth care work. *Journal of Child and Youth Care Work, 8,* 5–6.

CHAPTER 6

Developmental Practice Methods

Learning Outcomes

- Review the developmental practice methods domain of CYC practice.
- Apply the domain and competencies to field examples.
- Engage in discussion with colleagues about the domain and competencies.
- Identify areas of strength and development.

The Child and Youth Care Certification Board (2016) indicates that:

> Practitioners recognize the critical importance of developmental practice methods focused in child and youth care practice: Genuine Relationships, Health and Safety, Intervention Planning, Environmental Design and Maintenance, Program Planning and Activity Programming, Activities of Daily Living, Group Work, Counseling, Behavioral Guidance, Family (Caregiver) Engagement, Community Engagement. These are designed to promote optimal development for children, youth, and families including those at-risk and with special needs within the context of the family, community and the lifespan.

A. FOUNDATIONAL KNOWLEDGE

- Health and safety
- Intervention theory and design
- Environmental design

- Program planning and activity programming, including:
  - Developmental rationales
  - Basic strategies of program planning
  - Specific developmental outcomes expected as a result of participating in activities
  - Principles of activity programming (e.g., activity analysis, adaptation, strategies for involving youth in activities)
  - Relationship of developmental processes to the activities of daily living (e.g., eating, grooming, hygiene, sleeping, rest)
  - The significance of play activities
  - Community resources for connecting children, youth, and families with activity and recreational programs
- Behavioural guidance methods, including conflict resolution, crisis management, life space interviewing
- Behaviour management methods
- Counselling skills
- Understanding and working with groups
- Understanding and working with families
- Understanding and working with communities

B. PROFESSIONAL COMPETENCIES

The Child and Youth Care Certification Board (2016) divides the developmental practice methods domain into 11 areas:

1. Genuine relationships
2. Health and safety
3. Intervention planning
4. Environmental design and maintenance
5. Program planning and activity programming
6. Activities of daily living
7. Group process
8. Counselling
9. Behaviour guidance
10. Family and caregiver engagement
11. Community engagement

1. Genuine Relationships

"It's all about relationship." This is the mantra of CYC practice. The relationships CYCPs birth, grow, and maintain are with children, youth, families, and communities.

Relational-centred practice honours the collaborative meaning-making process that is so central to CYC practice (Bellefeuille & McGrath, 2013). This mantra is also about the relationships we share with other CYCPs and other members of our multidisciplinary teams, members of the child/youth/family/community's team, supervisors, and supervisees. CYCPs model for parents, children, youth, and communities a CYCP way of being (Brendtro & Ness, 1995; Garfat & Fulcher, 2011; Laursen, 2002). "Genuine relationships can also be loving relationships. Love is both a Noun—a feeling, and a Verb—a practice. The Greek word for love—agape—combines feeling and action. Love means to will the best for others and to do all we can to see that it happens for them. This is what we do" (Fox, 2017).

a. Recognize the critical importance of genuine relationships based on empathy and positive regard in promoting optimal development for children, youth, and families

Genuine relationships are integral to CYC practice. This genuineness is based on empathy and positive regard in promoting optimal development for children, youth, and families. CYCPs value working with others in a way that is authentic or real so we can attempt to see the world through another's eyes (Rogers, 1961).

How do you define genuine? How can you see genuine? How do you feel when something is genuine? Genuine can be hard to define, but when we see it, we know it. The children/youth and families we work with will be able to see and experience genuineness when it is authentically shared.

Empathy for others is tied closely to our attachment style (Bowlby, 1969/1999). When CYCPs are empathetic, we have a sense of the experience of the other from their perspective.

The idea of positive regard derives from the work of Carl Rogers. **Positive regard** means to provide care to a person irrespective of what they say or do (Rogers, 1980).

Discussion Opportunity 6:1

In a small group, please discuss someone in your life who demonstrates genuineness to others. Then, discuss what you think are the interactions or actions that children/youth/families look for in the CYCPs that work with them so they feel/believe that the relationship is genuine.

b. Forming, maintaining, and building upon such relationships as a central change strategy

Relationships are the central change strategy in our praxis, so all CYCPs strive to form, build, and maintain relationships with children, youth, families, communities, and colleagues. We support those we work with as well as identify who else can support them, who can challenge them, and who can become a family for them if there is no family available. CYCPs believe that relationships are the most important tool in our toolbox—"it is all about relationship."

Carl Rogers (1961) identified seven characteristics of a fully functioning person. Each of these characteristics enrich our ability to be in relationship with others:

1. A growing openness to experience—they move away from defensiveness and have no need for subception (a perceptual defense that involves unconsciously applying strategies to prevent a troubling stimulus from entering consciousness).

2. An increasingly existential lifestyle—living each moment fully—not distorting the moment to fit personality or self-concept but allowing personality and self-concept to emanate from the experience. This results in excitement, daring, adaptability, tolerance, spontaneity, and a lack of rigidity and suggests a foundation of trust. "To open one's spirit to what is going on now, and discover in that present process whatever structure it appears to have" (Rogers, 1961).

3. Increasing organismic trust—they trust their own judgment and their ability to choose behaviour that is appropriate for each moment. They do not rely on existing codes and social norms, but trust that as they are open to experiences, they will be able to trust their own sense of right and wrong.

4. Freedom of choice—not being shackled by the restrictions that influence an incongruent individual, they are able to make a wider range of choices more fluently. They believe that they play a role in determining their own behaviour and so feel responsible for their own behaviour.

5. Creativity—it follows that they will feel more free to be creative. They will also be more creative in the way they adapt to their own circumstances without feeling a need to conform.

6. Reliability and constructiveness—they can be trusted to act constructively. An individual who is open to all their needs will be able to maintain a balance between them. Even aggressive needs will be matched and balanced by intrinsic goodness in congruent individuals.

7. A rich full life—Rogers describes the life of the fully functioning individual as rich, full, and exciting and suggests that they experience joy and pain, love and heartbreak, fear and courage more intensely. Rogers's (1961) description of "the good life" is as follows: "This process of the good life is not, I am convinced, a life for the faint-hearted. It involves the stretching and growing of becoming more and more of one's potentialities. It involves the courage to be. It means launching oneself fully into the stream of life."

Relationships are reciprocal, so if we are being true to our relationships, and also ourselves, then we need to reflect on what we are getting out of our relationships (Matthews, 2005).

When we stop to ask why—*Reflective Practice in Action*—why do we do this work? Is it because we are open to experience or exercise creativity or that we trust our feelings when we work with others? Personal reflection and self-discovery need to be an ongoing growth process. It is one that is often coupled with peer consultation or supervision. We have to try to look at ourselves through the mirror held up for us by those we work with. We also have to accept that we only have control over ourselves, and if that is true, then we cannot change those we work with, but we can support their self-determined or self-actualized change (Burns, 2012).

Discussion Opportunity 6:2

If you were to create a chart that showed all the tools in your CYCP toolkit, what symbol would represent the skill of building relationships? Please share this with one or more individuals in your group.

Discussion Opportunity 6:3

When we work in a residential milieu, we must ask questions about safety. What is the minimum number of times the CYCP should check that the smoke detectors are working? When should batteries in smoke detectors be changed? Thinking of your work/practicum/placement experience site, is there a policy that communicates these fire safety expectations? If not, how do you think this policy should be worded, and how do we ensure that staff adhere to it so children/youth/families/communities and team members are safe?

Life spaces need to be maintained to address local fire codes and enforce preventative safety measures. It's also important to make sure the right resources are in place should emergencies occur. Fire plans, exit points, and a designated meeting place to assemble when alarms go off (Samis, 2016) should all be communicated so everyone knows what to do in an emergency situation. Children should also have bedroom doors closed at night to ensure they have extra time to escape should a fire occur.

1. Participate effectively in emergency procedures in a specific practice setting and carry them out in a developmentally appropriate manner.

Wherever people live, learn, work, and play needs to be a safe environment. CYCPs ensure that they adhere to and implement effective emergency procedures that address the needs of the specific practice site they are working in with the population that they are working with. CYCPs need to be able to provide basic first aid interventions and also recognize when additional interventions are required. Fire drills, fire plans, and school safety drills are required to help all of us practise safe behaviours and responses to potentially unsafe situations (Office of the Fire Marshal, n.d.). The CYCP needs to be aware of whose needs are being met. A person who has survived a fire may need preparation that a fire alarm will be ringing as they may experience post-trauma symptoms and subsequent behaviours. A child with sensory integration challenges may need to practise fire safety with the children and youth so that they have some preparation if the fire alarm goes off, or they may need to be consciously absent when the practice happens until a better plan can be created (Fraser, 2015).

Discussion Opportunity 6:4

Have someone in your group/class look up the term *sensory integration challenges*. Discuss what a child with sensory integration challenges may experience when he/she/ze/they hear a fire alarm. What would you as that person's CYCP want to do to help him/her/hir/them feel as comfortable as possible?

It is important to be aware that this may also be a venue for CYCPs to advocate for those they work with. Some school environments will alert caregivers when lockdowns have occurred so parents can process the experience at home. If caregivers are not alerted, they may not be aware of why their children are reacting and also may not be able to preemptively provide support or preparation. CYCPs also need to reflect on how they are anticipating emergency procedures, especially if they have their own personal history with the anticipated or experienced event. We always need to be mindful of our own self-regulation and how it impacts co-workers, children, youth, families, and the communities in which we live, work, and love.

2. Incorporate environmental safety into the arrangement of space, the storage of equipment and supplies, and the design and implementation of activities.

Environmental safety addresses the space where equipment and activities will occur. There are mandated safety rules for publicly funded institutions such as schools, group homes, and recreation centres. Though fear of liability may underpin the creation of rules for safe environments in institutional milieus, CYCPs are nonetheless committed to creating healing environments. CYCPs are therefore cognizant about planning and facilitating environmentally safe activities in the spaces that we work, play, and live in with children, youth, families, and communities.

c. Health

1. Access the health and safety regulations applicable to a specific practice setting, including laws/regulations related to disability.

Around the world, CYCPs need to adhere to municipal, state, provincial, and federal laws and regulations. This means that we need to investigate what these are and follow them accordingly so that the needs of all community members are inclusively addressed. The CYCP also needs to recognize the vulnerable position that those they work with are in and advocate for change where required. For example, fire codes and fire risks/safety are not often thought of carefully until a fire occurs (Ontario Association of Children's Aid Societies, n.d.).

This is especially important when we are supporting individuals who have a disability that may not be visible to others. Are we ensuring that their rights are being honoured?

Discussion Opportunity 6:5

What might be examples of laws/regulations that are related to disability in community, education, justice, and residential settings?

Your instructor/professor may divide your learning community into four groups so each group can address this question for a specific setting/milieu.

2. Use current health, hygiene, and nutrition practices to support healthy development and prevent illness.

Current health, hygiene, and nutrition practices can include activities that may be taken for granted, such as handwashing. Handwashing may need to be modelled with the children and youth we work with. Sending a child to the shower without being clear about the expectations can be a set-up for a child who has never had anyone teach them how a cloth or soap is used for self-care. Privacy also needs to be taken into account, as well as the **developmental stage of functioning** in the moment. CYCPs are aware that a child can function in various domains all at the same time as a result of neglect and abuse. For example, a child can present as a mature 11-year-old but may regress to being 5 at bath time due to a history of sexual abuse that occurred in a bathroom.

Teaching **sexual safety** as well as universal precautions is important not only for children/youth with high-risk behaviours but for all youth (Hindman, 2006). Creating opportunities for such discussions on an ongoing basis ensures that children/youth do not perceive that these conversations are occurring as a result of their experiences. There are some health issues and information that can be shared with the whole team; other information may only be appropriate to share with residence staff versus day-treatment staff or teachers.

Discussion Opportunity 6:6

What might be examples of health information that can be shared with the entire staff versus certain teams or individual staff members?

3. Discuss health-related information with children, youth, and families as appropriate to a specific practice setting.

Knowing what is appropriate to a specific practice setting may require discussion, direction, and/or input from your supervisor or team members, as well as the families you work with. For example, if you are a CYCP working with street youth, it may be very appropriate to talk about healthy sexuality and informed consent. However, if you work in a junior kindergarten classroom, this may not be a discussion you initiate. Another example is the value of exercise and healthy food, which a CYCP might assume is an appropriate discussion for all ages. It may not be appropriate, however, if you are working with youth that have eating disorders. CYCPs can confirm what is a beneficial conversation by sharing ideas with team members.

Discussion Opportunity 6:7

In a small group, discuss fire drills that you experienced in school. Also share if you practised fire drills at home and any other safety measures your family took for fire prevention.

Environments also need to be emotionally and sexually safe for the children/youth and the families that they live with (Fraser, 2011). The environment can contribute to safety by ensuring that privacy is supported with doors; the availability of private spaces for toileting, calm-down needs, and hygiene practices; and so on. Historically, some children have been physically and sexually interfered with by other residents in residential programs (Giles, 1990; Michael, 1994). Residential programs need to consider decision-making practices regarding when, how, and if children can share sleeping spaces, particularly if they are in different age groups. The message children deserve to receive is "this is a caring and safe place. We will protect you and help you grow. Try us" (Michael, 1994).

Discussion Opportunity 6:8

We need to share with children why they are taking the medication that they are taking. Once we have done that, we can discuss what the side effects are and what the benefits are. In this way we are obtaining their informed consent. CYCPs need to consider the legal requirements for informed consent (which are dependent on their geographical location) and also ethical requirements for informed consent. CYCPs may need to educate and prepare parents to discuss health diagnoses with children. It is important to create space for children to safely discuss their physical and mental health with all the adults who are to be involved in these conversations.

> The recommendation to provide illness explanations in a climate of openness and support, and in a warm, empathetic manner, extends to delivering mental health diagnoses to children. Open discussion signals that adults value children's questions and respect their ability to take part in the conversation. (Bringewatt, 2017, p. 1967)

How can the CYCP communicate important health information to children and youth? Why is it important to be transparent about the use and side effects of medication?

4. Describe the rules and procedures for storage and administration of medication in a specific practice site, and participate as appropriate.

All jurisdictions have policies about medication storage and distribution. Medication (both prescribed and over the counter) needs to be locked up and tracked with medication forms. This is important in milieus where more than one caregiver is providing medication and also important so a clear health history is maintained. Medication can only be transferred from one carer or professional to another. In some geographical areas, blister packages are required for medication as they are separated for each day that the medication is required, and therefore errors or omissions are easily noticed. Other agencies require that two staff provide signatures before medication is dispensed.

For example, in the 1980s, a day-shift CYCP in a group home could send monthly stimulant medication to the school by way of the Grade 8 resident. When a relief worker observed this interaction, he expressed concern that the child could be robbed of medication on the way to school or medication could be lost or sold. Thereafter, staff dropped medication at the office of the school.

d. Infectious diseases

1. Access current information on infectious diseases of concern in a specific practice setting.

In Canada, public health departments usually post highlights of concerns; in the United States, this is one of the roles of the Centers for Disease Control (CDC). CYCPs should check with the relative health authorities in their area for current information about infectious diseases, such as current outbreaks as this protects children/youth/families/ communities and well as all who serve them.

2. Describe the components relevant to practice.

Components of infectious disease concerns can impact the population that the CYCP works alongside, as well as the milieu that the CYCP works in.

Discussion Opportunity 6:9

A youth is admitted into an adolescent group home and is Hepatitis B positive but wants this information kept confidential from other group home residents. He also engages in sexual relationships with other residents, and the staff are not sure if he is using standard precautions and protection. Staff are told they cannot share his health status with other residents. Staff solve the problem about how to share preventative information while respecting confidentiality by facilitating a group discussion on ways to keep safe in regards to informed consent, standard precautions, and protection without talking about specific members of the group home community.

If you were a CYCP working in a residential milieu and needed to create a prevention program, what agencies could you partner with to access accurate health information?

3. Employ appropriate infection control practices.

Standard precautions address handling body fluids, including saliva, breast milk, blood, semen, and vaginal secretions. CYCPs are required to wear gloves when in contact with any bodily fluids. Take care when handling sharp instruments. Immediately wash surfaces that come in contact with bodily fluids (CDC, 1988).

Discussion Opportunity 6:10

1. What are strategies CYCPs can encourage children/youth and families to practise to control and prevent infection?
2. What are strategies that CYCPs need to practise when working in various milieus?
3. What are prevention strategies that are practised universally?

2. Intervention Planning

a. Assess strengths and needs

CYCPs can assess the strengths and needs of the child/youth/family in the milieu that is to provide service. We can assess strengths and needs by listening to the stories of those we walk alongside without judgment, looking for resiliency within them. Without understanding a person's needs we cannot support, encourage, or help build skills. Listening to the person's needs is essential to helping achieve goals and desires. Every child, youth, parent, teacher, and worker with whom I have had the privilege to be in relationship taught me that I have a responsibility to hold their stories with a gentle embrace and an open heart without judgment (Ventrella, 2017).

For example, children placed in foster care require CYCPs to identify their strengths as well as needs. Their successful adjustment in foster care, as well as their future well-being, is largely dependent on how well their needs are met at this critical developmental time in their young lives (Scozzaro & Janikowski, 2015, p. 2564).

When reviewing history or referral information, it is important to identify any trauma history or medical diagnoses when working with children/youth and families. Have any other professionals worked with them in the past or are working with them currently? These factors will impact intervention planning because we need to address needs individually.

b. Plan goals and activities that take agency mission and group objectives, individual histories and interests into account

CYCPs take into consideration the needs of children, youth, families, and community, as well as interests and social location. Agency missions and objectives can provide the context for service. These can also provide necessary resources or, conversely, require a referral for another agency to provide the needed interventions.

A high level of understanding is required in order to assess the impact of individual histories and interests. CYCPs also need to consider what impact past trauma may have in the story of those they work with. Dr. Bruce Perry (cited in MacKinnon, 2012) states that for trauma healing to occur the intervention must be:

- Relational (safe)
- Relevant (developmentally matched to the individual)
- Repetitive (patterned)
- Rewarding (pleasurable)
- Rhythmic (resonant with neural patterns)
- Respectful (of the child, family, and culture)

The following is an example of a format to consider when planning an activity. CYCP Peter Hoag of Toronto, Ontario, shares his unpublished model of activity planning with students at Sheridan College. His colleague, CYCP Julie Jaglowitz, named his approach **"the Magic Formula."**

- Mr. Hoag encourages CYCPs to assess the population they work with (child, family, group, or community; age of population; culture; etc.). This assessment includes needs, strengths, skills, abilities, and challenges. The CYCP can be curious about why the individual/group has been referred to the program, and what their age, gender, and culture are. The CYCP can also ask about their beliefs and attitudes, as well as their life in the context of their life spaces and systems such as the **chronosystem** (Maslow, 1943).
- The CYCP is then to assess the activity. How will this activity benefit the population that the CYCP is working with? What is the goal of this activity? Fun is a "given," but what does the CYCP believe, think, or hope the population will get out of engaging in this activity? What do the children/youth/families or communities want to get out of engaging in this activity?
- Who is the person facilitating this activity? Why are you the best CYCP to facilitate? Would it be better for someone who shared the social location of participants or someone whom the population has a strong relationship with to facilitate?

- The last step of the Magic Formula is the assessment/review part of the process. How are you going to assess effectiveness? What happened? Is it what you hoped would happen? Did you meet your goal with this activity? Was the need addressed? Most importantly, did the children/youth/group or family get what they wanted out of the experience? What can you do differently next time? CYCPs always need to assess/review/debrief interventions before planning again (Hoag, personal communication, 2013).

Discussion Opportunity 6:11

Share with your group an activity that you have facilitated or have observed. What works well; what does not? What would you do now if you were going to facilitate the same activity today?

c. Encourage child/youth and family participation in assessment and goal setting in intervention planning and the development of individual plans

CYCPs involve children/youth and families in assessment and goal setting in intervention planning and the development of individual plans. In order to engage and encourage participation, we need to create relationships that are safe or attempt to create safety, as many who have come before us have caused damage and hurt. Safety includes physical safety, emotional safety, sexual safety (Fraser, 2011), environmental safety, and ideological safety (Burns, 2006). That said, CYCPs do our work in the life space.

d. Integrate client empowerment and support of strengths into conceptualizing and designing interventions

> Empowerment is a multifaceted social process that has effects not only at the individual level of analysis, but also at the environmental and community levels. At the individual level, empowerment is a process whereby individuals struggle to reduce personal powerlessness by having increased control over their lives. (Delamere, Morden, & Rose, 2006, para. 17)

Once we are aware of client strengths, needs, and goals we need to take the time and determine a way to not only include them in intervention planning but ultimately have *them* plan the intervention. Providing young people with innovative opportunities to participate in their care in relevant and meaningful ways cannot be based on the availability of staff, resources, or programs (Brown & Hann, 2018, p. 18).

Asking children, youth, and families, "What do you need right now?" is a powerful first question. It honours the belief that, inside, every person knows what they need, and it is the CYCP's job to create the space for them to honour, identify, and share this. Garfat (2001) identifies that, developmentally, CYCPs move from wanting to:

1. Do for another
2. Do to another
3. Do with another
4. Do together

Designing interventions together or taking direction from the child/youth/family/group contributes to increasing self-efficacy and currency.

> There is a growing body of evidence that human accomplishments and well-being require an optimistic sense of personal efficacy. This is because ordinary social realities are strewn with impediments, adversities, setbacks, frustrations, and inequities. People must have a robust sense of personal efficacy to sustain the perseverance needed to succeed. (Bandura, 2000, 21)

Many children/youth have skills at assessing incongruency, so if a CYCP is not emotionally ready to be there for the child in an authentic way, he/she/ze/they then become a threat in that child's life space. Every time you "can" yourself, you send yourself into activated sympathetic or parasympathetic response (Lisa Dion, personal communication, 2017). CYCPs sometimes prepare (without intent) for "**fight, flight, or freeze**" when entering into new situations or situations that we fear will be conflictual. We need to be calm and regulated before interacting with children/youth/and families.

e. Develop and present a theoretical/empirical rationale for a particular intervention or approach

The theoretical and empirical rationale for any intervention or approach is grounded in relational practices. According to Anglin (2014), CYC practice is not rocket science: it's far more complex than that. In our current practices, our interventions are informed by the needs of those we walk beside, the contexts in which we work, and the evidenced-based or emerging practices that are considered to be the best approach. Garfat and Fulcher (2012) highlight 26 characteristics that we need to consider in interventions and approaches. These are: participating with people as they live their lives; rituals of encounter; meeting them where they are at; connection and engagement; being in relationship; using daily life events to facilitate change; examining context; intentionality; responsive developmental practice; hanging out; hanging in; doing with, not for or to; a needs-based focus; working in the now; flexibility and individuality; rhythmicity; meaning-making; reflection; purposeful use of activities; family-orientated; being emotionally present; counselling on the go; strengths-based and resiliency focused; love; and it's all about us.

Relationships with those we walk beside are the biggest tool in our intervention toolbox.

f. Select and apply an appropriate planning model

One planning model that has been utilized in the United Kingdom and Canada is the Choice and Partnership Approach, created by Ann Richmond and Steve East Herts (Fuggle, McHugh, Gore, Dixon, Curran, & Cutinha, 2016; Wilson, Metcalfe, & McLeod, 2015; York & Kingsbury, 2013). This approach in service-delivery planning is to engage the child/adolescent and family in determining what they want to work on and how they want the external service to provide support. The treatment plan is directed by the needs and goals of the child/youth/family/community.

Discussion Opportunity 6:12

1. What are some planning models that you have observed in your practicum or place of work?

g. Select appropriate goals or objectives from plans, and design activities, interactions, and management methods that support plans in an appropriate way

Selecting appropriate goals and objectives cannot be accomplished alone. SMART (specific, measurable, attainable, realistic, timely) goals (Doran, Miller, & Cunningham, 1981) need to be identified in collaboration with the person we walk beside. It is not helpful to have goals determined by others. We are more likely to accomplish something if it is our own agenda. Once goals are identified, we can break down the action plan.

h. Work with client and team to assess and monitor progress and revise the plan as needed

CYCPs need to work with multidisciplinary teams and the child, youth, and family to assess and monitor progress and revise plans accordingly.

The voice of the child/youth and family is important to include and evaluate so that accommodations and changes can be made and they can continue to progress toward their goal.

This is why an assessment or reassessment can be valuable: to ensure that we are creating and revising the most helpful treatment plan. For example, a child who has sensory issues may require input from another member of the team, such as an occupational therapist. This professional will assess and contribute to the treatment plan, whereas another professional may see the child's behaviour in the face of sensory triggers as requiring behavioural intervention instead of the child requiring preventative environmental supports (Miller, 2014).

3. Environmental design and maintenance

a. Recognize the messages conveyed by environment

Environments communicate messages across the range of being open and inviting to being chaotic and unsafe (Burns, 2006). Organizations need to be aware of the messages they are conveying through their physical spaces. Does the space feel inclusive and engaging? Are people free to roam or are there restricted areas? Are doors generally kept closed? Are there private or quiet spaces for people to access? Be aware that your physical environment sends a message.

Discussion Opportunity 6:13

Observe hallways at your college/university or agency. What do the hallways say about those and to those who visit them? Are these hallways warm and inviting? Are they culturally welcoming? Who are the people in the environment? Do children/youth/families see others that look like them, or are all the staff representative of one cultural group, spiritual group, or gender?

Those we work with gain a sense of who visits the milieu by just spending time in it. The next time you go to a CYC space, look around. Is there decoration that is inclusive and welcoming? Do you see people dressed in various cultural clothing? Are there posters and indicators that the space is safe? Our environments communicate messages.

Discussion Opportunity 6:14

In a small group have a conversation about environments first. Please identify five things your team wants the environment to convey when it is visited by children/youth/families or groups. Then identify five things that the team can do to ensure these messages will be shared or shared more effectively than they are currently. This is a special topic. Be gentle with yourselves and each other. Then have a debriefing to assess how it went and what needs to be done differently next time.

1.

2.

3.

4.

5.

b. Design and maintain planned environments which integrate developmental, preventive, and interventive requirements into the living space, through the use of developmentally and culturally sensitive methodologies and techniques

In order to be able to design, maintain, and plan environments for youth, we need to include them in the planning. Understand who they are, as well as the contexts that they live in and require for success.

> Young people use public spaces just as much as anyone else, if not more. And yet, too often young people, or young adults between the ages of 12 to 25, are not included in the process of Placemaking and end up "loitering" in other spaces. Some communities frown upon loitering, which can create a negative image for young people and just contributes to the stigma surrounding them, especially those who are at risk. By being actively engaged in youth-friendly spaces, young people can feel like they have investment in their community and they can develop a strong sense of ownership in these places. (Millard, 2015)

If we can include those who utilize the spaces by making use of developmentally and culturally sensitive methodologies and techniques, then we will be more successful at creating spaces that meet the intended community's specific needs. Culturally sensitive methodologies can include researching best practices, seeking direction from cultural experts, and gaining input from the youth themselves.

c. Arrange space, equipment, and activities in the environment to promote participation and prosocial behaviour, and to meet program goals

Whomever the CYCP is working with needs to take into consideration space design. Is the furniture comfortable and appropriate for the activities that will be shared (Maier, 1987)?

Discussion Opportunity 6:15

Consider some of the following questions:

- Do we have the proper-sized scissors for the craft activity?
- Is the craft activity about Halloween when the children do not celebrate this holiday?
- Is there enough space for everyone to feel included?

These are all questions that need to be asked about the life spaces we will be working in. What are other questions we as CYCPs can ask when we are trying to meet program goals while encouraging inclusion, participation, and prosocial behaviour?

d. Involve children, youth, and families appropriately in space design and maintenance

The CYCP will always endeavour to involve children youth and families in the activities they will engage in and the places in which engagement occurs. Children, youth, and families are users of services and need to be as involved as other users. Their involvement ensures that there is better allocation, availability, and applicability of resources (Kirby, Lanyon, Cronin, & Sinclair, 2003).

4. Program planning and activity programming

a. Connect own childhood activity experiences and skills, and adult interests and skills, to current work

CYCPs can reflect on their own childhood activity experiences and skills prior to planning for others. This reflection can include how these experiences impact our values and beliefs about therapeutic recreation.

Discussion Opportunity 6:16

Genevieve is the eldest of seven children. Her family experiences food insecurity, and at the young age of 12, she began to babysit until she procured a part-time job at the age of 14. She purchases all of her own hygiene products, clothing, and school supplies and does the same for younger siblings. In her third year of CYC practicum, the staff team discussed providing the adolescent girls with a monthly budget of $80 for clothing. Genevieve disagrees and feels that this is too much money for the youth to practise with. After all, they will not be able afford this when they are aged out of care. Later, Genevieve comes to realize that her suppositions are based on her experience of lacking the developmentally appropriate support that many youth receive. She recognizes that her "tough-love" approach does not fit with the therapeutic goals the team are trying to address, which are to provide the youth with opportunities to practise, learn, and incorporate new life skills.

Adam is not an athletic teen. He dislikes team sports and exercise. However, now that he is in college, a girl he admires invites him to run with her. Adam doesn't own running shoes, so he purchases running shoes and running shorts. He then begins to run and looks forward to both how tired and energized he feels after running. Adam decides that this is a valuable self-care strategy. Adam begins a practicum in a junior high school. There are four boys that he works with that spend much time in the office and are in trouble. They cannot sit still, focusing is an issue during instructional times, and they are not able to participate in extracurricular activities outside of school for a variety of reasons, including finances, lack of accessible programs, and so on.

Adam proposes to the principal that he mentor these boys, and with permission he begins the first cross-country team. These boys not only attend practice regularly but also win medals in their school district. Adam follows the boys as they move on to high school, and three of four boys continue on the track team in high school. One teen also told Adam that he runs daily to feel better about life and will run more than once a day to avoid peer pressure, drug use, and so on. Another boy obtained a track scholarship at an American university. What youth or adult activity can you share in your CYC practice?

b. Teach skills in several different domains of leisure activity

Leisure activities are known to be important for mental wellness for all ages (Goodman, Geiger, & Wolf, 2017). We learn new skills, create, relax, and sometimes share a sense of belonging with other people who enjoy the same leisure activities.

Discussion Opportunity 6:17

Manpreet has a long trauma history and by Grade 6 has attended seven schools. More details of this aren't required, however; what is important to know is that she begins to attend a school that starts a pilot program teaching children leisure activities. This means that every staff person, including support staff, hosts a group activity time twice a week for children who have signed up for that activity. The groups are comprised of children from Grade 1 to 8, and they develop not only a new skill but also relationships with children in other grades. The school staff notice that overall, the school community has become more connected. Children are observed helping each other at recess, and the school janitor (who teaches wood carving) notices that less garbage is thrown outside and in the halls. This program clearly has individual and community benefits.

Manpreet signed up for crochet. She cannot afford the wool or crochet hook but loves the idea of making something, creating something. This skill motivates her to later learn how to sew and knit and quilt, but during long drives, watching television, or in times of depression or anxiety, Manpreet will crochet.

Discussion Opportunity 6:18

What are leisure skills that others have shared with you? What are leisure skills you can share with others? When are you most likely to engage in leisure activities?

c. Assist clients in identifying and developing their strengths through activities and other experiences

Being attentive to what youth are saying and noticing potential strengths are both important CYC skills. These are opportunities to pull out a basketball net or take youth swimming or encourage them to try a new sport or group.

Discussion Opportunity 6:19

Maurice works as a CYCP in a foster home. He is aware that one of the boys (Marcus) loves the movie *High School Musical*. When a *High School Musical (on Ice)* program comes to town, Maurice purchases tickets for everyone. The youth does not want to admit how excited he is, but afterwards shares how shocked he was that Maurice noticed that he likes the movie. He also appreciates that Maurice did not tell the other youth that he chose the show for Marcus. This is the first time someone did something like this for Marcus, and he is so happy!

d. Design and implement programs and activities which integrate age, developmental, preventive, and/or interventive requirements and sensitivity to culture and diversity

CYCPs work holistically because we need to take all of these factors into consideration when we are relating with the whole person.

> Child and youth care is work with children and youth, as whole persons, in order to promote their social competence and healthy development, by participating in and using their day-to-day environments and life experiences, and through the development of therapeutic relationships, most importantly the relationship with the particular child or youth who is the focus of attention. (Anglin, 2003)

CYCPs plan programs with the understanding that those who are in the program make it therapeutic (Fox, 2018).

e. Design and implement challenging age-, developmentally, and cultural and human diversity appropriate activity programs

1. Perform a needs assessment
2. Assess clients' interests, knowledge of, and skill level in various activities
3. Promote clients' participation in activity planning
4. Select and obtain resources necessary to conduct particular activity or activity program
5. Request consistent feedback and consider adapting and making changes accordingly

We know that stakeholders at any level are more engaged when they have input in the decision making. It makes sense! The same goes for the children, youth, families, and communities that we work with. Let's get input on what they are interested in, what they are good at, and what are growth opportunities. It also is an opportunity to help model time and money management; just because we want to go rock climbing every weekend doesn't mean that we can.

1. Performing a needs assessment will be different for each milieu that you work in. This will minimally require you to observe: Can the children/youth and families that you work with do the task? For example, if your activity involves reading, are reading skills present? The same assessment has to occur with communication, social skills, and physical abilities.
2. Assessing clients' interests, knowledge of, and skill level in various activities requires observation and interaction with those you walk alongside. There is no point spending lots of time creating a basketball activity if no one has any interest in basketball. Similarly, organizing a dance with adolescents that are not allowed to dance due to their faith creates conflict for the youth as well as their families.

3. As already discussed, the most successful activity planning occurs when we are engaging those we work alongside of. They will teach us what they like, can do, and are interested in doing and working on.

4. Select and obtain resources necessary to conduct a particular activity or activity program.

Selecting and obtaining resources also require resources. A newly hired staff person, Alex, wants to dazzle the youth and staff at her group home with a cooking activity. The staff person works in an inner city and does not own a car. Alex needs to purchase scallops to make Coquilles Saint-Jacques. She went from grocery to grocery by public transportation, and no one had scallops. She finally went back to the group home with no dinner planned and no activity planned. She didn't make Coquille Saint-Jacques, and her shift partner is not happy that the evening shift is not organized as agreed upon.

5. Perform ongoing (formative) and outcome (summative) evaluation of specific activities and activity programs.

Alex keeps telling herself that if she just finds the needed ingredients, she can get her shift back on track. If the next grocery has scallops, she can be back at the house, prep ingredients, begin laundry, make phone calls, and so on. She tells herself that if she just gets the ingredients at the next store, the day will get back on track. When the youth get home, she makes macaroni and cheese casserole, and they take a walk around the nearby lake. The youth are happy, but Alex knows that her shift partner is still not pleased. After the youth are in bed, Alex reviews the treatment goals for the activities that week and realizes that making dinner with the youth (using ingredients on hand) did address the proposed goals.

Additionally, she shares with the youth her disappointment that the activity (dinner preparation) did not go the way she had wanted. She then brainstorms ideas with them about what she could have done differently. This **summative evaluation** process helps not only Alex and the youth but also her shift partner.

Discussion Opportunity 6:20

Has an activity you planned ever not gone the way you had hoped? Share this example with your group members. Did you seek feedback from others at the time? What would you do differently now?

f. Adapt activities for particular individuals or groups

Adapting activities includes being cognizant of developmental stages, strengths treatment goals, social location, learning challenges, budget, facilitation resources, and milieu.

Child and Youth Care Practitioners need to assess, facilitate, reflect, and reassess every time they undertake an activity with a child youth or family. It is important to include the social location of staff in this assessment.

Discussion Opportunity 6:21

A CYCP student who is a member of a Jehovah's Witness faith community is scheduled to take a latency-aged youth out trick-or-treating on October 31. She brings this to her supervisor as a concern. The supervisor responds by assigning another staff to this activity. Other team members challenge this decision. Is it not important that the CYCP can put their own "stuff" on the back burner to meet client needs?

This absolutely is an approach that many might take; however, in this case, this little person had never gone out trick-or-treating before and is so excited. The supervisor feels that he deserves someone who knows what the holiday is about and can share the community cultural relevance with the child. The supervisor could have "forced" the CYCP student to follow through, but she doesn't share the cultural belief in this holiday tradition and may have strong feelings about it. Would that be fun for either the child or the CYCP student?

A Grade 8 classroom community is going to take swimming lessons as part of their gym class. The gym teacher facilitates these lessons yearly. The CYCP is also going as a support to the male youth in the class, so there is supervision in the boys' change room. The only challenge this year is that in this class there is a new student named Aidan. Aidan is a transgender male student who states that he doesn't feel comfortable changing in the male change room. Aidan also is not happy to have to share his identity with other students. The CYCP chatted with Aidan about how to adapt the change room part of this activity. Aidan could put his trunks on at home and then change in a private change room afterwards. Aidan hasn't had top surgery and is binding, so he doesn't want to just wear swimming trunks. Aidan decided not to go swimming.

The CYCP felt bad about this and suggested other activities that could occur during the weekly swimming time. Instead, Aidan and his mother told the office that he had a medical appointment until swimming lessons are completed. The CYCP discussed with his supervisor that sometimes we have to accept the decision of youth, even if we do not agree with this decision.

Discussion Opportunity 6:22

What is an activity that may be a total conflict of values for you in your practice? Have you talked about it with your supervisor? Have you thought about the impact of this on child/youth/family/community needs? What "hole" is created in the treatment plan if you cannot follow through?

g. Locate and critically evaluate community resources for programs and activities and connect children, youth, and families to them

Locating and critically evaluating community resources for programs and activities requires the CYCP to contact others. Are you comfortable making phone calls with agencies or folks that you do not know? Do you know how to search specific programs on a computer? Do you have an understanding of the barriers that this child/youth/family might experience due to strengths, challenges, or social location? If you are unsure of your ability to complete the above tasks, it is important to ask for help from your placement supervisor/instructor/professor or a colleague. After asking the children/youth and families to help identify interests, we seek out resources that will address needs and connect children/youth and families with the programs.

Have you had experience with evaluation? Whose opinion counts? Have you facilitated a conversation in advance with stakeholders to discuss what they want out of their community resources? We can't evaluate anything if we aren't curious about what we are looking for. We use our creativity to evaluate, problem solve, and connect people with resources (Ventrella, 2015).

5. Activities of daily living

a. Integrate client's need for dignity, positive public image, nurturance, choice, self-management, and privacy into activities of daily living

Everyone deserves dignity, positive public image, nurturance, choice, self-management, and privacy in their activities of daily living. Children/youth and families also have a right to confidentiality and autonomy. For example, Aidan, the student who is transitioning and decided to say home from swimming lessons, only wanted to share his story with those who needed to know. The CYCP and Aidan's teacher are aware of Aidan's transitioning process, as is the school principal. However, the only office staff person who is aware is the support staff who manages school records. This is important as all staff do not need to know. This is Aidan's story to tell in Aidan's time. Sometimes, there is a misconception that all adults who work with a child/youth or family need to know all the details of the child's life. Then we have policy and legislation that talks about "duty to report." The new CYCP needs to have opportunities to check out ethics, especially around confidentiality, so that information is only shared as needed and necessary.

b. Design and implement, and support family members and caregivers to implement, activities of daily living, which integrate age, developmental, preventive, and/or interventive requirements and sensitivity to culture and diversity

1. Age- and cultural and human diversity appropriate clothing.

Clothing that reflects age, diversity, and is culturally appropriate depends on where you are, how old/young you are, and what your experience is with culture and diversity.

CYCPs can support children and youth to choose and wear clothing that promotes their best self. For example, there may be concerns when fashions for young girls mimic those meant for adults. Conversely, there may be times when we encourage children and youth to wear clothing that their peers are also wearing. At other times, we need to be intentional about making space for creativity and self-expression.

It is important to ensure that children/youth have clothing available that will protect them from the elements of the weather. If you have youth wearing long-sleeved clothing and long, heavy pants in the summertime, what does this mean? Should you be curious about this? Is this style? Is this a way to hide self-harming behaviours, or is this because they are afraid of bugs? Is this because they aren't sure how to dress for the weather? How about clothing appropriate for the winter? Some children who have never been able to trust adults to meet their needs will not ask adults for clothing when they need it—even mittens or gloves during cold winter weather.

Discussion Opportunity 6:23

We have to assess what role dress codes play for the CYCPs as well as the children and youth we are responsible for. For example, is it okay for a residence to say that they are not purchasing G-strings for adolescent girls (with clothing money provided by a children's aid society)?

2. Pleasant and inviting eating times that encourage positive social interaction.

Eating together provides an opportunity to socialize, engage, and interact.

Many children and youth have not had the experience of eating with other family members for a meal. Young children learn more than 1,000 "rare" words as a result of participating in dinnertime discussions that include learning and practising vocabulary, listening to stories that result in acquiring general knowledge, and learning to interact in culturally appropriate ways (Snow & Beals, 2006). These experiences encourage positive social interaction.

3. Age and developmentally appropriate rest opportunities.

Sleep helps us to:

- Remember what we learned
- Organize our thoughts, predict outcomes and consequences
- React quickly
- Work accurately and effectively
- Think abstractly and be creative (Mindell & Owens, 2003, p. 3)

In order to create rest opportunities for children, it is recommended that their regular schedule allow for adequate sleep. Where they sleep will also support sleep or wakefulness.

Experts will say that children sleep and rest well when they practise healthy sleep hygiene, which includes turning screens off at least 30 minutes before bedtime and not permitting computers/televisions/screens in sleeping spaces (American Academy of Pediatrics, 2016).

4. Clean and well-maintained bathroom facilities that allow age and developmentally appropriate privacy and independence.

Bathroom facilities in all life spaces need to be clean and well maintained and allow for age and developmentally appropriate privacy and independence.

CYCPs need to ensure that there are clean bathrooms in good repair for children and youth to utilize. To support privacy, cameras cannot be in bathrooms. Children and youth should have the opportunity to be independent in bathrooms where this is developmentally appropriate. Little folks will need to have help getting their hair washed, and

Table 6: The National Sleep Foundation recommends the following for age and developmentally appropriate rest opportunities

Age	Recommended	May be appropriate	Not recommended
Newborns	14 to 17 hours	11 to 13 hours	Less than 11 hours
0–3 months		18 to 19 hours	More than 19 hours
Infants	12 to 15 hours	10 to 11 hours	Less than 10 hours
4–11 months		16 to 18 hours	More than 18 hours
Toddlers	11 to 14 hours	9 to 10 hours	Less than 9 hours
1–2 years		15 to 16 hours	More than 16 hours
Preschoolers	10 to 13 hours	8 to 9 hours	Less than 8 hours
3–5 years		14 hours	More than 14 hours
School-aged Children	9 to 11 hours	7 to 8 hours	Less than 7 hours
6–13 years		12 hours	More than 12 hours
Teenagers	8 to 10 hours	7 hours	Less than 7 hours
14–17 years		11 hours	More than 11 hours
Young Adults	7 to 9 hours	6 hours	Less than 6 hours
18–25 years		10 to 11 hours	More than 11 hours

Source: National Sleep Foundation, 2019. How much sleep do babies and kids need? Retrieved from https://sleepfoundation.org/excessivesleepiness/content/how-much-sleep-do-babies-and-kids-need

sometimes CYCPs need to ensure kids are showering when they say they are but their aroma says otherwise. Creative CYCPs will take children/youth swimming or even suggest that they put their bathing suit on to shower. Gender-neutral bathrooms need to be available for children/youth who feel more comfortable using these.

5. Personal space adequate for safe storage of personal belongings and for personal expression through decorations that do not exceed reasonable propriety.

Every child and youth deserves to have personal space where their things are stored safely. They also need to have some ability to decorate their spaces in a meaningful manner. Lack of safe storage is often a complaint made by children/youth who are in residential care. "In our current social context, residential care/treatment is plagued with significant concerns that have the potential to infringe on young people's rights and their participation in the care that they receive" (Brown & Hann, 2018, p. 8).

Children and youth are placed in bedrooms with other children/youth, often without their expression of interest. These children and youth can be vulnerable victims. It is quite surprising that children who have trauma histories (known or unknown) are put in spaces that are unsupervised and unsupported. On occasion, residential group homes or foster homes place younger children and older children together. This too can be a prelude to problems. This is not to infer that older children will hurt younger children; however, one needs to consider healthy sexual development. It is normal for adolescents to masturbate, and they should have the privacy of their bedrooms and bathrooms to do so. It is also important for the children and youth to claim the spaces that they live in. Can they choose their paint colour if they cannot choose their furniture? How about choosing their bedding? Is there a place to post their posters? Can residents have input on bathroom design? Helping children/youth claim their spaces assists them in investing in these spaces being a home (Burns, 2006).

The area of concern regarding this competency item is the responsibility of the CYCP to ensure safety in the home or foster home. This means that CYCPs need to follow policy and protocol when going through youth rooms, as well as common spaces, to ensure that there is no fire-setting equipment, weapons, or drugs stored so to ensure that all children/youth who live in the space are safe, but that their privacy is still respected. This can be a double-edged sword when looking at the needs of all. A youth reports the following:

> Safety can be the key. There are times in both foster and group home where I feel threatened and unsafe. My belongings are often stolen. The stolen items range from nail polish, clothes and an IPOD touch. I tell the staff but they told me there is nothing they could do. It distresses me greatly that my personal belongings are taken and yet there is nothing anyone could do. (Chung, 2017)

This is a common complaint of youth in care, and it is the responsibility of all who work with children/youth to address these concerns proactively and preventatively.

c. Design and maintain inviting, hygienic, and well-maintained physical environments and equipment and supplies, which positively support daily activities

We need to create life spaces that are clean, inviting, and in good shape. When first reading this competency, the reader may assume that the environments are not in good physical shape to begin with. However, there are children and youth we live with who have never experienced a living space as positive or clean, or have never felt that they are "home" in their own home. For example, Liam lived in six foster homes. He had a complex trauma history. Within a short time of moving into his foster home, he broke all the furniture in his room and carved holes past the drywall into a vapour barrier, right to the outside wall underneath his posters. He didn't do these acts of destruction in anger; rather, when bored, he would break things.

d. Encourage development of skills in activities of daily living
1. Personal hygiene and grooming skills.

Encouraging personal hygiene and grooming skills needs to be a daily support process that we also model as CYCPs. However, this can be a sticking point among CYC teams.

Who decides when youth need haircuts? Where do youth get haircuts? Hair is not the same between children of various cultures. Some youth may want to have hair braided, have dreads, shave their head, grow hair long, or keep it short.

Discussion Opportunity 6:24

Phyllis, a foster mom of black Jamaican heritage, believes that children should have neat hair. Boys specifically should have their hair short and well combed daily. Enrique (the children's worker) believes that youth should be able to grow their hair as long as they want, as long as it is washed and clean. A youth wants to grow his hair, which became an embarrassment for Phyllis, especially within her church community. This disagreement eventually breaks down the placement, because Phyllis feels that she should have parental decision making in the areas of hygiene and grooming for the Crown wards that live with her. Enrique saw the youth making the decision about their hair as a way for the youth to have some power and control over their life.

Raj is placed with a Caucasian foster family, who cut Raj's hair before they discussed this with other members of the treatment team. The foster parents lack the understanding that his culture supports long hair for male community members. They instead see this as an indication of caregiver neglect.

CYCPs need to ensure that youth have their hair cared for and by individuals who understand the youth's culture and the cultural implications of hair care. Youth also need to have hair products that support their type and style of hair. Hair discussions (and values) need to be addressed with youth and their caregivers to ensure that one team member's beliefs do not overshadow the child's rights (Ontario Association of Children's Aid Societies, 2016).

Showering is also an important hygiene practice that many youth may need support in scheduling. CYCPs may also need to be aware that youth may never have been taught to shower adequately. It may be important to remind youth to use soap on underarm areas and genital areas. If a youth has been sexually abused, has felt unsafe in bathrooms, or has sensory challenges with water temperature, the showering process may be anxiety provoking. CYCPs may need to work with the youth to create a showering opportunity that is less pain-based for them.

2. Developing and maintaining areas related to daily living (e.g., maintaining living space, preparing and serving meals, clean-up).

Chores, chores, chores! How do we maintain living areas, teach life skills, and also ensure that we aren't spending all of our time cooking and cleaning? On some days, this will mean that the adults take on the cleaning duties. On other days, children and youth complete daily chores. It is often best is to maintain living space, prepare and serve meals, and clean up collaboratively. When we work together, children and youth not only benefit from a clean space but also learn valuable life skills.

3. Socially appropriate behaviour in activities of daily living: respecting others' privacy, expected grooming, and dress for various occasions.

Part of a CYCP's role in whatever milieu they work in is to model and teach socially appropriate behaviour in activities of daily living, which includes respecting the privacy of others, and grooming/dressing for various occasions. Fraser (2011) states that adults discuss with youth emotionally safe living spaces, physically safe spaces, and sexually safe spaces. This means that no matter who is in the space, rules include:

- Knocking on doors before opening them
- Only one child/youth using a bathroom area at a time (like when brushing teeth), unless supervision is provided
- Dressing in more than a towel when going to or from the bathroom
- Asking before going into sleeping spaces so adults know where all youth are when in the life space
- Asking before sharing affection and not assuming that the person you want to hug is in a space to receive affection

In regards to appropriate dress, this is often handled with identified dress codes in school settings and house manuals in residential or foster settings. Adults and youth can follow the consistent expectations that match the life space. For some youth, this means wearing dress clothing for church or a uniform for school.

6. Group process

a. Assess the group development and dynamics of a specific group of children and youth

Assessing the group development and dynamics of a specific group of children and youth is an ongoing task for the CYCP. "The role of group work can be seen as one which places emphasis on sharing of thoughts, ideas, problems and activities" (Harte, 2007, para. 7). CYCPs can assess group development using the stages of group development: forming, storming, norming, performing, and mourning/adjourning (Tuckman, 1965). This information then is balanced with an understanding of the dynamics of children and youth based on their development, social location, gender, culture, special interests, and so on. For example, a CYCP working with an adolescent group may sit back and encourage group members to facilitate the group process. When working with eight-year-olds, the same CYCP will take on a group leadership role until the group is at the norming phase, where they are identifying and agreeing on group norms/rules (Tuckman, 1965). See Chapter 3 for a chart that provides examples of group stage activities.

b. Use group process to promote program, group, and individual goals

CYCPs use group process to promote program, group, and individual goals. This can be achieved formally in therapeutic groups and informally during dinnertime conversation at a group home dinner table. "Group work may simplistically be described as the study and application of the processes and outcomes experienced when a small group comes together" (Harte, 2007).

c. Facilitate group sessions around specific topics/issues related to the needs of children/youth

CYCPs can organize sessions around specific topics that meet the needs of children/youth. Group topics might include weekly house or family meetings or topics that align with specific groups, such as parenting groups or social skills groups. CYCPs can use group process to provide both group and individual growth opportunities by engaging group members. Opportunities can including discussion, sharing, or even co-facilitating discussions. When children/youth have the opportunity to develop group leadership skills, this enables them to feel connection with others (Quigley, 2006).

d. Mediate in group process issues

CYCPs require the skills to mediate during group process activities to ensure that there is safety and equal opportunity for all members to participate. Groups provide members the opportunity to learn, experience, and process conflict. Conflict is part of group dynamics and learning. When successful, the group benefits from learning new skills, gaining new knowledge, and sharing feedback (Harte, 2007).

Many CYCPs may want to avoid group work, given their need for more experience in how to mediate conflict and potential aggression. Specific incidents of aggression also need to be explored via the context in which they occurred.

> Aggression can often seem unpredictable or unprovoked, but there is always a reason for it. If we can identify risk factors or triggers for the aggressive behavior, we can reframe aggressive outbursts as an opportunity for learning and for helping the aggressive child get the help he or she needs. (Haddad & Gerson, 2014, p. 13)

7. Counselling

a. Recognize the importance of relationships as a foundation for counselling with children, youth, and families

Relationship building and maintenance is key to CYC practice. Relationships are foundations for counselling with children/youth and families. People remember you based on your relationship skills. A popular saying, sometimes attributed to Maya Angelou, is that people may not always remember what you say or what you do, but they will always remember how you made them feel (Goalcast, 2017).

b. Has self-awareness and uses oneself appropriately in counselling activities

The CYCP use of self requires intentional reflection and sometimes support. "The child and youth care professional (CYCP) connects with children/youth by means of the heart—an emotional, personal, and sensory connection. In order to work from the heart, the CYCP must have a strong and healthy connection to his/herself" (Burns, 2012). Building on this self-awareness, "we inform our intentionality through theory which helps to provide the framework necessary to promote voice, autonomy and choice with the young people we work with. Intentionality also supports the ethical standards that are created to protect both the young person and the practitioner" (Brown, 2017, p. 28).

c. Able to assess a situation in the milieu or in individual interaction and select the appropriate medium and content for counselling

A CYCP needs to assess situations within milieu or within shared interactions so as to select the medium that best meets the need of the person or system while adhering to the Code of Ethics.

This is the life space interview (Redl, 1959). For example, if a teen discloses that they are cutting or self-harming, this is a more appropriate conversation for a private office or quiet area, whereas discussing the recent basketball game might occur in the presence of others in a busy hallway. If the teen is cutting, the CYCP may discuss triggers and strategies, whereas if the teen indicates they are suicidal, then the conversation is being moved toward an emergency room.

d. Able to make appropriate inquiry to determine meaning of a particular situation to a child

CYCPs need to be curious with children and youth in order to learn how a situation is experienced by that child. All situations are grounded in stories (experiences): the child's, the CYCP's, and the context in which they occur. Some of these stories are happening now, some happened in the past, and some are yet to occur but may feel current. Sometimes these stories, whether experienced or imagined, provide the foundation for our beliefs about ourselves, and they are not always accurate or productive. CYCPs want to support those they walk beside to narrate new stories for themselves that communicate strength. They are capable, hopeful, and free (Phelan, 2009).

e. Assist other adults, staff, parents, and caregivers in learning and implementing appropriate behavioural support and instruction

CYCPs model lifelong learning and attempt to assist other adults, staff, parents, and caregivers in implementing appropriate support and instruction.

Professors and supervisors need to model a CYCP way of being with students and supervisees. This can feel like a fine line sometimes, especially if a student is a trainee of a professor. Though it is outside of the scope of a professor's role to be the CYCP to their students and provide supports such as counselling, professors have a responsibility to model relational practice. If we are going to "talk the talk, we have to walk the walk." Students can be encouraged to ask professors and field practicum supervisors:

- what their child and youth care background is;
- what their educational history is;

- what their experience in the CYC field is;
- if they are members of their local CYC professional association;
- if they take updated training; and
- if they identify as a CYCP or as another member of the multidisciplinary team.

Once we understand the context of the feedback, we can begin to ascertain how to integrate it. As a profession, we also have to advocate and encourage each other to continue engaging in training and clinical supervision. It is powerful learning to review interactions shared with a youth. Children/youth and families are often our very best teachers and mentors.

f. Employ effective problem-solving and conflict resolution skills

CYCPs have the privilege of teaching and modelling problem-solving and conflict resolution skills with children, youth, families, and communities. These opportunities arise within the life space.

In order to effectively problem solve, the CYCP must have a clear understanding of the need of the child, youth, families, and communities. Once we understand the need, we can then brainstorm and build skills, knowledge, actions, and resources that will lead to meeting the need. The repercussions of not addressing the need include increasing risk factors and reducing the chances of problem solving successfully. CYCPs need to teach, practise, teach again, practise, then implement skills that promote effective problem solving. It is a circular process, not a linear one. Effective problem solving increases skill development, knowledge, self-awareness, and resiliency.

Effective problem solving involves steps. We identify the needs, issues, or problems; assess how these impact all stakeholders; brainstorm options; evaluate the options; pick an option; and identify how we will know if the chosen option will be successful or not.

CYCPs are committed to an effective conflict resolution process. All relationships will experience conflict at some point. CYCPs value the importance of teaching, practising, and reflecting on conflict resolution. Relational practice includes resolving conflict, learning about the self, and discovering how we relate to others while in relationship.

Conflict resolution skills need to include:

- Responding to the need(s) and issue(s)
- Being respectful to self and everyone involved
- Listening to the meaning of the other person's experience
- Verbal and nonverbal communication
- Empathy toward other people's perspectives
- Creating safe relationships and environments
- Regulation of emotions, thoughts, and reactions
- Commitment to the resolution and relationships involved
- Creative problem solving to meet the need(s) or issue(s)

If conflict cannot be resolved, it is important to seek supports, consultation, supervision, persons of faith, and so on.

Strategies that teach conflict resolution include:

- Organizational programming: schools, communities, judicial institutions, and residential care can create self-regulation spaces.
- Play offers direct teaching opportunities (Fraser, 2013).
- Team relationship-building opportunities: CYC teams, multidisciplinary teams, sports, art classes, band, meditation groups, theatre, cooking, praying, retreats, and so on.
- Promoting teachable moments in one's life space.
- Making space and time in the environment to resolve conflict.
- Reflective practice, during and post–conflict resolution.
- Organizations can create conflict resolution policies.
- Peer mediation, which means helping children/youth identify how to problem solve issues among themselves where possible.
- Curriculum can create psycho-educational opportunities.
- Creating peaceful (safe) classrooms or micro-environments.
- Creating peaceable (safe) schools or macro-environments (Olive, 2006).
- Ongoing reflection, feedback, and evaluation.

Essentially, CYCPs have the opportunity to employ the tools and create the environments that model nonviolence in order to prevent both self-destructive and conflictual behaviours and instead create healing and safe milieus that promote resolving conflict.

8. Behaviour guidance

Behaviour guidance is a process through which the CYCP and the child/youth/family reflect on their behaviour to find a path that builds on their abilities, aspirations, and needs. Behaviour guidance is strength-based. Workers strive to build community without using tactics of exclusion or domination (Skott-Myhre & Skott-Myhre, 2007). CYCPs are guiding, not dictating. Behavioural guidance opportunities are opportunities to learn new skills and increase knowledge. CYCPs invite opportunities for behaviour guidance because this increases the development of self-awareness, **intrinsic motivation**, and self-determination. We translate interactions (Fraser, 2011) and events, then communicate expectations clearly in such a way that the child/youth or family connects the benefits and/or disadvantages of a situation. Behavioural guidance discussions assist the individual to creatively make meaning of the challenge they are experiencing in the life space (Ventrella, 2015).

a. Assess client behaviour, including its meaning to the client

Assessing client behaviour and its meaning can take lots of time and is a relational, if not clinical, experience. We can observe behaviour and hypothesize what may be going on, but it is dangerous to assume anything unless child/youth/family confirmation is procured. At times, those we work with may not be conscious of the meaning of behaviour, just as we may not be conscious of the underlying reasons for our own behaviour. That is sometimes to be determined by reviewing past experience and current contexts, often within the safety of relationships. We can begin by being curious. Curiosity helps to say to the other, "I see you, I hear you, and I want to get to know you."

b. Design behavioural guidance around level of client understanding

When we design behavioural guidance around the child/youth or family's level of understanding, we are aware of the amount of detail that is necessary to share for the child/youth we are working with. For example, we do not need to tell an eight-year-old in the group home that a safety rule we have is that we do not play in each other's bedrooms because we have residents who act out sexually. Instead, we may say, it is important that I know where all of you are at all times, so please ask before you attempt to go into the room of a peer. Or we will all play together in common spaces of the house. There is a fine line between engaging a child and youth fully in the treatment plan by providing all details versus having a team discussion and agreement on what information is age applicable. Even better, we can consult the folks who know the child best (their caregivers) so we can seek their wise counsel.

We also can help parents understand that keeping routines consistent will assist children/youth to feel safe and connect this plan with life examples. This can provide a teachable moment for the family. Lastly, it is important to engage the child or youth in designing behavioural guidance interventions so they have an understanding of why rules, routines, and expectations are designed the way they are.

c. Assess the strengths and limitations of behavioural management methods

In order to assess strengths and limitations of **behaviour management methods**, we have to be clear on the goals we hope to achieve.

"When using token economies, CYCPS need to assess the strengths and limitations of the program" (Rauktis, 2016, p. 100). Assessing behavioural management methods involves curiosity and comparing past behavioural communication with current behavioural communication, all within the context of the milieu. Instead of applying behavioural management strategies, we should be advocating for **behavioural guidance interventions**, so as to increase intrinsic personal control and efficacy for those we walk alongside.

d. Employ selected behavioural management methods, where deemed appropriate

Selecting and employing behavioural management methods is a skill for CYCPs. CYCPs have long practised good care by investing in strong therapeutic alliances and relationship building, coupled with an understanding of relational practices, development theory, and attachment theory. Behaviour guidance methods are strength-based and refer to a belief that children/youth are in charge of themselves and, instead of managing them, we want them to practise self-determination.

When we do need to manage behaviour, we need to consider who has the best relationship with the child or youth. It is always best to give children/youth forewarning of the expectation and be aware of their strengths, challenges, and the context of the expectation. Is the expectation realistic? When children or youth do not follow expectations, it can also be helpful to discuss with them what they think they need in order to be successful in the future. Natural and logical consequences are more likely to support expectations than punishment. Specific behavioural approaches may be employed, such as time outs or time "ins," when a child is not in a place to interact and needs a place to "reset." Current parenting resources (Fraser, 2011) talk about parents (or CYCPs) being "regulated" before attempting to help children to become the same. Our interventions need to be in response to the child/youth's needs versus our needs as a reaction to their behavioural choices and presentation.

e. Assist other adults, staff, and parents and caregivers in learning and implementing appropriate behavioural guidance techniques and plans

Assisting others in both learning and implementing appropriate behaviour guidance techniques and plans requires a CYCP to be versed in a variety of plans, strategies, and interventions. These techniques and plans need to be culturally and developmentally sensitive and respectful.

For example, a residential youth centre had a levels model of programming called **GAS—Goal Attainment Scale** (Weinstein & Ricks, 1977). Youth and their primary youth worker can identify a goal area and break this down into a SMART goal so the youth can verbalize what it could look like, sound like, and feel like if they were working on and achieving their goal. Points are achieved daily for functioning, and youth can earn privileges based on what level they are on. Consequences and privileges work the same way—all are based on a level system.

Discussion Opportunity 6:25

One Sunday, Katie comes on shift to hear that Warren has moved to an earlier level, so he is no longer entitled to snack. Given today is Warren's birthday, this means he cannot have birthday cake even though the other kids are having it. Katie could not follow through with this as the behaviour demonstrated by Warren happened yesterday. Today is his birthday, and she could not imagine not allowing him to have birthday cake, although this is the program requirement. Katie changed the consequence, and then the other staff brought it to a team meeting to discuss consistency. After this team meeting, the team decided that using food as a consequence was not helpful to the prognosis of the goal areas for the children and youth that they worked with. It also wasn't helpful for relationship building, especially when working with children who had experienced neglect.

In many geographical areas, child welfare agencies have policies against using food as a behavioural intervention.

Discuss with your group how to intervene effectively without using food as a consequence in the following scenarios: A teen returns after running away from a group home; A 9-year-old has been caught taking lunches from other students; A 12-year-old is eating all the cheese in his foster home in the middle of the night.

f. Give clear, coherent, and consistent expectations; set appropriate boundaries

Giving clear, coherent, and consistent expectations in order to set appropriate boundaries can feel "mean." If we are not comfortable with conflict, being direct with children/youth/families and communities can be a learning curve. On some occasions, we may ignore behaviour not as planned ignoring, but because certain actions avoid being directive, while we hope that the behaviour extinguishes itself. Setting good boundaries is important, as it creates safety for all members within the therapeutic milieu. Carol Stuart (2008, p. 165) writes:

> Like the actor, the practitioner has to enter and exit a professional world of pain and ugliness and must make strategic decisions about where to place boundaries at a particular point in time, while maintaining a strong and open self. Tapping self brings the professional character forward in relation to the demands of the script and the reaction of the audience.

g. Evaluate and disengage from power struggles

Evaluating and disengaging in power struggles helps to maintain relationships, yet power struggles are so easy to invest in! They are an interaction where no one truly will "win." For example, many toddlers engage in power struggles with their parents around food (Spock & Needlman, 2012). Children and teenagers will also engage in power struggles, especially when they are being asked to do something or adhere to a rule that they disagree with. CYCPs are skilled at recognizing that such behaviour is a form of communication that says, "I do not need or want to listen to you." From the adult perspective, by engaging in power struggles, CYCPs are saying, "You have to listen to me, I am the one who has the keys. I am in charge."

> Programs based on controlling behavior typically are problem-focused and describe the goals for youth as eliminating the specific behaviors which are problematic. Treatment plans are quite linear, detailing problems and describing how the youth will be ready to leave when the problematic behavior has ceased to occur and programs that believe in behaviour management establish rules so that self-control . . . not good behaviour is the overall aim of the program. (Phelan, 2006)

h. Employ genuine relationship to promote positive behaviour

Relationships are reciprocal in child and youth care practice and demonstrate authentic caring within the relationship. It can be hard to draw the line about when to care, how to care, and how not to care. Our code of ethics needs to be adhered to, and we need to often refer to colleagues for peer consultation or our supervisors for administrative or clinical supervision. It is also important, when employing genuine relationships to promote positive behaviour, that the CYCP promotes self-determination.

> It is not helpful for staff to solve problems for children/youth, because it reinforces for the child/youth that he or she can't. It is more important that adults teach problem-solving skills; that coaching is provided, not interference. When peers are having trouble with each other, work with them to solve it, but don't solve it for them. (Fox, 1995)

So in creating a genuine relationship, we encourage positive behaviour and problem-solving skills and also believe that the child/youth will demonstrate positive behaviour.

i. Employ developmental and cultural/diversity understandings to promote positive behaviour

CYCPs always attempt to employ their knowledge and assess developmental functioning when promoting positive behaviour. Developmental age can be different than chronological age. Looking at the developmental strengths of children and youth is important in creating expectations for behaviour. We want to have reasonable expectations of what the child is capable of demonstrating. As well, understanding the child's cultural context and experiences help to ensure that expectations match identity and needs.

j. Employ planned environment and activities to promote positive behaviour

CYCPs have long recognized that planned environments and activities promote positive behaviour. Activities include daily routines for mealtimes, wake ups, and bedtimes. Other activities can include therapeutic recreation, which meets the specific needs of individuals as well as the overall needs and supports the overall development of those we walk alongside. Setting children and youth up to be successful can be achieved by establishing an environment that affirms positive choices while utilizing a consistent approach to communicate expectations and rules (Durrant, 2007).

k. Employ at least one method of conflict resolution

In order to determine what method of **conflict resolution** we wish to employ, we need to hear what the child/youth/group or families are saying is the experience that they are struggling with. Listening to what the challenge (and sometimes the underlying message) is can be the first step to addressing and preventing a crisis. "Successful engagement is paramount. The formation of a therapeutic alliance is essential before any interventions can be successful" (Sainsbury Centre for Mental Health, 2007). Once we understand the context of the conflict, we can work toward resolution. The five steps to conflict resolution are: identifying the source of the conflict; looking beyond the incident (CYCPs call this context); brainstorming solutions; identifying ones that all parties can agree or buy into, and lastly; agreeing on next steps. Creative problem-solving models such as the Torrance Incubation Model (Torrance & Myers, 1970) can teach children/youth/families and communities how to problem solve before things become a crisis. This model is explained more fully in Chapter 7.

l. Employ principles of crisis management

1. Describe personal response to crisis situations.

People respond to crisis in personal ways. CYCPS can be asked to describe a personal response to a crisis situation in a job interview. Crisis brins up the best and the worst in us. After a crisis, some of us are described as calm, cool, and collected. Some people jump into managing crisis and afterwards respond with a delayed sad/angry/fearful response. Some sensations in our body immobilize us in crisis.

CYCPs are challenged to carefully review the interactions and experiences that they define as being a crisis situation. These are beneficial to review in supervision. Some CYC teams will review what led up to a crisis event and how it is managed as a peer consultation and peer learning process. Understanding how we contribute and perpetuate crisis is part of the learning process.

2. Describe personal strengths and limitations in responding to crisis situations.

We all need to be able to describe our personal strengths and limitations in responding to crisis situations. CYCPs who have a trauma history may be able to respond to impending crisis situations in a proactive manner or in a healthy manner, while others may be triggered by the crisis situation. This is why there is a great focus on the safe and effective use of self in CYC programs. Supervision is another wonderful place to discuss our personal strengths and limitations as they relate to responding to crisis situations.

3. Take self-protective steps to avoid unnecessary risks and confrontations.

The following story is an example of how one staff person took self-protective steps to avoid unnecessary risks and confrontations.

Martha arrived at her group home to find a staff person standing at the top of the back split stairs with her back to the stairs. In front of the staff member stood a teen who was screaming at the staff person while waving her arms around. Martha could imagine the teen pushing the staff member backwards. If this occurred, the staff person could have most certainly been hurt, if not killed. Martha jumped up the stairs and asked the teen, "What did you eat for lunch?" to divert her attention as Martha took the elbow of the staff and guided her sideways.

When we work with children and youth and families, we always need to be concerned with:

- Who is in the room
- Where the exits are
- What the special benefits or limitations are
- What items in the room could cause harm or health
- What the tone of the environment is in the space that you are joining with others
- The power imbalances between people and an understanding of the impact of oppression on feelings of safety

4. Dress appropriately to the practice setting.

CYCPs work in schools, custody settings, group homes, foster homes, and community settings. They need to be prepared to dress appropriately for the milieu in which they are employed; however, they also need to be prepared to take on other duties that come up. For example, a group home CYCP may need to attend a doctor's appointment, court appearance, or school meeting; hence it is important to always have court clothes in a backpack or the car. Conversely, after attending meetings, more casual clothes may be required, so casual pants and shirts are appropriate. The CYCP also needs to present professionally even in casual clothing, so they need to be mindful of slogans on clothing, top buttons or lack thereof, and ensuring that underclothing is not visible. This is especially important for the younger-looking CYCPs who verbalize that they feel they are not taken seriously. It is important to dress the part of the professional if we want to be regarded as such.

5. Employ a variety of interpersonal and verbal skills to defuse a crisis.

Interpersonal and verbal skills can defuse a crisis. **Crisis intervention** or crisis prevention training is often a condition of employment for the graduating CYCP. They also may be required to take specific certification approved for a specific milieu or organization. Each certification may have some differences and teach the CYCP to recognize that a crisis is coming. Specific skills are often taught to defuse a verbal crisis before it becomes a physical crisis. Skills that are effective in this intervention can include affirmation, acknowledgment of feelings, provision of physical and emotional space, and so on. There are many programs available, including Understanding and Managing Aggressive Behaviour (UMAB), de-escalation training, non-violent crisis intervention training, and those from the Crisis Prevention Institution (CPI).

6. Describe the principles of physical interventions appropriate to the setting.

CYCPs need to be familiar with the non-violent prevention and physical intervention policies/practices that are endorsed by the organizational and milieu requirements in which they work. In an interview, it is appropriate to ask what best practices are for the organization and what the history or statistics of intervention are for the specific organization that you wish to work at.

7. Conduct a life space interview or alternative reflective debriefing.

Reflective debriefing and life space interviewing are different than counselling skills. Life space work means that you are working without a safety net in various natural life spaces (Phelan, 2009), including where people live, learn, and have fun. In order words, the CYCP is not controlling the environment or what is going on in the environment. However, the CYCP can facilitate activities and encourage positive interactions and opportunities that support the goals of all in the life space.

The life space concept is attributed to Fritz Redl (1959).

Fritz Redl developed the Life Space Interview as a therapeutic tool. The environment of the traditional individual therapeutic session is artificial and too far detached from a child's reality. He says scheduling 50 minute therapy sessions are impractical in helping troubled children who are living in a group residential setting. In its place he identified the need to develop a set of techniques for residential child care workers that can allow them to provide what Redl called therapy on the hoof. (Sharpe, 2009, para. 8)

The goals of the life space interview are:

a. Use of daily events to enrich the experience and create insights in the young person.

b. Encourage young people to recognize reality when they are socially near-sighted to the events they are involved in.

c. Foster socially healthy areas in the young person to show that benefits through secondary gain as a result of acting-out or any anti-social behaviours are not, in the long run, satisfactory.

d. Increase the young person's self-esteem by stroking and encouraging those part of the young person's persona that are seen as having positive value.

e. Seek out alternative acceptable defences to any socially unacceptable ones the young person may use so that their adaptational skills are widened.

f. Encourage young people to move across the boundaries of self by helping them to expand the boundaries so that they include and show respect for other people, benign adults, the peer group, and the wider community.

g. By creating insight, encouraging social awareness, nullifying benefit through secondary gain, increasing self-esteem, finding acceptable defences and expanding self-boundaries; to build personal confidence to the extent that painful issues from the past, perceived as malign, may be faced, coped with, or resolved.

The life space interview makes use of a series of momentary daily spontaneous life experiences in order to extract from them a level of insight within healthy relationships, which makes it possible to achieve long-term therapeutic goals. (Sharpe, 2009, para. 12)

9. Family and caregiver engagement

a. Communicate effectively with family members

Communicating effectively with family members involves, including:

- verbal communication;
- nonverbal communication;
- social location;
- cultural competency;

- understanding of historical factors, including intergenerational trauma;
- understanding of the experience of oppression;
- roles, rules, and boundaries;
- and let's not forget relationship!

b. Partner with family in goal setting and designing and implementing developmental supports and/or interventions

The CYCP that can partner with a family in goal setting, designing, and implementing developmental supports and/or intervention is promoting inclusion.

Discussion Opportunity 6:26

When Thomas comes into foster care, his mother shares that he regularly gets into many accidents. She does not want him to engage in any physical activities where he could potentially get hurt. This has resulted in a 12-year-old who is quiet and often is isolated from his peer group. Thomas has a low tolerance for risk when learning new skills. He desperately wants to learn how to skateboard and saves up his allowance for over a year to purchase a skateboard, helmet, knee pads, and elbow pads.

In order to ensure safety, his group home CYCP team compromises and decides that he can use the treasures (that took him so long to obtain) on the back deck away from roads and potential traffic. Then, if he continues to have interest and refines his balancing skills, they will have a discussion with his mom about "taking it to the street." His mother is not happy when told and predicts accidents to come.

Unfortunately, while practising one afternoon, the skateboard flies up and clips Thomas in his testicles. Ice is applied, and when he says he has to use the washroom, the CYCP provides him with a cup and suggests that a urine sample be saved. When blood is discovered in the urine, he is taken to the hospital, where it is determined he needs to have surgery. Luckily, he subsequently does not become sterile.

This example (which could also be used in the relationships and communication domain) demonstrates a CYCP who manages a medical situation effectively, preventing long-term physical impairment in a situation that could have happened to any male 12-year-old learning how to skateboard. But it is not any 12-year-old. It is a 12-year-old whose parent is not in support of the activity that ultimately caused him harm. In the moment, the CYCP had to immediately put the youth's needs first versus their own guilt/shame/shock that the parent predicted a problem with an experience that does not cause damage in most children/youth who skateboard. The CYCP also needs to facilitate conversations between youth and mom to navigate and compromise for future rules around activities.

A child or young person's sense of belonging is enmeshed in family genealogies and social histories. Through participation in decision-making, family members are both encouraged and challenged to participate in restorative practices which at the very least enhance diplomatic relations between a child or a young person and family members. Starting to notice opportunity moments that can be nurtured in families requires preparation, purposeful use of activities and planned interventions offering restorative relationship experiences. (Fulcher & Garfat, 2015, p. 42)

In this case, the CYCP put the youth's health needs at the forefront and processed the other fears in supervision. Share an example of when you or a colleague partnered with family in goal setting, designing, and implementing developmental supports and developed interventions for the child or youth.

c. Identify client and family needs for community resources and supports

The most successful way to identify client and family needs for community resources and supports is to ask! An example was posted in a community newspaper. A Rwandan community leader was happy to have mental health support workers come in to assist in the work with their precious children. Unfortunately, many tried to set up one-on-one appointments with vulnerable and high-risk youth.

> The Rwandan prescription for Depression: Sun, drum, dance, community. We had a lot of trouble with western mental health workers who came here immediately after the genocide and we had to ask some of them to leave. They came and their practice did not involve being outside in the sun where you begin to feel better, there is no music or drumming to get your blood flowing again, there is no sense that everyone had taken the day off so that the entire community could come together to try to lift you up and bring you back to joy, there is no acknowledgement of the depression as something invasive and external that could actually be cast out again. Instead they take people one at a time into these dingy little rooms and have them sit around for an hour or so and talk about bad things that had happened to them. We had to ask them to leave. (Solomon, 2013)

d. Support family members in accessing and utilizing community resources

After we know what a family wants, it is our job to help them access and utilize community resources. CYCPs may also have to create resources. Jade Medeiros, a CYCP in St. Catharine's, Ontario, Canada, will often reach out to the community to find mentors for youth. She will post social media requests such as: "is there anyone that has small business experience" or "knows how to play a harp?"

Creating connections such as these finds informal supports that may help the family grow in the direction they hope to without feeling pathologized (Medeiros, personal communication, 2017). Mentors help families to build community.

e. Advocate for and with family to secure and/or maintain proper services

CYCPs advocate for and with family to secure and/or maintain proper services. Many families benefit from having a CYCP attend school or medical meetings with them. Even if the CYCP says nothing, their emotional support helps a family so they do not feel alone or outnumbered when the official system they are dealing with has many people around the table. Additionally, it is beneficial when the CYCP understands the legislation the system is working under.

10. Community engagement

a. Access up-to-date information about service systems, support, and advocacy resources, and community resources, laws, regulations, and public policy

The CYCP that accesses up-to-date information about service systems, public policy, laws, and regulations has the necessary tools to engage with the community. Understanding how to access service systems, support, and advocacy resources ensures that the CYCP can utilize these to meet the needs of community members.

Discussion Opportunity 6:27

A CYCP accompanies a youth and his foster family to court. The youth is charged with a provincial crime, yet the duty counsel lawyer told the family that they are going to be heard in federal court. The CYCP believed the matter could be dealt with in the provincial court, which would have meant it was resolved before the youth went home that night. The matter could have been heard in the morning, and he could have entered a plea of not guilty earlier in the day. Instead, the youth and family waited for four hours for the case to have an initial hearing. The youth also had to travel back to the youth facility five hours away and had to return to court the next morning. He felt both overwhelmed and frustrated. The youth gathered more charges as a result of being in conflict with another incarcerated youth. The duty counsel lawyer later admitted to the CYCP that she was correct and duty counsel was wrong. Upon reflection, the CYCP didn't feel confident asking questions more strongly. She later found out that although the lawyer looked mature, it was his first week on the job as a duty counsel lawyer.

In a group find an example from your community of an advocacy resource that assists youth who are involved with the legal system. Next, discuss a recent government direction or policy that might negatively impact children and youth you are in contact with.

b. Develop and sustain collaborative relationships with organizations and people

It is important to develop and sustain collaborative working relationships with organizations and people. It is a small working world. Once a CYCP has been working in the field, they will meet others that they have previously worked with. Therefore, it is important to remember that your first day in formal CYC education is the beginning of your profession, it is the beginning of your reputation as a CYC, and it is the beginning of your opportunity to treat other CYCPs like family members. This means that it is important to provide peer support when it can be provided, for not only your peers and colleagues but also the children/youth and family that they work with, when you are called upon to do so. This creates a web of CYC support where we are happily interdependent on each other.

c. Facilitate client contact with relevant community agencies

CYCPs facilitate client contact with relevant community agencies. A wise CYCP wants to work themselves out of a job. This is done by not only fulfilling the treatment plan but also connecting the child/youth or family with community agencies that can provide supports when the CYCP has closed the "file" or completed the identified interventions. "In traditional Native society, it is the duty of all adults to serve as teachers for younger persons. Child rearing is not just the responsibility of biological parents but children are nurtured within a larger circle of significant others" (Krueger, 1991).

Chapter 6 Learning Outcomes Evaluation

- Do you have a greater understanding of the competencies noted under the developmental practice methods domain of CYC practice?
- Are you able to apply the domain and competencies to field examples?
- Are you able to use the language of the competencies in discussion you share in and outside of the classroom/workshop with colleagues? Which ones?
- What are some areas of strength (competencies) that you have in this domain?
- Do you have artifacts that provide evidence of this strength?
- What are competencies that you can develop in the developmental practice methods domain of practice? (You can use Appendix A as a resource.) Develop a SMART goal in relation to one competency.

REFERENCES

American Academy of Pediatrics. (2016). *American Academy of Pediatrics supports childhood sleep guidelines*. Retrieved May 27, 2018, from https://www.aap.org/en-us/about-the-aap/aap-press-room/pages/American-Academy-of-Pediatrics-Supports-Childhood-Sleep-Guidelines.aspx

Anglin, J. (2003). Child and youth care: A unique profession. *CYC-Online: E-journal of the International Child and Youth Care Network (CYC-Net)*, (35). Retrieved from https://www.cyc-net.org/cyc-online/cycol-1201-anglin.html

Anglin, J. P. (2014). Child and youth care is not rocket science: It's FAR more complex than that! *Relational Child and Youth Care Practice, 27*(2), 58.

Bandura, A. (2000). Self-efficacy and the construction of an optimistic self. *Reaching Today's Youth, 4*(4), 18–22.

Bellefeuille, G., & McGrath, J. (2013). A relational-centred international education partnership: A phenomenological inquiry into the lived experiences of child and youth care/social care students and faculty. *Contemporary Issues in Educational Research, 6*(3), 279–288.

Bowlby, J. (1999). *Attachment. Attachment and Loss* (vol. 1, 2nd ed.). New York, NY: Basic Books. (Original work published 1969)

Brendtro, L., & Ness, A. (1995). Fixing flaws or building strengths. *Reclaiming Children and Youth, 4*(2), 2–7.

Bringewatt, E. H. (2017). Delivering diagnoses: Parents as translators and withholders of children's mental health diagnoses. *Journal of Child and Family Studies, 26*(7), 1958–1969. doi:10.1007/s10826-017-0709-5

Brown, S. (2017). What if child and youth care is not rooted in relationships? *Relational Child and Youth Care Practice, 30*(4), 24–29.

Brown, S., & Hann, K. (2018). TheirNet. *Relational Child and Youth Care Practice, 31*(1), 6–22.

Burns, M. (2006). *Healing spaces: The therapeutic milieu in child and youth work*. Kingston, ON: Child Care Press.

Burns, M. (2012). *The self in child and youth care*. Kingston, ON: Child Care Press.

Centers for Disease Control. (1988). Perspectives in disease prevention and health promotion update: Universal precautions for prevention of transmission of human immunodeficiency virus, hepatitis B virus, and other bloodborne pathogens in health-care settings. *Morbidity and Mortality Weekly Report, 37*(24), 377–388.

Crismon, M. L., & Argo, T. (2009). The use of psychotropic medication for children in foster care. *Child Welfare, 88*(1), 71–100.

Child and Youth Care Certification Board (CYCCB). (2016). Developmental practice methods. College Station, TX: Author. Retrieved from https://www.cyccb.org/competencies/developmental-practice-methods

Chung, I. (2017). From a young person's perspective: Towards a better residential care system for youth. *CYC-Online: E-journal of the International Child and Youth Care Network (CYC-Net)*, (218), 11–19. Retrieved from http://www.cyc-net.org/cyc-online/apr2017.pdf

Delamere, F. M., Morden, P. A., & Rose, H. A. (2006). Promoting resilience in youth through facilitating leisure engagement in self-determined community-serving projects. *Journal of Child and Youth Care Work, 21*, 18–28.

Doran, G., Miller, A., & Cunningham, J. (1981). There's a S.M.A.R.T. way to write management goals and objectives. *Management Review, 70*(11), 35–36.

Durrant, J. E. (2007). *Positive discipline: What it is and how to do it*. Ottawa, ON: Save the Children.

Fox, L. (2017). Connections: Examining the personal and philosophical "glue" that connects us to our profession, each other, and the children, youth and families we serve. *CYC-Online: E-journal of the International Child and Youth Care Network (CYC-Net)*, (218), 20–37. Retrieved from http://www.cyc-net.org/cyc-online/apr2017.pdf

Fox, L. E. (1995). Exploiting daily events to heal the pain of sexual abuse. *Journal of Child and Youth Care, 10*(2), 33–42.

Fox, L. E. (2018). Using what we know for sure to keep hope alive. *CYC-Online: E-journal of the International Child and Youth Care Network (CYC-Net),* (230), 7–27. Retrieved from https://www.cyc-net.org/cyc-online/apr2018.pdf

Fraser, T. (2011). *Adopting a child with a trauma and attachment disruption history.* Ann Arbor, MI: Loving Healing Press.

Fraser, T. (2015). Creating trauma focused educational milieus. *Relational Child and Youth Care Practice, 28*(4), 57–68.

Fuggle, P., McHugh, A., Gore, L., Dixon, E., Curran, D., & Cutinha, D. (2016). Can we improve service efficiency in CAMHS using the CAPA approach without reducing treatment effectiveness? *Journal of Child Health Care, 20*(2), 195–204.

Fulcher, L., & Garfat, T. (2015). *Child and youth care practice with families.* Cape Town, South Africa: CYC-Net Press.

Garfat, T. (2001). Developmental stages of child and youth care workers: An interactional perspective. *CYC-Online: E-journal of the International Child and Youth Care Network (CYC-Net),* (24). Retrieved January 5, 2017, from http://www.cyc-net.org/cyc-online/cycol-0101-garfat.html.

Garfat, T. (2008). Characteristics of a child and youth care approach: An exploration of their possible relevance and their contextualization in the South African reality. *CYC-Online: E-journal of the International Child and Youth Care Network (CYC-Net),* (115).

Garfat, T., & Fulcher, L. (2012). *Child and youth care in practice.* Cape Town, South Africa: CYC-Net Press.

Garfat, T., & Fulcher, L. (2011). Characteristics of a child and youth care approach. *Relational Child and Youth Care Practice, 24*(1–2), 7–19.

Goalcast. (2017). 25 Maya Angelou quotes to inspire your life. Retrieved May 27, 2018, from https://www.goalcast.com/2017/04/03/maya-angelou-quotes-to-inspire-your-life/

Goodman, W. K., Geiger, A. M., & Wolf, J. M. (2017). Leisure activities are linked to mental health benefits by providing time and structure: Comparing employed, unemployed and homemakers. *Journal of Epidemiology and Community Health, 71*(1), 4–11. Retrieved May 27, 2018, from https://www.ncbi.nlm.nih.gov/pmc/articles/PMC5643199/

Haddad, F., & Gerson, R. (2014). *Helping kids in crisis: Managing psychiatric emergencies in children and adolescents.* Washington, DC: American Psychiatric Publishing.

Harte, S. (2007). Groups and groupwork. *CYC-Online: E-journal of the International Child and Youth Care Network (CYC-Net),* (104). Retrieved from https://www.cyc-net.org/cyc-online/cycol-0709-harte.html

Hindman, J. (2006). *There is no sex fairy: To protect our children from becoming sexual abusers.* Alexandria, VA: Alexandria Associates.

Kirby, P., Lanyon, C., Cronin, K., & Sinclair, R. (2003). *Building a culture of participation: Involving children and young people in policy, service planning, delivery and evaluation.* London, UK: National Children's Bureau.

Krueger, M. (1991). Central themes in child and youth care. *Journal of Child and Youth Care, 5*(1).

Laursen, E. K. (2002). Seven habits of reclaiming relationships. *Reclaiming Children and Youth, 11*(1), 10–14.

MacKinnon, L. (2012). Neurosequential model of therapeutics: Interview with Bruce Perry. *The Australian & New Zealand Journal of Family Therapy, 33*(3), 210–218. Retrieved from http:// childtrauma.org/cta-library/interventions/

Maier, H. W. (1987). *Developmental group care of children and youth.* New York, NY: Haworth Press.

Maslow, A. (1943). A theory of human motivation. *Psychological Review, 50,* 370–390.

Matthews, C. (2005). Reflective practice. *Relational Child and Youth Care Practice, 18*(2), 49.

Millard, C. (2015). Young people and placemaking: Engaging youth to create community spaces. Retrieved from https://www.pps.org/article/young-people-and-placemaking-engaging-youth- to-create-community-places

Miller, L. J. (2014). *Sensational kids: Hope and help for children with sensory processing disorder (SPD).* New York, NY: Penguin Group.

Mindell, J. A., & Owens, J. A. (2003). *A clinical guide to pediatric sleep: Diagnosis and management of sleep problems.* Philadelphia, PA: Lippincott Williams & Wilkins.

Office of the Fire Marshal. (n.d.). Fire safety planning guidelines for residential care facili- ties. Retrieved June 24, 2018, from http://www.ingersoll.ca/docman/fire-service-links/ documants/130-residential-care-facilities/file

Olive, E.(2006). The milieu teaching conflict resolution. Retrieved April 23, 2019, from https://www .cyc-net.org/cyc-online/cycol-0306-conflict.html

Ontario Association of Children's Aid Societies. (2016). *One vision, one voice: Changing the Ontario child welfare system to better serve African Canadians. Practice framework part 1: Research report.* Toronto, ON: Author.

Ontario Association of Children's Aid Societies. (n.d.). *Fire safety and prevention a resource guide for child welfare professionals.* Toronto, ON: Author.

Phelan, J. (2006). Controlling or managing behaviour: A crucial decision. *CYC-Online: E-journal of the International Child and Youth Care Network (CYC-Net),* (86). Retrieved from https://www .cyc-net.org/cyc-online/cycol-0306-phelan.html

Phelan, J. (2009). The wounded healer as a helper and helped: A CYC model. *CYC-Online: E-journal of the International Child and Youth Care Network (CYC-Net),* (121). Retrieved from https://www .cyc-net.org/CYC-online/CYConline-mar2009-phelan.html

Quigley, R. (2006). Positive peer groups: "Helping others" meets primary developmental needs. *CYC-Online: E-journal of the International Child and Youth Care Network (CYC-Net),* (85). Re- trieved from https://www.cyc-net.org/cyc-online/cycol-0206-quigley.html

Rauktis, M. E. (2016). "When you first get there, you wear red": Youth perceptions of point and level systems in group home care. *Child and Adolescent Social Work Journal, 33*(1), 91–102.

Redl, F. (1959). Strategy and technique of the life-space interview. *American Journal of Orthopsychiatry, 29*(1), 1–18.

Rogers, C. (1961). *On becoming a person: A therapist's view of psychotherapy.* Boston, MA: Houghton Mifflin.

Rogers, C. (1980). *A way of being.* Boston, MA: Houghton Mifflin.

Samis, M. (2016, October 7). Let's practice our fire drills. *Safe Kids Worldwide.* [Blog Post]. Retrieved from https://www.safekids.org/blog/lets-practice-our-fire-drills

Sainsbury Centre for Mental Health. (2007). *Crisis resolution.* London, UK: Author.

Skott-Myhre, H. A., & Skott-Myhre, K. S. G. (2007). Radical youth work: Love and community. *Relational Child and Youth Care Practice, 20*(3), 48–57.

Scozzaro, C., & Janikowski, T. P. (2015). Mental health diagnosis, medication, treatment and placement milieu of children in foster care. *Journal of Child and Family Studies, 24*(9), 2560–2567. doi:10.1007/s10826-014-0058

Sharpe, C. (2009). Fritz Redl and the life space interview. *CYC-Online: E-journal of International Child and Youth Care Network,* (129).

Snow, C. E., & Beals, D. E. (2006). Mealtime talk that supports literacy development. *New Directions for Child and Adolescent Development, 2006*(111), 51–66. doi:10.1002/cd.155

Solomon, A. (2013). Depression, the secret we share [Video]. Retrieved from https://www.ted.com/talks/andrew_solomon_depression_the_secret_we_share?language=en

Stuart, C. (2008). Shaping the rules: Child and youth care boundaries in the context of relationship. In G. Bellefeuille & F. Ricks (Eds.), *Standing on the precipice: Inquiry into the creative potential of child and youth care practice* (pp. 164–165). Edmonton, AB: MacEwan Press.

Spock, B., & Needlman, R. (2012). *Dr. Spock's baby and child care* (9th ed.). New York, NY: Gallery Books.

Torrance, E. P., & Myers, R. E. (1970). *Creative learning and teaching.* New York, NY: Harper and Row.

Tuckman, B. W. (1965). Developmental sequence in small groups. *Psychological Bulletin, 63*(6), 384–399. doi:10.1037/h0022100.

US Fire Administration. (n.d.). USFA position on home smoke alarms. Retrieved June 24, 2018, from https://www.usfa.fema.gov/about/smoke_alarms_position.html

Ventrella, M. (2015). Nurturing creativity in child and youth care practice: It's not what we think but how we think! *Relational Child and Youth Care Journal, 28*(2), 48–56.

Ventrella, M. (2017). The power of surrendering to mindfulness teaching in child and youth care. *Relational Child and Youth Care Practice, 30*(3), 56–77.

Weinstein, M. S., & Ricks, F. A. (1977). Goal attainment scaling: Planning and outcome. *Canadian Journal of Behavioural Science/Revue canadienne des sciences du comportement, 9*(1), 1–11. doi: 10.1037/h0081604

Wilson, S., Metcalfe, J., & McLeod, S. (2015). Comparing choice and partnership approach assumptions to child and adolescent mental health services in NHS Greater Glasgow and Clyde. *International Journal of Health Care Quality Assurance, 28*(8), 812–825.

York, A., & Kingsbury, S. (2013). The choice and partnership approach: A service transformation model. Exeter, UK: Short Run Press.

CHAPTER 7

Nurturing Creativity in Child and Youth Care Practice

Learning Outcomes

- Review how to nurture creativity in the CYC practice.
- Identify LEAP skills that you possess.
- Identify LEAP skills you will develop personally and professionally.
- Develop SMART goals for these LEAP skills.

Creative thinking is not a talent; it is a skill that can be learned. It empowers people by adding strength to their natural abilities, which improves teamwork, productivity, and where appropriate, profits. (De Bono, 1994)

Creativity is defined as the production of novel, useful ideas or solutions to problems in order to serve a purpose (Amabile, 1983; Puccio, Murdock, & Mance, 2005; Stein, 1974). The common theme in definitions of creativity is that the creator has a relationship with the process, and the product is novel and useful to the environment (Langer, 2005).

Creativity is considered the most desirable twenty-first-century skill and vital to the life of an organization; therefore, successful Child and Youth Care Practitioners recognize that creativity is critical in any relationship or organizational environment. Creative approaches to care require that practitioners think differently. Working creatively in relational work means seeking out other points of view; because relational work is inclusive, practitioners are not limited to their own ideas or bags of tricks. Everyone—colleagues, young people in care, friends, family members, and communities—is a potential creative resource (Ventrella, 2015). Unless CYCPs incorporate creativity in their practices, they will habitually act mindlessly and develop patterns that stifle creativity in children, youth, families, and communities. When familiar routines become embedded in organizations, the result is outdated behaviour that suffocates its members (Ray, Baker, & Plowman, 2011). Creative novelty is the capacity to develop new, effective, high-quality ideas and gain acceptance of them within and outside of the organization (Matthew, 2009); therefore, organizations need CYCP leaders who allow employees the freedom to propose creative novelties (Wang & Casimir, 2007). When there is supportive CYCP leadership that promotes creativity, employees become more inspired (Mathisen, Einarsen, & Mykletun, 2012). The flow of creativity depends on the absence of judgment or oppression, which encourages people to express themselves in relationships.

HOW IS CREATIVITY FUNDAMENTAL TO CHILD AND YOUTH CARE PRACTICE?

Creativity in relational practice enhances "in-the-moment" approaches and self-development through novel interactions within systems and promotes effective problem solving.

CREATIVITY AND RELATIONAL PRACTICE

In a field where relationship is everything, practitioners need to find novel ways of "doing with and doing together" (Garfat, 2001). Creativity goes above and beyond regular patterns and builds on something novel in ways valuable to the task at hand (Amabile, 1996; Sternber & Lubart, 2006). In CYCP practice, there is information that can be applied variously to different children in different situations—sound therapeutic principles that underlie application—but CYCP work also demands innovation and creativity (Curry, Lawler, Schneider-Munoz, & Fox, 2011).

Discussion Opportunity 7:1

In what ways did you experience creative relational responses with a friend or someone in your community, such as a teacher, a person of faith, someone from customer service, a government system representative? How did creativity meet a need or make a difference in the relationship?

"IN-THE-MOMENT" PRACTICES AND CREATIVITY

Creativity is possible in any moment in a relationship: how we interact, how we welcome someone, how our verbal and nonverbal communication is made inclusive to all. Relational practices are always presenting us with new interactions; how we respond makes the difference between promoting the needs of the relationship or not. How we respond to challenges in the moment can be influenced by our creative responses. One of the most effective skills of the CYCP is the ability to respond to a moment, which can make the difference between the child feeling supported or feeling overwhelmed. Think of a moment where a creative response made a difference in a relationship you had or witnessed.

Discussion Opportunity 7:2

You are a CYCP working at a school program, and you walk the children to their school bus. You receive a message that the school buses will be 20 minutes late. What are creative responses to meeting the children's needs?

Self and Creativity

A core principle of CYCP practice is that understanding oneself is fundamental to the process of building relationships; therefore, attending to self-development is foundational preparation for practice (Ward, 2013). A relational perspective involves knowledge and awareness of self in the moment of interaction (Stuart, 2013). The focus shifts from simply having a relationship to being in relationship (Garfat, 2008). In light of the fluid nature of relationships, self-awareness on the part of each worker is essential. Adapting to the continual change in relational work involves generating creative, even novel, responses and ideas essential for adapting to change (Grivas & Puccio, 2012).

Discussion Opportunity 7:3

What are some creative "in-the-moment" self-care strategies you can integrate during a shift? Come up with alternative ways to practise self-care. Do not include journaling or supervision. How can you add creativity in your personal life? How do these practices promote your interactions with children, youth, and families?

SYSTEMS AND CREATIVITY

Systems must include creative ways to interact that embody the values of different systems and meet the needs of all people involved in them. Systemically prescribed relationships promote rigid boundaries, regulated roles, and stereotypical power-based relationships that limit the potential for the relationship to grow and promote oppression. A systemic culture that values creative responses ensures systems push limits and institutional thinking to best meet the needs of children, youth, and families. Systemic change is challenging but essential in order to respond to the many challenges—working with children, youth, families, communities, cultures, and economic and environmental factors—faced by CYCPs on a daily basis.

Discussion Opportunity 7:4

How has systemic rigidity impacted you as a student and/or a CYCP? What systems you have experienced that have reduced your ability to be creative? In what way can systems promote creativity in children, youth, and families?

CREATIVITY AND EFFECTIVE PROBLEM SOLVING

When using creative and novel approaches, CYC practitioners support children and families in new ways of problem solving, being together, and doing things, and in considering new responses in relationships. Each relationship between a child and parent benefits from creative novelty, meaning that what works for one child will not necessarily work for another. Helping families develop new ways to respond interrupts ineffective patterns that have not been meeting the needs of individuals and sets up exploration into alternative responses that are more likely to meet their needs.

Discussion Opportunity 7:5

Reflect on a previous problem you did solve, but explore other potential ways you might have solved it. Try using creative problem solving in the following situation.

A CYCP is supporting Alex at a youth shelter. Alex is struggling with finding reliable housing. Neither the CYCP nor he have been successful in finding him a space after contacting extended family, a friend, and local shelters.

Try to make at least 20 suggestions. Share the question with your group and do not affirm or disagree with any suggestion. Let the creativity flow and build on each other's ideas. What is the most effective intervention?

EDUCATORS AND CREATIVITY

Educators need to value creative practices and build an educational paradigm that models best creative practice within the realities of current work (Shaw & Trites, 2013). Lieberman and Langer (1997) reported that students who asked to make their material meaningful showed better retention and increased creativity in essay writing when compared with students asked to memorize material. CYC education can be a challenge to creativity. Traditional educational approaches value the right answer, and of course, students seek to do well academically. It can be difficult as an educator to enable students creatively while still ensuring they also learn the basics needed for practice-based work (Ventrella, 2015). Creative teaching that leaves space for student creativity opens students to the learning potential of their own experiences and promotes greater willingness to deconstruct thoughts and categories while encouraging the reframing of personal responses. When teaching methods include contemplation, reflection, and introspection, students can find more of themselves in their courses (Barbezat & Pingree, 2012). Educators and students both need to construe meaning from creative interactions in the education system and then promote creativity as a skill among children, youth, and families.

Discussion Opportunity 7:6

Outline the meaning you derived from some creative educational experience from your past. Suggest how what you learned might be handed down to children, youth, and families.

Your professor asks you to teach the concept of relational practices to the class. With a budget of $200, share some ideas about making the lesson evocative and meaningful for the class.

CREATIVITY MODEL—TORRANCE INCUBATION MODEL (TIM)

Many consider E. Paul Torrance one of the most prominent scholars of creativity (Torrance & Safter, 1999). When the **Torrance Incubation Model (TIM)** is applied to child and youth care practices, creative "**LEAP skills**" can be taught and applied to relationships without losing the fundamental principles of CYC practice. There are three important stages to teaching or implementing creativity (Torrance, 1979).

STAGE 1: HEIGHTENING ANTICIPATION

The goal of Stage 1 is to get the child or youth's attention, stimulate curiosity, and inspire motivation for learning and change. Encouraging the child or youth creates a desire to know more about a skill or area of interest. Goals include having the child or youth anticipate how expectations will benefit them, getting the child to be curious about their process, allowing them to imagine and wonder, and giving them purpose and motivation. Anticipation may include relating to themselves or others.

Discussion Opportunity 7:7

Have you ever been curious about a vacation destination or in taking up art, music, carpentry, fishing, photography, web design, or other courses? Did you ever wonder what you could learn from a new skill or experience, and how what you learn transfers to another part of your life? A sense of wonder gives rise to a broader range of experiences and skills.

STAGE 2: DEEPEN EXPECTATIONS

Stage 2 is where CYCPs create and develop meaningful learning. The challenge is clearly identified. CYCPs can develop a list of actions or metaphors that outlines the development process. As you do this, keep in mind the saying "That is the tip of the iceberg; go beyond the surface." Take the time to discover what is missed in looking forward and what it means to the child or youth. Then brainstorm solutions and actions that will address the problem or point in a new direction.

Discussion Opportunity 7:8

Louis is so anxious about writing his school exams, he says he will not attend and will accept a zero grade. What was missed in the initial interaction with his CYCP is that he had previously had a panic attack during a test, for which some of his peers teased him for years.

Come up with an action that addresses the problem in areas that can help Louis deepen his learning experience. What metaphors and images might encourage Louis to write the exam and avoid getting teased?

STAGE 3: EXTEND THE LEARNING

During Stage 3, the CYCP supports the child or youth in carrying out the learning in real-life context by encouraging the child or youth to take the lead and apply the solution or skills. For example, if Louis's solution is to write his exam alone in a quiet room, ask him to imagine the scenario, then visit the room and meet who will be supervising. CYCPs walk beside the child and youth and support them in taking the lead, confident that their needs will be met and that they have a safe relationship where they can take risks on the way to meeting their goals.

Discussion Opportunity 7:9

Imagine that you have successfully completed some ambition of yours and discuss how you subsequently extended your dream, image, or goals in real life.

What relational skills can you develop with a child or youth that can be applied to solve other relationship challenges in that child or youth's life?

Each of these stages—of heightening, deepening, and extending the learning—is essential to a meaningful creative process.

CREATIVE LEAP SKILLS FOR CHILD AND YOUTH CARE PRACTITIONERS

TIM developed LEAP skills to promote creative teaching that can be implemented with children, youth, families, systems, and students (Torrance & Safter, 1999). LEAP skills challenge you to go beyond your comfort zone in order to try different skills. You might gravitate toward certain LEAP skills more than others. We ask many of the children, youth, and families that we work with to try and implement many things with which they may not be comfortable. The goal is to be aware of creative skills and explore ways to mindfully integrate them in relationships and problem-solving strategies with children, youth, families, and systems. Remember to consider the obvious, but also think outside the box.

Be Original

Have you ever had a problem that comes up over and over again? Have you noticed that a solution works for someone else but does not work for you? In relationships, do you always experience the same challenges with different people? Have you ever started behaving the same way as the people with whom you interact? Have you ever tried to solve a problem without success? Trying new approaches interrupts habitual patterns of thinking and acting and opens up the possibility of new and more effective perspectives and actions.

Ways to encourage originality in children, youth, and CYCP students

- Record 10 approaches that did not work and explore original ways to make them work
- Promote the courage to be original
- Present an object and ask for different ways the object could be used
- Come up with different ways one might travel to a destination
- Provide a variety of clothing items and explore different ways to wear them
- Provide children with toys and have them invent a solution to a community problem
- Explore different ways a person might say hello to someone
- Create a t-shirt that identifies a group's originality
- Find an original way to send a message to someone (without a phone or paper)
- Take the lines from a painting to develop a new image

Be Flexible

Have you ever been in relationship with someone who believes there is only one way of solving a problem? It is important for us to create a variety of content and have different perspectives. The way a 15-year-old understands bedtime curfew and the way a parent might are very different. People from different cultures may have different value systems. How can we be flexible in allowing different perspectives and still maintain meaningful relationships? Being flexible allows us to understand that all people in relationships need to be flexible to make room for exchange that is creative and nourishing to all.

Ways to encourage flexibility with children, youth, and CYCP students

- Read children a short story and ask them to create several alternative endings
- Have children develop different ways in which they can participate in a school trip
- Make a list of values that you believe you cannot change and question the purpose of each value
- Try a restaurant that serves a different culture's food that is different from what you usually dine on

- Make a list of alternate ways to complete chores
- Identify flexible ways to play with others during recess
- Identify flexible ways a child in residence might maintain contact with their family
- Come up with different ways parents and children might say good night
- Teach a class from the back of the room or remove the desks
- Ask students to post their reflections on their learning on a social media site that can be read by everyone

Produce and Consider Many Alternatives

Have you ever reacted too quickly or solved a problem, then realized the problem is not effectively solved and you may even have created another problem? Do you wish you had considered alternative ways to solving the problem or meeting your needs? If you have a need or problem, it is important to produce and consider many possible solutions. Proposing a variety of possibilities is an opportunity for children and youth to build on each idea and come up with a well-thought-out decision. During the process, no idea can be considered a bad one or dismissed out of hand. The skill of considering alternatives is an effective means to creative problem solving.

Ways to encourage producing and considering alternatives with children, youth, and CYCP students

- A parent is struggling financially and might not be able to send their child on the school trip. Come up with alternatives to solve the need or the problem.
- What are different ways you can use straws?
- Read a paragraph out of a book and change 10 words. Explore how the meaning of the paragraph has changed.
- Share a problem and develop a story about the problem. Create five different titles for your story.
- Four youths at a party notice that people are using a lot of drugs. They feel scared and uncomfortable. Develop alternative ways they might respond.
- The principal of the school witnesses a child being aggressive during recess and requests the CYCP discipline (not punish) the child. What are several ways to discipline the child?
- Discuss different ways people can communicate with each other.
- Make a comic strip to illustrate a concept your professor/instructor has taught.
- Give a word to a person and explore different ways that word can be understood.
- List ways in which we listen to someone and identify alternative ways to hear the message.

Be Aware of Emotions

Understanding what you may be feeling or others are feeling matters to relationships. It is important to recognize both verbal and nonverbal cues. Identifying, trusting, and using feelings appropriately provides us with better understanding and leads to acceptance and productivity. Integrating emotional awareness in the creative process augments mere logic. Have you ever had an idea that created emotions of excitement, joy, anticipation? Emotions fuel the creative juices, and those of others provide great feedback on your ideas. Emotional intelligence is the awareness that the regulation and discriminating application of emotions is integral to the creative process (Sundararajan & Averill, 2007).

Ways to encourage being aware of emotions with children, youth, and CYCP students

- Identify emotions before and after an event and indicate if they are the same or different.
- Create new and different emojis.
- Read a story and ask what emotions it evoked.
- Watch a movie and explore what a character might be feeling.
- Spend some time with a pet or watch a video of an animal and explore what feelings arise.
- Read inspirational quotes with an awareness of your emotions and if emotions change.
- Take pictures of yourself expressing different emotions. Note the transition as your emotions change.
- Observe colours in your environment and pay attention to any feelings they evoke.
- You are working for an outreach program when a youth you are approaching appears to be high, slurring her words, having difficulty standing, and not answering your questions coherently. What emotions might you be feeling? What information are your emotions conveying to you and to her?
- In class, what happens emotionally when you "check out"? When you freeze or become numb, does it provide you with valuable awareness?

Elaborate—But Not Excessively

Elaborating on a task is important. At the same time, it is essential that the process is on task, as spouting excessive information tends to alienate listeners. It is important to be considerate of how much others can take in at one time. Concise and meaningful information allows a larger audience to take it in.

Ways to encourage elaboration that is not excessive with children, youth, and CYCP students

- Share three things about your day and how they were meaningful for you.
- Listen to a piece of a podcast and share it with another person in three sentences.
- Watch a clip of a movie and explain why you do or do not recommend watching it in under one minute.

- Read a children's book and share how the main themes can promote child development.
- Try to convince someone to travel to a unique destination in fewer than five sentences.
- Identify a self-care strategy that supports your ability to relate to others more effectively.
- Read a short poem and discuss if the poem is a satisfying experience, or if it left you needing more to understand its meaning.
- You have been subpoenaed to court for a case you are currently working. The lawyer asks you to elaborate and be concise, asking you not to provide any extra information that can be used against the family. Practise what you say.
- You are working with children who have experienced grief and loss. Develop questions that will help the children elaborate yet provide them a focus.
- Ask persons of a different culture, socioeconomic status, sexual orientation, learning ability, or faith to tell about their experiences and what they embrace about their diversity.

Combine and Synthesize

Combining and synthesizing ideas and experiences makes connections and develops new meanings, outcomes, and approaches. The combination of ideas allows for something new to transpire, which may feel strange at first, then later be seen as the beginning of something formative and valuable. In CYC practice, we combine many skills and synthesize how these skills can be transformed into novel practices. Practising social skills with a CYCP can be synthesized with transferring the skills to social relationships. An example of synthesis is the combination of a treadmill with a computer desk: exercise synthesized with work, health with making a living—a creative way of solving a timely problem for many. Another example might be a 14-year-old, Kyle, who had to ride in a cab for one hour each way to school every day. He developed a relationship with the cab driver, who became one of his greatest supports. Their creative relationship developed out of the synthesis of two needs.

Ways to encourage combining and synthesizing with children, youth, and CYCP students

- How do education and creativity work together?
- Combine a guitar with another object and discuss how the object can help play the guitar.
- Jasdeet is in Grade 4 and struggles with reading. Her strengths are singing and poetry. Discuss how her need to develop reading skills could be combined and synthesized with her strengths.
- Dante does not attend school and spends most of the day in his room playing video games, because socializing makes him very anxious. How can you combine and synthesize the need for education and social development?

- Identify two common recipes and develop a new recipe with the combination.
- Explore different forms of prayer, then combine two or more different forms and develop a new way to pray.
- Identify two mediums of art, then combine them and label the new form of art you have developed.
- Explore different ways cultures greet each other, then combine different forms of greeting and develop a new way to greet others.
- Plan a school trip for Grade 8 graduation by combining two destinations in one so that a new place is created where teens might want to socialize.
- A CYCP is planning for supervision and needs to combine self-care with case consultation. Create for her a new way to experience supervision.

Highlight the Essence

The problem we identify is not always the quintessential problem. Identifying what is most important and absolutely essential, and disregarding irrelevant information, leads to focus on the meat of the issue. Focusing on only part of or indirectly on the problem perpetuates aspects of the problem we are overlooking.

Winnow is afraid of failing her college exam. The essence of the problem turned out to be pressure from the potential loss of financial assistance, which could lead to loss of her housing and the end of her ambition to be first in her family to graduate from college. In another example, a CYCP working in a residential treatment centre has a new intake tell her that he hates her. On the surface, it appears to be a relationship issue between that staff member and the youth, but later the youth admitted his outburst stemmed from fear, since this was his third group home. The above cases show how the essence of a problem may be hidden on first examination.

Ways to encourage highlighting the essence with children, youth, and CYCP students

- Review the lyrics in a song and circle five words. What is the essence of the five words and meaning in the song?
- Record 8–10 words that describe your strengths. What is the essence of the words?
- List the last three purchases you made. Develop a commercial about the essence of the products you have purchased.
- Cook a meal with children and ask them to explore the essence of cooking and eating together.
- Record several traditions from different cultures and highlight the essence of traditions and the importance to relationships.
- Explore different forms of multimedia and electronics and how have these changed the essence of relationships.
- Meditate for five minutes and become aware of the essence of being in a quiet place and connecting to your breath.

- Google your name and explore if your name has different meanings. What parts of the search highlight the essence of who you are?
- Reflect on a course or class you have taken and reflect on the essence of the concepts and Child and Youth Care practices.
- Highlight the essence of what it means to you to become a Child and Youth Care Practitioner.

Put Your Ideas in Context

Understanding your experiences in a bigger framework means connecting them together in meaningful ways, regarding yourself, your relationship to others, and your relationship to systems. When we understand our history we can connect the past to the present and to our vision of the future.

Ways to encourage putting your ideas in context with children, youth, and CYCP students

- Identify a personal problem. Create an idea that might be of benefit to you.
- After a car accident, Dionne's mobility is dependent on a wheelchair. Prior to the accident, Dionne spent lots of time kayaking, paddle-boarding, and canoeing. Being on the water is very important to Dionne's self-care and socialization. Come up with creative proposals to enable Dionne to have these needs met.
- Take an idea that works in one context and demonstrate how it will not work in another context.
- How can you use Lego at a children's party? A board meeting? While fishing? On a drive to Seattle?
- How can a cellphone be used to build relationships? In school? At places of faith? In travel and finances?
- Imagine you are building a sculpture out of clay. Draw your sculpture, and discuss what the sculpture means to you and what context the sculpture could be used in.
- You are a reporter who is going to interview adults who grew up in care. Develop a creative way to interview them that is respectful to the context.
- Develop a ride for a new amusement park. How will it add meaning to the relationships of the community?
- You work in a day-treatment school program and you want to start a garden program, but you cannot garden outside the grounds. How can gardening be valuable in the context of education and relationship? What will you propose?
- You are a CYCP and your task is to create a documentary. What is the title of the documentary? What themes will be highlights in this documentary that will hold meaning to children, youth, families, and the profession?

Stay Open

Have you ever made a decision and realized later that you needed to consider other alternatives? Did you make a choice that was the quickest but not necessarily the most effective option? When exploring creative ideas, it is important that you are not premature in coming to conclusions. It is important to be open to all options before making a decision, because openness values relationships and new and even opposing ideas. The environment needs to be a safe place for people to propose ideas without being judged.

Ways to encourage staying open with children, youth, and CYCP students

- Share how you have recently solved a problem and invite feedback. Keep an open mind when listening to different ways you could have solved it.
- Share a story that did not end well for you. Reflect on the positives that came from the experience.
- Share a conflict you had with someone who is important to you. What is the other person's perspective? What do you think mattered to them, and why?
- Get into pairs. Have each person scribble on a piece of paper. Pass the image to your partner, who will add to the image, and then discuss the new image.
- Find a research study with whose findings you disagree. Keep an open mind and explore what you can take away from the research.
- Make a list of personal goals that you believe might be impossible. Stay open to your goals.
- What was life like for your parents and grandparents? Your great-grandparents? What is their legacy to you?
- You're going to write a screenplay. List some themes that are different from any film you have seen.
- What different ways can homeless people be housed?
- You are working at a community program with a $1,000 budget to encourage and support the diversity of the community. Develop some projects that promote diversity.

Visualize It—Richly and Colourfully

Visualizing your dreams, projects, goals, plans, solutions, relationships—whatever is important to you—is an active process. Extend your creative process to include details that are appealing to all five of your senses. Visualize the shapes, colours, lines, feelings, smells, sights, and taste, and the relationship to each sensation.

Ways to visualize richly and colourfully with children, youth, and CYCP students

- You are working at an agency, and your responsibility to is organize a summer camp for children ages 12 to 16. How do you provide an experience that addresses all the senses?
- You are working at an agency that wants to plan a special trip for the children and youth in the program. Visualize fundraising opportunities you can create and implement.
- You are supporting Samantha, a 17-year-old who is the first person in her family to consider attending college. She is very scared and shares that it is easier to not

go to college and instead find a job in her small town. Explore creative ways in which Samantha could visualize a rich and colourful future if she attends college.
- Create a poster that reflects your value system as a CYCP.
- Write three quotes that are an inspiration to children, youth, and CYCPs.
- You are supporting a 10-year-old Spanish boy named Hugo, who did not share much in his last two visits. Can you visualize ways for Hugo to express himself without words?
- Visualize a change in systems that you believe would be more supportive to children, youth, families, and communities.
- Visualize what you want your CYCP career to look like in 3, 5, and 10 years.
- Record a dream and visualize the dream as part of your life.

Make It Swing! Make It Ring!

You might remember your times tables because your Grade 3 teacher taught them by singing, or your passwords by reciting them over and over again. You may have had the experience of relationship through dancing or drumming as a community. Have you ever had an intense feeling throughout your body with any words? Swing and Ring is about using kinesthetic and auditory senses through sound and movement as part of the creative process.

Ways to encourage making it swing, making it ring with children, youth, and CYCP students

- Donna is a 16-year-old Canadian female who has been using drugs and recently discovered she is pregnant. A child protection agency is involved in her family's life. Donna takes care of her two young siblings when her parents are at work. She loves her maternal grandparents and worries they are going to be disappointed. In a team, have each person represent a system that may impact Donna. Try to come up with at least 15 systems.
- Get in pairs and face each other. Make facial expressions that clearly describe an emotion. Have fun exaggerating the emotion without words.
- Listen to different genres of music and feel the different emotions each evokes.
- Have students or teams participate in a lesson/team meeting while walking. How is the experience different from sitting?
- Listen to the lyrics of a song and change the words to make it more meaningful to your life.
- Have your students/team greet each other in different ways than saying hello or shaking each other's hands.
- Have someone become a sculpture. Or "sculpt" all the students/team members together to create one large sculpture. Discuss in groups/teams what the sculpture will represent.
- You and an eight-year-old child are baking a cake together. Discuss how baking together can build a relationship.

- What is something kinetic you can do that promotes self-care?
- We are drawn to listen to the sounds of words or sounds around us. Take a few moments to listen to the silence between the sounds.

Look at It Another Way

What if you were born in another country? How does location change your values and belief systems, traditions, or language? Think of your favourite movie. What if the main character were a different gender? How does that change the story? Reflect on your favourite romance movie. What if the movie depicted a same-sex relationship? What if you invented a product that could change people's lives? How does this impact your life? What if your favourite song was sung by an opera singer? How does the singer change your relationship to the song? What if there were no colour green on the Earth? How would that change our relationship with nature?

Allowing yourself to brainstorm alternatives imagines how different relationships could change. Looking at things from a different perspective is important to the creative process and creative problem solving, because different approaches support change and build on concepts that already exist. Challenge yourself to look at your values, beliefs, habits, solutions, relationships, culture, challenges, dreams, and goals in other ways and embrace the creative process.

Ways to encourage looking at it another way with children, youth, and CYCP students

- Ask everyone to bring in an item and explore different ways you can use that item.
- Form groups of four and explore ways you can make a tower out of straws and paper.
- Have children, youth, or students lie outside on a day with fluffy clouds. Ask them to share their impressions of the images they see.
- Reach out and shake someone's hand. List five different ways you can interpret this action.
- Reflect on your last disagreement or argument and explore the other person's views in new ways.
- The cellphone is no longer just a phone. How else can you look at it?
- Take several pictures and share your story through these pictures.
- Tell a child a story or movie, with the ending first.
- What are your values about self-care? Try to look at self-care in a new way.

Enjoy and Use Fantasy

Watching a five-year-old pretend they have superpowers, can fly to the moon, or are building the "tallest" tower, or act as a teacher, magician, or artist, is magical. When do we stop enjoying fantasy? As children develop, we promote logic over imagination and fantasy. As CYCPs, we need to embrace fantasy as part of the creative process. Ask youth to fantasize about their futures in detail. They can look at home, school, career, and relationships: what do they look, feel, and sound like? Ask a child to imagine happiness or where they see themselves in five years. Eight years? Ten years? Ask them to create a new job that has never been invented. Ask a group of children to create a fantasy children's movie—who knows, they might just create the next blockbuster! Fantasy needs to be part of play and relationship building in the child and youth life space. Model for parents the importance of imagination in relationship and attachment. Teach children, youth, and families to express and show care, love, and kindness with imagination, and the sky is the limit. The experiences of early life have the profound ability to shape the infant, child, adolescent, and ultimately the adult. Each child has their own unique genetic potential, yet this potential is expressed differentially depending upon the nature, timing, and patterns of developmental experience (Perry, 2001, 2002).

Ways to encourage enjoying and using fantasy with children, youth, and CYCP students

- How would life be different if everyone could fly? What laws would change? How would children learn in school?
- Imagine that you can use a time machine, once in your life. Where would you go and to what era? How would this trip change your life?
- Ask children and youth to imagine their text and email transfers visually. What would it look like?
- Imagine a new food. What would it look and taste like?
- Imagine you are a scientist and you could invent anything. What would it be, and how would it serve communities?
- Imagine there is no oppression or racism. How would the world be different?
- Draw a comic strip of happiness.
- Imagine you could change a system issue in the field. What would you change and how would it benefit children, youth, and families?
- Tell a story from the perspective of a youth who has been incarcerated for eight years for a crime committed when he/she/ze/they were 17 years old.
- Imagine a job that you could create as a CYCP. Imagine your career and the legacy you want to leave behind as a CYCP.

Breaking Through—Expand the Boundaries

Have you ever been part of a system with rigid policies? Ever try to resolve an issue with a company that responded by saying, "Sorry, it's against policy"? Inflexibility in the face of needs is very frustrating. Child and youth care once did not include children in their own goal development. In the past, many agencies worked in isolation. Now agencies support and interact with the community. Child and youth care has already broken through many barriers and needs to continue breaking through other barriers that stand in the way of best practices. Boundaries need to be flexible and open to change to keep up with evolving relationships.

Ways to encourage breaking through and expanding the boundaries with children, youth, and CYCP students

- What impact does open adoption have versus closed adoption?
- What would residential care look like if parents lived in residence with their children?
- What would happen if CYC faculty trained Indigenous people in their communities as CYCPs who could then support their communities?
- Reflect on CYC breakthroughs that have changed CYCP practices.
- What are the risks of not reflecting on CYC practices and not encouraging breakthroughs?
- What are breakthrough strategies we can develop for other disciplines to recognize our value as a professional body more?
- What breakthrough practices can we develop to ensure placement continues to be essential learning?
- How can supervisors promote breakthrough changes with CYCPs?
- Brainstorm breakthrough changes to CYC practice that can continue to demonstrate creative ways of providing care.
- Create a list of breakthrough ways you and teams can demonstrate self-care.

Let Humour Flow and Use It

Have you ever laughed with someone and felt the joy in the relationship? Have you ever surprised someone and their response was a radiant smile? Ever sat by a camp fire, told jokes, and sensed the communal connection? Have you ever seen a child laugh at the discrepancies between the meanings of words? Have you ever seen youth create their own language and laugh at the conversation? Laughter is contagious and humour an important skill in building joyful relationships, because it lightens up communications, which in turn provide a sense of safety. Humour and play are related when it comes to interactions between people, groups, and communities.

Ways to encourage letting humour flow and using it with children, youth, and CYCP students

- Watch a funny video with children and youth. Listen to the silence before the laughter and then hear the synchronicity of the laughter.
- Ask your own parents to share a funny story about you when you were little. Or ask other parents to tell stories about the funny things their children said or did.
- Act out a story without using words. Try to express yourself with your face and body.

- Get in small groups and tell silly childhood jokes. For example, how did the chicken cross the road?
- Watch a children's movie and follow the humour to explore how humour builds a relationship and connection to a funny character.
- Share your favourite comedy movie and how you felt, thought, and reacted.
- Discuss how your family shares humour. Can you remember a time when there was little humour and how that impacted relationships?
- Get in small groups and share how humour can be an effective way to build relationships.
- How can humour be used for team development?
- How can humour promote self-care?

Get Glimpses of the Future

What are some glimpses of your personal life in the future? Where do you see yourself working in 5, 10, 20 years? What do you want your contribution to the CYCP field to look like? In what age groups and milieu do you see yourself working? In what will you specialize? If you could create and develop a future agency, who would you serve and what programs would you provide? If you can imagine fulfilling a dream, what would that look, feel, taste, and smell like? Getting a glimpse of your future is about making a prediction and imagining things that you want in your life. Be creative and predict things that do not yet exist. The possibilities are endless for you personally and professionally.

Ways to encourage glimpses of the future in children, youth, and CYCP students

- What do you predict communities will be like in 10 years? How will the changes impact or influence CYC practices?
- Imagine you are a supervisor of an agency. Write a proposal that develops a program to support diversity and decrease oppression in communities.
- If you could create a robot that would meet the needs of children, what would it look like and what functions would it provide?
- What do you believe will not change in CYC practices in the future? How will you protect the concepts to ensure they remain part of CYC practice?
- Explore how media will change in the future and how the change will impact or influence children's development in the future.
- Imagine that, in 10 years, you have developed an evidence-based intervention that supports children with attention deficit disorder, obsessive compulsive disorder, anxiety, depression, or any other mental health challenge. What does your intervention look like, and how would the intervention support future children and youth?
- Imagine how CYCP conferences might be different in the future. How can professional development continue provincially or internationally on a regular basis?

- Imagine creating a mobile program for children and youth that visits communities. What does your mobile program look like, and what community needs could you meet?
- Visualize an agency that incorporates self-care stations in the agency. What would they look like, and what needs do they meet for CYCPs?
- Glimpse your future in terms of the actions you need to take to move in the direction of your dreams.

The preceding 16 creative skills were developed by Torrance and Safter (1999). Burnett and Figliotti (2015) added four more creative problem-solving skills that contribute to creativity: curiosity, embracing the challenge, mindfulness, and tolerating ambiguity.

Have you wondered how community trends change? Have you had the desire to visit another country? Ever wonder what it takes to be famous? CYCPs are lifelong learners and keep learning to teach from different perspectives. Is there a gap in the system that makes you ask questions? How might we be communicating in 10 years? How might neuroscience change how we intervene with others? Curiosity is the fountainhead of knowledge, and a passion for learning for its own sake makes life more fulfilling and balanced. CYCPs practise nurturing curiosity in children and youth because we know it is key to developing the child's passion for living. Curiosity is for life.

Curiosity

Ways to encourage curiosity in children, youth, and CYCP students

- Explore your food: the ingredients, the shapes, the colours, flavours, and scents. Where do they come from? How they are grown?
- Explore some behaviours that are problematic in public. What causes them? What contributes to them? What needs are being met?
- Share a few amazing facts about a unique spot in the world. Explore the questions that made you curious about that place.
- Watch a 10-minute segment in the middle of a movie. What do you think happened before and after?
- Examine some pictures of people and wonder about each person's story, their dreams, their challenges.
- Put objects in a box or bag, then have people explore them by shape, by weight, by touch, and by feel.
- Go on a walk and be curious about what you see, hear, feel, and smell. Take pictures and make a memory board of your experiences.
- Be curious about how social issues impact others globally.
- Be curious about an issue that adolescents are facing today. What skills and strengths do they have today compared to those in the early 1950s, for example?
- Be curious about yourself and what you have to offer the CYCP field.

Embrace the Challenge

In relationship, it is important to welcome challenges because they lead to learning new skills and show us areas that need to develop further. Reflect on a challenge you have had in your life that contributed to making you stronger and wiser. Challenges can be painful, frustrating, and stressful, but we can learn about ourselves when we view challenges not as problems but as opportunities for discovering our own strengths. Children, youth, and families can be taught to reach out for resources and build support networks when faced with challenges.

Ways to encourage embracing the challenges with children, youth, and CYCP students

- In small groups, share a personal challenge you have overcome and what you learned about yourself.
- Share a professional challenge as a CYCP and how the experience added to your skill set.
- How do the challenges adoptive children and adoptive parents face teach them about safe relationships?
- If you have a limitation in an area of academic learning, what resources might support your handling the challenge?
- What milieu can you find most challenging to work in? What support can help you work outside your comfort zone?
- Celebrate a challenge that you have embraced and the new skills you acquired.
- Watch a video about someone who demonstrated courage and conquered their challenges.
- You are supporting a foster family. On your visit, the foster youth is screaming and using foul language to express their anger. You can sense your anxiety increasing. Discuss how you can embrace the challenge and use in-the-moment intervention to build relationship and teach new skills of relating.
- You are supporting a teacher, and you notice that she is referring to a student with criticism and negativity. She expresses that this child will only be trouble in the future, and your relationship with the child has been very different: open, humorous, and positive. How will you support both the teacher and the child so that all three relationships can be sustained and nurtured?
- Many CYCPs say they do not have time for self-care. Embrace that challenge and explore ways to incorporate self-care using minimal time.

Mindfulness

Have you ever sat on a beach and had your breath connect with each wave? Paid attention to the words of a meaningful song? Eaten your favourite food and be reminded of your mother? Heard a baby laugh and felt yourself smile? Been with a youth who struggled academically and watched them work through their fears, or worked through a family's grief and felt their pain? These are examples of mindful attunement. An essential component of mindfulness is how it affects attitude, cognition, and behaviour.

Mindfulness is also applied to challenges, such as setting aside your wish to end your shift in order to support a family in transition during your home visit or to work with an angry child by taking three deep breaths. Mindfulness is paying attention to the present moment and suspending judgment as the experience unfolds (Kabat-Zinn, 2003). Pausing to reflect on the moment without judgment to yourself is to be in relationship with yourself and others. Mindlessness lacks conscious control of actions that go unquestioned (Langer, 1989). If we are not mindful, then we are mindless (Langer, 2005).

Mindfulness is an active state of awareness in the present context and is guided by rules and routines (Langer, 1989, 1997, 2009). Mindfulness is a teachable skill that can be nurtured by taking responsibility for attention and attitude (Langer, 2005). Mindfulness begins by organizing thoughts, ideas, and perceptions without judgment or suppression (Nyanaponika, 1972). By slowing down thoughts, a higher quality of attention minimizes interference from emotions, judgment, and impatience and broadens perceptions.

Mindfulness theory in practice benefits business, education, and social services and leads to creative teamwork that overcomes the initial effort of novel tasks (Grant, Langer, Falk, & Capodilupo, 2004). Improved perspective leads to improved performance (Langer, Hefferman, & Kiester, 1988; Lieberman & Langer, 1997) and increases creativity and decreases burnout (Langer, Hefferman, & Kiester, 1988). Students are asked to make their material meaningful rather than memorize it; the result is better retention of lessons and increased creativity in essay writing (Lieberman & Langer, 1997). Greater attention, enjoyment of tasks, and improved memory are the benefits to children, college students, and the elderly when asked to notice new things mindfully (Langer & Bodner, 1995). Mindfulness is a skill we need to teach and integrate in child and youth care education programs (Ventrella, 2017).

Ways to encourage mindfulness in children, youth, and CYCP students

- Go for a walk with a child and ask him/her/hir/them to look at details he/she/ze/they have never noticed, such as veins on a leaf, the kinds of trees, new colours, smells, and so on.
- Take five minutes of silence and focus on your breath. Observe your thoughts and sensations in your body.
- Conduct a drumming circle (or bang on desks, tables, or buckets) and listen to the sounds and intervals of silence.
- Set a timer for a minute and try to pay attention moment to moment.
- Reflect on how CYC education has changed your values, beliefs, and actions.
- Sit with someone who may have the same or different culture and exchange on your influences.

- Reflect on a challenging experience, a difficult time, or an overwhelming emotion and find reasons to appreciate the experience in terms of a lesson you learned from it.
- Stand in front of another person and mirror each other's movements. Pay attention to each movement and the sensations in your body (Munns, 2008).
- Challenge yourself to meditate for 15 minutes before your start your day. Record a journal on your experience at the end of the day.
- Record 10 things for which you are grateful before you go to bed.

Tolerate Ambiguity

Remember a time when you felt at odds over a dilemma? Did the contradictions create anxiety that made you freeze or hold you back from reaching for a goal? When children go for home visits, they can feel ambivalent about the ambiguity of the situation. The uncertainty of your prospects of landing that job versus your excitement about getting it is an ambiguous situation. A CYCP can be ambivalent about their team or a supervisor's support when the messages are ambiguous. The world is ever-changing and full of things we do not know. Always having certainty does not leave space to explore what is not known. In order to risk taking on a challenge, it is important to accept and fully experience life's ambiguities, or at least tolerate them, because they are inevitable.

Tolerating the presence of ambiguity means letting in the questions despite the discomfort. To stay with the moment, mindfully, allows emotions to regulate and thoughts to clear. As a CYCP, tolerating ambiguity is a means to effectively respond to uncertainty in relationships. Creativity carries an essential component of ambiguity by always asking what, how, and why; that is, going deeper and beyond the status quo in our learning. What we do not know is equally important as what we do know, because human beings have the capacity for curiosity and changing their environment.

Ways to encourage tolerating ambiguity in children, youth, and CYCP students

- Create three metaphors that support children, youth, and CYCP in tolerating ambiguity.
- Watch a movie clip and push pause during the climax. Have a discussion about your thoughts, feelings, and reactions to waiting to know the ending.
- Send someone close to you a text or email. Ask them three questions. Ask them to respond after three days. What thoughts, feelings, and reactions do you have?
- Imagine you are a parent with a child with medical needs. You have a very important meeting with the school to discuss supports, but it is suddenly postponed for three weeks. How might you react? What skills are useful to work with the ambiguity?
- Share a time when you were very stressed, but after a time, the problem worked itself out.

- What skills can you teach children or CYCPs who struggle with tolerating ambiguity?
- Reflect on your high school graduation or another time when there was ambiguity in your life. How did you respond to the transition?
- Consider where you are in your development as a CYCP. What you are most ambiguous about working as a CYCP?
- Your own wellness is important. What do CYCPs need to incorporate to protect their self-care as part of their practice?
- Each relationship we build with children, youth, and families is different and unique, which makes CYC so exciting; however, how can diversity and uniqueness increase ambiguity?

CONCLUSION

Creativity must be at the forefront of child and youth care; we must support the creativity process in every relationship (Ventrella, 2015). Practising creativity allows for relational skills, creative problem solving, unique thinking, and practices. CYCPs need to be creative in relationships and interventions, and with systems, education, and practices. TIM provides concrete skills that can be learned and practised to incorporate as part of relationship development and change. Supporting mindfulness, curiosity, and tolerance supports the development of children, youth, and families.

Chapter 7 Learning Outcomes Evaluation

- Do you have a greater understanding of how to nurture creativity in your CYC practice?
- Do you already utilize some of the LEAP skills in your personal and professional life? Which ones?
- Identify LEAP skills you would like to develop. Why are these important to you?
- What are competencies that you can develop in the creativity domain of practice? (You can use Appendix A as a resource.) Develop a SMART goal in relation to one competency.

REFERENCES

Amabile, T. M. (1983). *The social psychology of creativity*. New York, NY: Springer-Verlag.

Amabile, T. M. (1996). *Creativity in context*. Boulder, CO: Westview Press.

Barbezat, D., & Pingree, A. (2012). Contemplative pedagogy; the special role of teaching and learning center. In James E. Groccia, & C. Laurar (Eds.), *To improve the academy: Resources for faculty, instructional, and organizational development* (pp. 177–191). San Francisco, CA: Jossey-Bass.

Burnett, C. & Figliotti, J. (2015). *Weaving creativity into every strand of your curriculum*. United Kingdom: KnowInnovation Press.

Curry, D., Lawler, J. M., Schneider-Munoz, J. A., & Fox, L. (2011). A child and youth care approach to professional development and training. *Relational Child and Youth Care Practice, 24*(1), 148–161.

De Bono, E. (1994). *De Bono's thinking course* (rev. ed.). New York, NY: Facts on File.

Garfat, T. (2001). Development stages of child and youth care workers: An interactional perspective. *CYC-Online: E-journal of the International Child and Youth Care Network (CYC-Net), (24)*. Retrieved from http://www.cyc-net.org/cyc-online/cycol-0101-garfat.htm

Garfat, T. (2008). Characteristics of a child and youth care approach: An exploration of their possible relevance and their contextualization in the South African reality. *CYC-Online: E-journal of the International Child and Youth Care Network (CYC-Net)*, (115). Retrieved from http://www.cyc-net. org/cyc-online/cyconline-sep2008-sbo.html

Grant, A., Langer, E., Falk, E., & Capodilupo, C. (2004). Mindful creativity: Drawing to draw distinctions. *Creativity Research Journal*, 16(2–3), 261–265.

Grivas, C., & Puccio, J. G. (2012). *The innovative team: Unleashing creative potential for breakthrough results*. San Francisco, CA: Jossey-Bass.

Kabat-Zinn, J. (2003). Mindfulness-based interventions in context: Past, present, and future. *Clinical Psychology: Science and Practice, 10*, 144–156.

Langer, E. J. (1989). *Mindfulness*. Philadelphia, PA: Addison Wesley.

Langer, E. J. (1997). *The power of mindful learning*. Boston, MA: Perseus Books.

Langer, E. J. (2005). *On becoming an artist: Reinventing yourself through mindful creativity*. New York, NY: Ballantine Books.

Langer, E. J. (2009). *Counter clockwise: Mindful health and the power of possibility*. New York, NY: Ballantine Books

Langer, E. J., & Bodner, T. (1995). *Mindfulness and attention*. Unpublished manuscript, Harvard University, Cambridge, MA.

Langer, E. J., Hefferman, D., & Kiester, M. (1988). *Reducing burnout in an institutional setting: An experimental investigation*. Unpublished manuscript, Harvard University, Cambridge, MA.

Lieberman, M., & Langer, E. J. (1997). Mindfulness in the process of learning. In E. J. Langer (Ed.), *The power of mindful learning*. Reading, MA: Addison Wesley.

Mathisen, G. E., Einarsen, S., & Mykletun, R. (2012). Creative leaders promote creative organizations. *International Journal of Manpower, 33*, 367–382.

Matthew, T. C. (2009). Leader creativity as a predictor of leading change in organizations. *Journal of Applied Social Psychology, 39*, 1–41.

Munns, E. (2008). In L. Lowenstein (Ed.), *Assessment and treatment activities for children, adolescents and families* (vol. 1). Toronto, ON: Champion Press.

Nyanaponika, T. (1972). *The power of mindfulness.* San Francisco, CA: Unity Press.

Perry, B. D. (2001). The neuroarcheology of childhood maltreatment: The neurodevelopmental costs of adverse childhood events. In K. Franey, R. Geffner, & R. Falconer (Eds.), *The cost of maltreatment: Who pays? We all do* (pp. 15–37). Binghampton, NY: Haworth Press.

Perry, B. D. (2002). Childhood experience and the expression of genetic potential: What childhood neglect tells us about nature and nurture. *Brain and Mind, 3,* 79–100.

Puccio, G. J., Murdock, M. C., & Mance, M. (2005). Current developments in creative problem solving for organization. *The Korean Journal of Thinking and Problem Solving, 15,* 43–76.

Ray, L., Baker, L., & Plowman, A. (2011). Organizational mindfulness in business schools. *Academy of Management Learning and Education Journal, 10,* 188–203.

Stein, M. I. (1974). *Stimulating creativity: Individual procedures* (vol. 1). New York, NY: Academic Press.

Sternber, R. J., & Lubart, T. I. (2006). Investing in creativity. *Psychological Inquiry, 4*(3), 229–232.

Stuart, C. (2013). *Foundation of child and youth care.* Dubuque, IA: Kendall Hunt Publishing Company.

Shaw, K., & Trites, J. (2013). Child and youth care education is child and youth care practice: Connecting with the characteristics of practice. *Relational Child and Youth Care Practice, 26*(4), 11–15.

Sundararajan, L., & Averill, J. R. (2007). Creativity in the everyday: Culture, self, and emotions. In R. Richards (Ed.), *Everyday creativity and new views of human nature* (pp. 195–220). Washington, DC: American Psychological Association.

Torrance, E. P. (1979). An instructional model for enhancing incubation. *Journal of Creative Behavior, 13*(1), 23–35.

Torrance, E. P., & Safter, T. (1999). *The incubation model of teaching: Getting beyond the aha!* Buffalo, NY: Bearly Limited.

Ventrella, M. (2015). Nurturing creativity in child and youth care practice. *Relational Journal of Child and Youth Care, 28*(2), 48.

Ventrella, M. (2017). The power of surrendering to mindfulness teaching in child and youth care. *Relation Child and Youth Care Practice, 30*(3), 55.

Wang, Y. K., & Casimir, G. (2007). How attitudes of leaders may enhance organizational creativity: Evidence from a Chinese study. *Creativity and Innovation Management, 16,* 229–238.

Ward, R. (2013). The importance of congruence in child and youth care education. *Relational Child and Youth Care Practice, 26*(3), 52–57.

CHAPTER 8

Competency Case Studies

Learning Outcomes

- Apply competencies to case study questions.
- Reflect on competencies that are strengths and opportunities for development.

This chapter has a case study for each CYCCB domain of practice, as well as the domain of creativity. When answering the reflective questions, please consider what competencies can assist the CYCP in addressing the issues cited in the case example. Review all domains of practice and provide competency examples using the Competency Chart in Appendix A. In our world of praxis, we do not respond using just one skill. We usually use many, and these not only interconnect but often build on each other. These case studies can be reviewed after each domain is studied or all at once by the student when all domains have been taught and discussed.

CASE STUDY #1: PROFESSIONALISM

Martin is a third-year student. He is working in a community placement where he meets with children and youth who participate in activities after school and on weekends. His supervisor is a CYCP who graduated from the same college five years ago. He has regular supervision and feels that he is learning a lot. His supervisor uses the competency checklist that Martin brought to supervision, and he is very interested in learning about the competencies.

Martin is in his last semester and is very excited to work after graduation. His supervisor indicates she will provide him with a reference that will hold him in good stead against competitors for an upcoming position. About six weeks before his graduation, his supervisor suggests they have supervision at a restaurant since they have had such a busy day.

While at the restaurant, she touches his hand and later his butt and makes comments that make Martin uncomfortable. He is very careful about giving clear messages and respecting work boundaries. He is confused to see his supervisor not modelling the same.

His supervisor is aware that Martin is married with a baby on the way. Before the end of the dinner, she reminds Martin that she intends to provide him with a good reference.

Martin decides to confide in a professor at school. He is worried that if he reports his supervisor, he will be let go from his practicum and then may be prevented from graduating.

His professor reassures him that he has support from her as he attempts to address this boundary violation professionally. She reminds him that someone touching him without consent could be considered a criminal act. Additionally, the professor is concerned about other students experiencing the same abuse if placed at this agency.

Discussion Opportunity 8:1

1. What policy does your college or institution have about unwanted advances and sexual interference between co-workers and supervisors?
2. If you were Martin, what would your next steps be?
3. Does the fact that Martin identifies as a homosexual male have any impact on his ability to lodge a complaint about a female supervisor?
4. Should he worry about voicing such a complaint so close to graduation?
5. Have you had discussions about student/front-line worker rights and responsibilities in your institution? Explore what frontline workers' rights and responsibilities are in institutions. How does knowing about these rights and responsibilities impact the relationships between CYCPs and youth?

CASE STUDY #2: PROFESSIONALISM

Preet is beginning her second practicum in a group home with two other students from her college. One is another second-year student, and the other a third-year student.

After shift change one day, the older student states that he has to go to work. He doesn't finish his shift note and asks another student to complete his documentation and sign his name. The other student agrees. Preet wants to intervene on the grounds of ethics, but doesn't want to sound bossy.

She worries the other students will think she's being too "by the book," but she knows if the student who completes the note is ever subpoenaed to court, she would have to commit perjury or admit that she completed the documentation.

Discussion Opportunity 8:2

1. What does Preet have to do to address this ethical code violation?

2. What competencies does this example require under the domains of professionalism and relationship and communication?

CASE STUDY #3: CULTURAL AND HUMAN DIVERSITY

Re-examine Case Study #1 with this additional information: *Martin is black, and his supervisor is white. In addition to the unwanted sexual advances, she has made racialized comments about black men in relationship with white women.*

Discussion Opportunity 8:3

1. Should Martin do anything different?
2. Is the college responsible for any preventative communication?
3. What competencies need to be considered when managing this situation?
4. What competencies can assist Martin in managing his experience? Please review all domains, and cite a few examples from each domain.

CASE STUDY #4: CULTURAL AND HUMAN DIVERSITY

The night caretaker at a smaller, rural elementary school transitioned from male to female. Some of the parents are complaining to the principal about the impact of this caretaker's presence in the school community. The Child and Youth Care Practitioner (in the presence of other teachers and a vice-principal) overheard students making mean comments about the caretaker. Though senior staff are present, no one identifies the comments as transphobic or concerning.

Discussion Opportunity 8:4

1. How could the CYCP address the students' comments?

CASE STUDY #5: APPLIED HUMAN DEVELOPMENT

The Khawaja family are Syrian refugees who arrive in Canada. The family consists of father, mother, 14-year-old Fatima, 10-year-old Nahia, and 8-year-old Alki. The family is so grateful for the support they have received. They have temporary housing and minimal financial support. They have connected to a place of faith and receive support from their community. The family has connected with another Syrian family, and they have been spending a lot of time together. The parents struggle with engaging in community programs due to lack of finances/transportation and language barriers.

Fatima has been attending high school for four months. She enjoys singing and writing poetry. Fatima has expressed that she would like to write her story of coming to Canada one day. She is struggling with academics and making friends. She eats lunch alone most days or sits in the library. Mr. Peterson has reached out to Fatima and encouraged her to speak to the Child and Youth Care Practitioner of the school. Fatima shared with the CYCP that she has to help her family and takes care of her siblings. She expresses that she feels safest when she is in bed with all her siblings. She feels loved, and her family means a lot to her. Fatima has shared that communication is a barrier because she is worried about her English and sometimes finds slang or facial expressions confusing. Fatima feels safe in Canada but continues to have trouble sleeping because of flashbacks and hearing louds sounds of bombing and shooting. Fatima would like to meet with the CYCP weekly to gain more information about Canadian culture, and she would like to make new friends. Fatima has also agreed to meet with a peer tutor to go over her academics and assignments. The CYCP has introduced Fatima to the school librarian, and a connection has been made. Fatima and her family are in transition and look forward to finding a safe place to live and yet continue to miss their culture, as well as the family and friends they left behind.

Discussion Opportunity 8:5

1. What strengths does the family, and Fatima in particular, display?
2. What can the CYCP do to support Fatima's psychological, social, emotional, and behavioural development?
3. How can the CYCP support the family from an ecological perspective?
4. What can the CYCP learn from Fatima and her family?
5. What systemic barriers may present themselves, and how can you creatively problem solve the limitations?
6. Think of all of the domains of practice and identify competencies from each domain that could be utilized when working with this family.

CASE STUDY #6: APPLIED HUMAN DEVELOPMENT

Joan is a single mom who adopted three children, who are 5, 9, and 15 years of age. The CYCP who works with Joan is assisting her in creating an evening routine structure that meets both her needs and the needs of her children. Joan identifies that she needs an hour before bedtime to organize the morning clothing, lunches, and knapsacks, but finds that by 9:00 p.m., she is exhausted.

Discussion Opportunity 8:6

1. If you were the CYCP working with Joan, what suggestions could you share with her?
2. Is there anyway the children could be involved in these preparation tasks?
3. If so, what tasks would be developmentally achievable for a 5-year-old, 9-year-old, and 15-year-old?

CASE STUDY #7: RELATIONSHIP AND COMMUNICATION

Andreas and Joseph are two brothers who attend the same school. Andreas's teacher, Ms. Smitz, contacts child protective services because she is concerned with the children's cleanliness. Andreas shares that they have minimal food at his house. Andreas's lunches consist of one slice of bread. Andreas can complete assignments at school but very rarely completes homework. Andreas has shared that he has chores and needs to take care of his brother Joseph. The child protection agency indicates that the family needs some supports for meeting basic needs, routines, and structure.

Mom has been diagnosed with depression and also has told Ms. Smitz that she feels very anxious about being in large groups, so she cannot attend parent-teacher nights. She shares that she has become more withdrawn since her husband left her with minimal notice. The father occasionally visits the children but does not have a consistent schedule. Many times he has indicated that he will pick up the children and does not show up. Andreas and Joseph feel very sad. Sometimes they will withdraw to their room, and sometimes they will have outbursts of anger. Their mother is caring and shows affection to her children. When she is feeling well, she enjoys taking the children to the park. The mother has a supportive sister who helps her when she can. The aunt loves Andreas and Joseph and enjoys having them spend weekends with her family. Mom would like some support and would like to have more routines and structure in her home. She would like support for the children. She is engaging and is very grateful for any support.

The CYCP attends the home weekly. On most days, mom and the children look forward to the session. Occasionally, the mother is in her bed and struggles with getting ready for their time together. The CYCP has met in the family home for five weeks. The mother and children have demonstrated some changes, such as improving evening routines and making time to complete homework. Their basic needs continue to be a challenge. The mother's depression has improved, although in the last three weeks she has spent most of her time in her room. Andreas seems to be arguing more with Joseph and refuses to do chores. The children have not seen their father in four weeks.

Discussion Opportunity 8:7

1. What competencies could the CYCP utilize to work with mom and the children?
2. Think of the five domains and identify a few that can be helpful from each domain.

CASE STUDY #8: RELATIONSHIP AND COMMUNICATION

Samuel is a CYCP student and is new to the group home team. He finds team meetings stressful as there appears to be underlying conflict between other staff. Samuel will only be at the group home for 12 weeks, so he is not sure how to communicate how he is feeling.

His college colleagues and professor have suggested that he bring his concerns to his placement/practicum supervisor. Instead, he mentions his observations to other staff on shift and provides examples.

When Samuel gets to supervision, his supervisor brings up that staff have expressed concern about his patterns of communication and lack of confidentiality.

Discussion Opportunity 8:8

1. What can Samuel do now to address how he has communicated?
2. What patterns of communication of the culture of the group home?
3. How did the system of the group home support Samuel's behaviour?
4. Are there team building activities that the supervisor could initiate to address the team boundary concerns?

CASE STUDY #9: DEVELOPMENTAL PRACTICE METHODS

Antar works in a residential treatment centre. There are two locations, one that works with latency-aged boys and one that works with adolescent girls. One weekend, his supervisor requests that he cover shifts at the adolescent residence as staff have food poisoning.

Antar is nervous. He has sisters and has always found that they are quick to argue with him. He knows what to do with the boys. He often takes them out to engage in lacrosse or street hockey. He is not sure what to do with the girls. He arrives on shift and is greeted by Jaylene, a 14-year-old with many piercings and a tattoo on her arm. She is taller than Antar.

His shift mate, Nargis, is a female CYCP he has met at an all-agency meeting. The girls are all in the kitchen creating a menu for the coming week. Antar joins them after pouring himself a cup of coffee. He quietly observes the group until the girls make comments about him probably not knowing how to cook. He starts to feel his face get red. He knows how to cook. Nargis wonders if the girls are assuming that because Antar is Sikh, he expects women to make things for him. He offers to cook a vegetarian meal for them the next night when he returns, so he provides them with a list of items that he requires when they go shopping.

Jaylene then makes a comment under her breath about Indian males. Antar had a little bit of hesitancy confronting this as she appears to be an angry teen, and he is used to working with 10-year-olds.

Discussion Opportunity 8:9

1. What developmental practice methods competencies could Antar focus on in this new role?
2. If you were Antar's shift mate, what feedback would you share about his activity planning?
3. What feedback could you share about his ability to confront and share observations with youth on shift?

CASE STUDY #10: DEVELOPMENTAL PRACTICE METHODS

Wolfgang is excited to be hired at the community centre that supports youth who live on the streets.

Some of the youth struggle with food insecurity, emotional/physical/sexual safety, and exposure to street drugs such as fentanyl.

Discussion Opportunity: 8:10

1. If you were Wolfgang, what would you want to research before you go to work for the first time?
2. What questions do you have for your supervisor?
3. What items (relationally and concretely) would you like to have in your toolbox in order to support the youth you meet?

CASE STUDY #11: CREATIVE LEAP SKILLS

Kim is aging out of her group home. She is looking for affordable housing but is struggling to find a place that she can pay for. Landlords do not want to rent to an 18-year-old.

Discussion Opportunity 8:11

What LEAP skills could a CYCP apply that could assist Kim in procuring housing? If you are working in a group, remember to not be judgmental about group member ideas so you can build on all discussed options.

CASE STUDY #12: LEAP SKILLS

You are facilitating a parenting group for parents who have children who struggle with focus, paying attention, planning, and organizing their belongings.

Discussion Opportunity 8:12

What LEAP skills could you teach the parents that they could apply in their interactions with their children? What LEAP skills could the children utilize to assist with focus, planning, and organization?

Chapter 8: Learning Outcomes Evaluation

- Were you able to apply competencies to case study questions?
- Can you identify which competencies are strengths and opportunities for the CYCPs named in the case study?

CHAPTER 9

Supervision: Integrating Competencies

Learning Outcomes

This chapter will help you to meet the following objectives:

- Discuss developmental and discrimination models of CYC practice in supervision.
- Integrate domains of practice with supervision.
- Discuss activities that can be utilized in supervision.
- Apply the domain and competencies to field examples.
- Engage in discussion with colleagues about the domain and competencies.
- Identify personal areas of strength and development.

SUPERVISION

Models of Supervision

Supervision is a learning process, if not the cornerstone of training (Barnett, Erickson Cornish, Goodyear, & Lichtenberg, 2007) for most helping professionals, including CYCPs, psychologists, psychotherapists, social workers, and counsellors. The supervision process often takes a **developmental model approach**, assessing the current stage of practice of the supervisee (Drewes, 2008; Phelan, 2017). In child and youth care, many supervisors also utilize a **discrimination model** (Bernard, 1979, 1997) where the supervisor observes the student when they intervene, discusses how the student conceptualizes what they observe happening around them, and identifies how they can adapt their way of being to the meet the needs of the child/youth/family or community while understanding how all of this impacts them. The supervisor then provides the student or new practitioner with information based on the supervisee needs. They may need wisdom about paperwork completion, how to intervene with an angry child, or how to debrief with teammates after a particularly challenging shift. Supervisors will often utilize the model that matches their approach working as a CYCP (Garfat, 2001).

Discussion Opportunity 9:1

What kind of questions can you ask your new supervisor at placement/practicum or volunteer experiences?

CYCPs of all developmental phases can approach the supervisory experience with curiosity, recognizing that this relational opportunity is an investment in not only their healthy professional development but also the quality of care those that they work alongside receive (Fraser & Ventrella, 2016). Supervisors will often ask new supervisees what their previous experience has been in supervision in order to create a conversation about needs, agreements, and opportunities. Incorporating competencies within discussions between supervisee and supervisor can create a road map for the supervisory process (Fraser, 2019).

The Role and Skill Set of a Supervisor

Understanding the role of a supervisor can assist a developing CYCP in understanding what they can request and depend on in the supervisory relationship, knowing that the needs of the population they work with are addressed first (Poole, 2010). Effective supervisors have many skills and qualities, including flexibility, knowledge, experience, and the ability to be supportive/empathetic, as well as organizational skills (Kilminster & Jolly, 2001).

The first skill a supervisor demonstrates is building a safe relationship. To be able to support the development of a relationship, it is important to recognize that there is an inherent power imbalance between supervisor and supervisee, so this needs to be addressed transparently. The CYC supervisor will need to discuss the many hats he/she/ze/they wear within the supervisory relationship, including that of teacher (Fox, 2017; Maier, 1985).

Discussion Opportunity 9:2

Do you prefer weekly, semi-weekly, or in-the-moment supervision?

In addition to being **mentor** and training planner, the supervisor may be an administrator, program supervisor, evaluator, and also a supervisee in their own supervisory relationship.

Establishing Relationship Rules/Agreements

Establishing relationship rules and agreements meet the needs of both supervisor and supervisee. These need to include what each person in the dyad is hoping for in the allotted supervisory time. The frequency and scheduling of supervision is also established. Additionally, other support persons are often identified so the supervisee has back-up leaders they can approach for support/direction in the absence of a formal supervisor's presence. Examples of supervisor needs may be that the supervisee is on time and comes prepared for supervision, with an agenda of topic discussions and specific questions they need consultation on (see supervision chart).

Discussion Opportunity 9:3

What types of needs do you and your group members have about supervision? For example, how often you will meet, what type of topics are on the agenda, and so on? Imagine creating a supervisory contract. What might you want to see reflected in this contract?

Agreements can include the concept of supervisory confidentiality. A contract might also say supervision will occur weekly (or biweekly) except in cases of illness or emergency. Supervisees and supervisors who do not share the same profession can discuss and agree on what ethical code they adhere to. This is especially important if a CYCP is being supervised by another discipline professional and a situation of conflict occurs in ethical decision making. Supervisor and supervisee also can identify a dispute agreement. What happens if the supervisor recommends something? Is the supervisee bound to follow this recommendation as a directive, or is the recommendation more like a consultation? What are next steps if there is still disagreement about case direction?

Goal Setting

Part of supervision can also involve the supervisees identifying short-term and long-term goals (SMART goals where possible) so the supervisor can provide supplementary learning opportunities or resources. Errors made, misconceptions, or queries are also opportunities for learning. We have all made mistakes "on the floor" in our practice, and it is important to debrief or deconstruct these so they can be avoided in the future. We may be lucky enough to have colleagues and "shift" partners to debrief interactions with, but it is also valuable to process these scenarios with our formal supervisors, especially if competency themes arise.

Our field prides itself on being primarily relational. The relationships that we share with our supervisors are remembered and motivate us to be our best CYCP selves. Additionally, our early supervisor's words are often repeated when we move into a supervisory role ourselves.

Reciprocal Supervision

The supervisory relationship is relational and therefore reciprocal. The supervisee learns from the discussion, identified challenges, and consultation in order to build strengths in the various CYC domains of practice. The supervisor also gains knowledge, experience, challenge, and opportunity from this relationship. This reciprocal relationship therefore promotes the development of both individuals personally and professionally. Therefore, the supervisor also needs to be cognizant of not only their relationship with the supervisee but also the impact that the supervisee has on their own development (Delano & Shah, 2015; Hawkins, Shohet, Ryde, & Wilmot, 2012).

The CYCCB domains are an integral part of the supervisory relationship and experience. We define **supervision** as the relationship of a person assigned the role of supervisor, mentor, team, or individual for the purpose of supporting your development as a CYCP. Remember that some of our best teachers and supervisors, who can support a CYCP's development, are the children, youth, and families with whom we engage; therefore, carrying what they teach us into the supervision process and advocacy is good use of our experiences in the field. Supervision relationships must remain respectful of each other's development stage, culture, and diversity.

The intention of any relationship in CYC practice is to build on each other's strengths, empower successful functioning in life, and explore further relational practices that meet the needs of children, youth, families, and communities. It is important that supervision relationships provide a safe place that allows exploration without judgment and promotes reflection and creativity while building the capacities of everyone involved. In this process, the CYCP takes active part in individual and team development. We often say that CYCPs plant the seeds in those with whom we work, and because our work is relational, they also plant seeds within us. *Supervision is reciprocal.* The student teaches the teacher, and the teacher teaches the student.

Let's explore how the supervisor and the CYCP can utilize the competencies in the CYCB domains of professionalism, cultural and human diversity, applied human development, relationship and communication, and development practices methods. It is here we will discover strengths and opportunities.

Professionalism

Supervisors and those being supervised need to have a safe, honest, open, and secure relationship in which the participants are willing to take risks and have open dialogue. The frequency of scheduling supervision and informal check-ins affect the opportunity of relationship building: they must be regular and dependable. Important to creating a sense of safety is having discussions about confidentiality, boundaries, and what each person values about the relationship if it is to be supportive and encouraging. It is also important to determine in this supervision contracting phase what happens if there is a disagreement between supervisor and supervisee. Are the supervisor's directives binding or more consultative?

As already stated, supervision includes developing short- and long-term goals and implementing resources to build on the CYCP's strengths. The supervisee needs to be self-directed to encourage taking personal initiative. A supervisor can promote the CYCP to follow their personal interests, passions, creative impulses, and continuous learning, all of which will contribute to their own and the field's development. A supervisor can promote not only the independent work of a CYCP but also their functioning as part of a team. The relationship needs to encourage dialogue about the code of ethics and law and regulations, and support the development of the profession and practice within them. Dialogue can explore common trends and challenges children, youth, families, and the professional are currently engaging. Supervision needs to encourage participation in professional associations, regulating bodies, conferences, and other training. Strategies need to be in place to keep current with the literature and research on evidence-based practices. Because CYCPs spend a lot of energy attending to the needs of others, it is important that supervision includes discussion of self-care and well-being, and the strategies needed to maintain professional and personal life balance. Professional development and behaviours need to be addressed. Supervision is a relationship that promotes the importance of self-awareness and creates a safe place for CYCPs to explore their own values, beliefs, and attitudes that direct how they relate to children, youth, and families. Supervision is effective if it allows the CYCP to evaluate their own performance and receive feedback that will encourage further development and empowerment.

The role and organization duties of the CYCP and their boundaries need to be clearly outlined. Other areas that need to be clarified and benefit from regular feedback are: workplace expectations, attendance, recording, reporting, and workload balance. It is the supervisor's responsibility to provide the CYCP with policy manuals, laws, and regulations that are relevant to their community; recording formats; legal report of abuse or neglect; and, if there is crisis, consent forms, confidentiality, and functional clothing. A supervisor brings their experience of how to communicate with other organizational systems, how to arrange transportation, how to maintain safety for everyone, how to budget, and how to form a team and engage in systemic communication.

Self-awareness is a fundamental component of CYC practice that promotes personal development and self-care. Together, the supervisor and supervisee will learn to recognize their strengths, areas of development, and personal needs. Discussion is useful for supporting and encouraging the development of skills and knowledge, and identifying those resources that promote development. Self-care needs to be a continuous concept in reflection because best practice means integrating wellness practices in the CYCP's personal as well as professional life. The supervisor needs to ensure that stress management and support networks are part of the team and organization. Without support, stress will challenge a CYCP's capacity to continue effectively and mindfully with others.

Discussion Opportunity 9:4

A CYCP struggling to balance the needs of her aging parents plus the responsibility of shift work at the residential treatment centre is an example of someone who needs their supervisor to accommodate and support them in feeling safe and confident in their program.

Consider what support you might need from your supervisor if you feel it is difficult to be present at work and you are experiencing a high level of stress. What support would be needed by a colleague who just came back from maternity leave and has only been sleeping four hours the last three nights?

A fundamental responsibility of the CYCP is advocating for children, youth, and families. Supervision needs to highlight the importance of advocating on their behalf with other disciplines, systems, policies, and government, which includes awareness of the Convention on the Rights of the Child, and continuing discussions about policies and actions that educate, advocate, and promote the well-being of all children, youth, and families.

Discussion Opportunity 9:5

You are a CYCP working with a family where both parents experience depression that interferes with their ability to function. They have two daughters, aged 12 and 14, who are making meals and doing housework themselves in addition to completing their homework. The last time you visited, the girls told you that their parents have been asleep for days. The school calls you because the girls have lice again, for the sixth time this year. The teacher has noticed that their current life experiences are affecting their social development. You have notified a child protection agency, but you were told it is not a protection issue. How might you engage your supervisor in exploring ways to advocate for the development and well-being of these children?

Culture and Human Diversity

Celebrating our strengths and acknowledging areas of development and, in some cases, recognizing our limitations regarding cultural and human diversity are prerequisites to reducing risk to, or oppression of, vulnerable populations. The supervisor may need to assist the supervisee in identifying cultural awareness (Drewes, 2008). Culture and human diversity exists within all relationships. Embracing different cultures and subcultures in all their diversity enriches a relationship and society. Identity, age, class, race, ethnicity, level of ability, language, spiritual/faith belief systems, educational achievement, gender identity, and gender differences are all areas that need to be considered in the relationship between individuals, supervisors, and teams.

Supervision is a good place to explore biases, beliefs, and cultural and other values that can influence your effectiveness when relating to children, youth, families, and communities.

Discussion Opportunity 9:6

You are a CYCP meeting with an Italian family on a weekly basis, and you notice a power imbalance in the marriage. You suspect the wife and children are being abused. You believe the wife could divorce her husband because he is abusive, but she says she does not want to. In what way might you explore her belief system with your supervisor or team?

Discussion Opportunity 9:7

A new CYCP grad is very excited about being hired for her first a full-time position at a residential centre. On the third day, an eight-year-old child screams, "I hate you, you are fat and ugly!" The CYCP feels hurt and notices that she is reactive toward the child. The supervisor observed the interaction and, at the end of the shift, checks in with the CYCP. Initially, the CYCP shares that she is fine and is not upset about the interaction, but after a few minutes admits she felt the child had been rude and is not respectful to adults. The supervisor validates the CYCP.

How might the supervisor begin a conversation that will explore the supervisee's beliefs, bias, and culture and how these impact her effectiveness?

Discussion Opportunity 9:8

Mitis is a CYCP who, in supervision, talked about meeting a family that does not speak English fluently. Mitis asks his supervisor how he might overcome the language barrier and still value the family's culture.

Think back to supervisors or teammates who have either supported your development or hindered you. What cultural values and beliefs do you possess that need a supervisor's support and understanding in specific ways to make you feel validated and encouraged?

Supervision allows a relationship to recognize and prevent stereotyping. Using cultural resources and embracing the ways they are a support system to children, youth, families, and community is best practice for a CYCP. The conversation in supervision needs to continuously address issues regarding respect, honour, and the consideration of cultural and human diversity so that what culture brings to enrich our relationships, families, and community is celebrated.

Child and Youth Development

It is the mandate of CYCPs to promote optimal development of children, youth, and their families. Family life span needs to be considered when relating to others. Supervision needs to include how to support the development of relationships, skills, knowledge, self-awareness, and strengths. During supervision, a developmental-ecological perspective needs to be applied when discussing, consulting, or evaluating the relationship between the CYCP and children, youth, and families. Exceptionality in development, such as trauma, abuse, neglect, and developmental disorder, needs to be taken into consideration during supervision.

The developmental needs of the child, youth, or family need to guide how we relate to the person verbally and nonverbally. The better we understand a person's developmental stage or needs, the more effective and supportive will be the goals and interventions designed for them. This understanding assists a CYCP in engaging and building together these goals and interventions. The foregoing factors also apply during supervision, which emphasizes relationship building within the profession. Only if the CYCP and the supervisor consider development will the CYCP be able to recognize the current abilities of a child, youth, or family, and implement appropriate supports.

Discussion Opportunity 9:9

John is a CYCP employed at a day-treatment program. Joey, a student there, is creative, brings his humour to the class, and is willing to help the teacher and John. Though he is 13, Joey's reading level is Grade 4. John notices that when the teacher assigns comprehension lessons, Joey becomes very agitated, or he puts his head down on his desk and reports that he is not feeling well. The teacher wants Joey to improve his reading, so she has been challenging him with Grade 6 academics. John and his supervisor discuss with the teacher how they might support Joey at his development stage of reading abilities. The multidisciplinary team is able to discuss Joey's strengths and incorporate creative lessons, such as drama, bulletin boards, and singing, as effective ways to help him succeed. This occurred after they considered his developmental stage and needs.

Have one group member share a challenging example about a youth they have worked with currently or in the past. All group members are reminded not to share identifying information such as location/age, names, and so on. Ask other group members for insight about how to support the developmental needs of the child/youth presented for discussion.

When the team at a children's residential centre is organizing camps, they need to discuss the level of abilities of each participant in order to design programs that accommodate everyone's needs. Factors that are considered include socialization, cognition, and family development. Families are discussed from an ecological perspective that considers all the systems impacting the family.

Discussion Opportunity 9:10

Emanuel is a CYCP working with a mother who has just given birth and is also caring for her 18-month-old baby. He discussed her struggles with his supervisor, asking her about this family's developmental life span, applicable ecological factors, and their impact. He wants to know what community resources can support the development of each person in the family and the family as a whole. Together with his supervisor, he explores how he can relate to a family and each of its members depending on their development.

Reflect on how Emanuel might greet a 4-year-old within a family versus a 17-year-old. Also, how can he engage with a 4-year-old that he knows is on the autism spectrum and is nonverbal, as compared to a 14-year-old diagnosed with anxiety and attention deficit disorder, even though both showed behaviours of rocking, outbursts of yelling, and roaming during session?

Relationship and Communication

Relationship and communication competencies are integral to CYC practice with children, youth, and families, and colleagues and even supervisors. Effective communication is essential to building a safe relationship. Dialogue needs to be respectful, non-judgmental, and a safe place to have uncomfortable and challenging exchanges. A conversation on a power imbalance between a supervisor and supervisee needs to be addressed transparently, as does the most effective way to address triggers, and how to connect with difficult youth about celebrating their accomplishments; these are all good examples of communication challenges. Exploring cultural differences in communication styles between a supervisor and CYCP requires embracing the diversity with understanding. Styles of communication also need to be explored on teams, identifying communication patterns between team members and the supervisor. Reflection on the strengths and avoidance behaviour in communication will help overcome many roadblocks to effective, constructive, creative, and positive relating.

The supervision relationship is an ongoing developmental process that must include self-reflection as well as reflection on the relationship between supervisor and supervisee. Considering what you *bring* to a relationship with your supervisor, at the beginning, at regular intervals over the course of a year, and perhaps beyond, is as crucial to success as considering what you *need* from a supervisor during the same interval.

Discussion Opportunity 9:11

Joseph has been a CYCP for three years, and he just started a new job at a justice centre, where a probation officer is his supervisor. Joseph shares with him that he has witnessed many staff reacting and punishing youth who are only expressing their needs. Joseph is struggling with staying true to his CYC principles and code of ethics while developing relationships with colleagues. Along with their strengths, having a supervisor from a different discipline may pose some barriers and impact the development of a CYCP.

Role play how Joseph can share his concerns with his supervisor.

Supervision includes working with multidisciplinary teams and other systems that can impact children, youth, families, and communities. Supervisors need to model, teach, practise, and support how and when to work with different disciplines, even as they continue to advocate for CYC practices and principles. Some examples of issues to address include: confidentiality, consent for release of information, record keeping, how to meet the needs of families with programs that have different mandates, maintaining boundaries, and dealing with limits in delivery of specific services.

Discussion Opportunity 9:12

Clarissa works at a residential assessment home. The children are about to attend a community winter festival and are very excited about going on dog sled rides, seeing ice sculptures, skating, and tobogganing. The children have followed the program, worked hard at completing their chores, and are packing lunches for everyone when a child protection worker calls asking to meet Simon, one of the children. When Clarissa tries rescheduling, the worker insists it is the only time available for her, and Clarissa decides to delay the winter fest for an hour. One boy becomes so upset, he runs off to his room, swearing at staff, and another starts to yell at Simon, blaming him for the delay. At their next meeting, Clarissa asks her supervisor how to balance and support the needs of two different systems and also addresses her own needs in an incident as difficult as this one.

If you were the supervisor, what ideas might you have to share with Clarissa?

Supervision needs to include supporting CYC professional development, continuous learning, following the code of ethics, certification, and encouraging concepts and principles of CYCP practices. Recall the case of Emanuel, a CYCP who works in a family program and wants to develop better family relational skills. Consider how the supervisor can provide him with opportunities to develop further skills.

Developmental Practice Methods

Supervisors and CYCPs are constantly considering the development of children, youth, and families throughout the life span. Supervision needs to build safe relationships wherein to explore evidence-based practice methods that empower, encourage, support, and build positive relationships so that the children, youth, families, and communities can live their full potential. The supervisor and CYCP relationship needs to have open discussion on methods being used and their effectiveness in building stronger relationships. Supervisors need to regularly review and together recognize strengths or areas that may need further development. Supervisors need to continuously have discussions about relationships, health and safety, intervention planning, environmental design and its maintenance, program and activity planning, activities for children, youth, and families, life space, group work, behavioural guidance, counselling, and family and community engagement.

Regarding health and safety, it is important to consider general policy, procedures, documentation, and reporting policies in order to ensure children, youth, families, the community, and CYCPs are safe and at minimal risk, *if any*. Supervisors need to ensure medication training and documentation thereof are clear and followed, including clarification of policy on transporting and storing medication.

Discussion Opportunity 9:13

You are a CYCP taking children to camp, and you have several bottles of medication that need to be stored in a cool place locked away from the children. Brainstorm creative ideas of how to store medication and travel with the medication to the camp.

Discussion Opportunity 9:14

You are working with Leah, who is living on the streets. On some days, she sleeps in an abandoned building with other youth. What information might you provide Leah to reduce her risk of infectious disease?

The above sample situations highlight the need for consistent discussion with supervisors on prevention and intervention planning in order to stay current with the conditions surrounding children, youth, and families, and their assessments of them, based on understanding their needs and strengths, their goals and passions. Supervision also needs to encourage CYCPs to make best use of their own strengths and talents, and to take initiatives in program and intervention planning. What unique strengths and talents of yours are assets when engaging children, youth, and families? How do your strengths build relational intervention and practices?

A CYCP who enjoys camping outdoors or playing an instrument might consider using one of these activities as part of an intervention. Supervision needs to recognize the great value of using a multidisciplinary approach in which each person brings their own perspectives and expertise. Inclusion and consideration of others, including children, youth, families, and communities, is essential to interventions, goals, missions, and plan and process review. Supervisors need to ask questions in a way that supports inclusion and promotes the voices of the children, youth, and families. If you are working with a family that just emigrated from Syria, how can you draw out and engage their strengths, passions, culture, and voice to ensure they are part of the intervention planning?

Environmental design and maintenance are important considerations throughout supervision. Designs need to be inclusive and support diversity. Children, youth, and families need to have accessibility. Programs and activities that promote the family life space and integrate resources are essential. Supervision needs to include designing and maintaining programs that allow CYCPs to share the life space of children, youth, and families—in other words, to walk alongside them in real time.

Discussion Opportunity 9:15

Try brainstorming creative programs that can encourage inclusiveness.

For example, with a budget of $100, what creative program could you develop at a high school that promotes prosocial behaviours?

Discussion Opportunity 9:16

During supervision, a CYCP discusses some youth in his care that are siblings. One of the siblings is demanding a lot of their parents' attention. The parents say both children are doing well at school, with no negative behaviours. When he reaches out to the sibling who does not need immediate attention, she hides away in her room to spare her parents the stress. The other spends very little time at home in order to cope, saying she is tired of the fighting and has thought about running away.

Do you think the CYCP believes the siblings have needs that are not being met? If you could design a program for this family, what kind of program would it be?

An agency identifies a camp program for the sibling that had not been identified as needing services and who really needed a break. The response is overwhelming from everyone attending. Some children share that it is the first time they feel they are noticed and how difficult it is to live with family members who are coping with mental health issues. Some share that they self-harm quietly in their rooms to cope. Some of the children say camp was "too much fun!" Program design needs to consider all parts of a family and community. Program planning and activities need to promote development and build skills, knowledge, and awareness of self. Supervisors and CYCPs need to include program designs that consider activities in daily living as part of supervision.

A skilled supervisor promotes and demonstrates team effectiveness and development. CYCPs very rarely work in isolation. Working as part of a team and group is a very important part of supporting children, youth, and families. Supervision needs to promote and support group programming, facilitate groups that meet participants' needs, develop skills, and increase knowledge and self-awareness. Consider what needs of children can be met more effectively in a group setting. During your next supervision, you might write a proposal for a social skills group for high school students. What support do you need from your supervisor? What strengths do you have as a group facilitator, and what areas do you believe you will need to develop? How can your supervisor support your development?

Relationship development is the fundamental foundation to working with children, youth, families, and communities. Supervision must include discussions about the CYCP's beliefs, thoughts, feelings, and reactions to each child, youth, and family they are supporting. Supervision needs to be a safe place wherein the CYCP can explore self-awareness. When this is possible, the relationship between the supervisor and CYCP is better able to develop meaning from such awareness and realize its value to the relational process. Supervisors need to ensure that CYCPs have effective problem-solving skills to promote resolution and, very importantly, to demonstrate these skills with CYCP and teams. The supervision process needs to assess, guide, support, and teach the skills and knowledge of behaviour guidance. What support do you need from your supervisor to disengage from a power struggle? How can a supervisor support a CYCP during a crisis? What do you need from your supervisor or team during a crisis? How will reflecting and debriefing support a CYCP and team?

Supervisors are responsible for not only the CYCP and the team but also the families and communities they serve. They need to consider the holistic needs of all so inclusion is practised.

Discussion Opportunity 9:17

An agency works with a family that does not have transportation. The team struggles with balancing confidentiality and helping the parents reach out to the community to find resources that can help them. Initially, the parents cancel several appointments. A phone call made on their behalf finally provides them with some community resources they can utilize. The mother finds someone from a church who is happy to drive them every week in exchange for her grass getting cut. From this, a friendship develops, and the family receives the support they want and desperately need.

Are you aware of community supports available to families in your community? How would you go about finding ones for the family seeking transportation?

Supervision needs to explore many systems that can support the family. The more community supports the family has, the quicker a celebration of CYC service termination can happen. Supervisors need to support CYCPs in building relationships with families.

That may translate to working flexible hours or being out in the community or visiting at a church or donut shop or library. Programs and supervisors need to encourage CYCPs to engage with families and the community.

As already stated, supervision is a reciprocal relational process. Supervisors and CY-CPs are responsible for assessing the developmental stages of the CYCP and providing support, skill, knowledge, and self-awareness so that the CYCP can continue their professional development. A past supervisor of mine, Paul Vella, used to say that if we take care of the CYCP, then they can do their best work with children, youth, and families, and it helps to have a supportive, empowering, encouraging supervisor in your corner. CYC supervisors are an essential part of CYCP development, and having the common language in relational practices provides a safe place to grow as an individual, as a team, as an agency, and as a profession. Supervision is a fundamental responsibility for supporting CYCPs, so that they in turn can transfer their learning and relational skills to children, youth, and families.

The use of activities in supervision can provide opportunities for both supervisor and supervisee to engage and experience openness to transformational learning.

> With transformational openness we begin new ways of thinking and talking and making space for wider concerns. Now other voices join the supervisory pair (or group) in the supervisory room—the quiet, unspoken voices, the powerless voices, the underprivileged voices, the abused voices, the hurt voices. (Carroll, 2011, p. 26)

Please review the following activity ideas in a small group, and discuss which ones you think you might like to engage in with your class or team members as practice for a future supervisory experience.

Supervisor Genogram

Genograms (McGoldrick & Gerson, 1985) help to understand the familial connections we share.

Creating a supervisor **genogram** can be a wonderful opportunity for the supervisor to share the historical wisdom he/she/ze/they received from his/her/hir/their own supervisors when he/she/ze/they were growing or new in the field. In this activity, the supervisor acknowledges all previous supervisors and what their areas of expertise were and are (Aten, Madson, & Kruse, 2008). This information is then shared with the supervisee, including the expertise/CYC passion that the current supervisor wishes to share.

The Tree of Life

The Tree of Life is a narrative activity attributed to Michael White's Dulwich Centre Foundation (https://dulwichcentre.com.au/the-tree-of-life/). It has been utilized worldwide with communities, families, and individuals (Denborough, 2008). We have adapted it here as a supervisory activity. CYCPs first draw a tree. In the roots, they identify from whom they inherited their relational skills, values, beliefs, and skills. These are the things that are gifted to them. The trunk of the tree represents the skills and strengths that the individual brings to the "work." Examples could be athletics, musical ability, self-regulation, a sense of humour, and so on. The branches then represent helpers to the practitioner. Who assists them in being the best that they can be? Who helps them, supports them, challenges them, and so on? The leaves identify future dreams and goals. This activity is a great starting point when establishing the supervisory relationship.

Ecomaps

Team ecomaps (Hartman, 1995) can be valuable for individuals, as well as entire teams. If all team members are listed at the centre of the ecomap (as can be done in a familial ecomap), then support systems and strategies utilized by individual team members can be acknowledged. After this is completed, themes in a variety and cadence of supports can be identified. It is also a great way to illustrate the many systems that team members are engaged in. After completing this activity, the whole team, as well as individual team members, are often able to recognize gaps in self-care and then utilize this awareness to create SMART goals.

Drawings of Safety

In many trauma interventions, such as **structured interventions** for children, adolescents, and parents (SITCAP; Steele & Kuban, 2013; Steele & Raider, 2001) or **rapid eye movement** desensitization (Shapiro, 2001), protocols include a starting place that helps the individual determine how he/she/ze/they define and how he/she/ze/they create **safety** in his/her/hir/their life spaces. Having a supervisee consider what he/she/ze/they need to feel safe can be very powerful. Supervisors, however, need to be aware that it can also be very difficult if the supervisee lacks past safe experiences (Fraser & Ventrella, 2016).

Directions could begin with "Let's use the pencil to create a drawing of your safe place or the safest place that you can imagine." Questions that can be posed include:

- What do you want to have in a "safe" space?
- Can anyone else be there for you, and if so, who?
- Are there self-care tools that you want to have in your safe space?

It may be too early in the supervisory relationship for the supervisee to share their drawing with their supervisor; however, the supervisor may invite the supervisee to really get to know this place and visualize this space. It might also be helpful for the supervisee to imagine themselves in this space, so he/she/ze/they have time to breathe and feel in control and self-regulated prior to entering stressful situations or engaging in stressful/challenging conversations. Supervisor and supervisee also need to consider that some individuals may not be in a developmental/emotional place where they can define/identify or create safety. This then becomes a very important supervision question.

Breathing Exercises

Breathing deeply and slowly is known to help us slow our heart rate and breathing. It helps us to ground ourselves in the here and now and even slow the stress hormones running through our brains (Drewes, 2008). Supervisors may need to teach and practise breathing with supervisees so they can practise this skill with the children/youth and families that they work with. Breathing can be reviewed using a real stethoscope. This can help not only supervisees but also children/youth and families connect breathing to heart rate. Making this connection can help someone with anxiety use breathing techniques when they feel their heart is pounding, so they can feel calmer and more in control. If someone gets angry, they can recognize this and take a moment to calm themselves before continuing in a stressful conversation, instead of having an outburst.

Journaling

Journaling daily or weekly reflections can be a useful tool for both supervisor and supervisee. Specific questions can be posed to track themes that show up day-by-day or week-by-week. Instead of using words, supervisees can also be asked to draw their weekly experience. If the supervisee finds it difficult to start writing or drawing, he/she/ze/they can pick a movie title or song title that describes his/her/hir/their best learning for the week (Fraser & Ventrella, 2016).

Expressive Arts Activities

Where words fall short, expressive arts activities can help to communicate feelings and ideas during individual or group supervision (Bratton, Ceballos, & Sheely, 2008). Here are a few examples of expressive arts activities that can be incorporated in supervision:

- Collages created on card-size cardboard or mural paper. Both can serve to archive the experiences of the developing CYCP. Directions can be provided, such as "Let's collage how we feel about beginning to say goodbye (separation) to the children." A more general prompt might be "Let's collage how we feel in this moment."
- Create sculptures using model magic or modelling clay (Fraser & Ventrella, 2018).
- Use miniature toys to role play shared interactions (Morrison & Homeyer, 2008).

In each of these activities, the supervisee can be invited to look at his/her/hir/their current experiences and also envision the experiences that he/she/ze/they hope will come. Taking photos of his/her/hir/their product can serve to archive the experiences for current and future supervision sessions.

Team Gratitude

Safety must be built in the team. Asking the team to stand beside someone who supports their development and sharing appreciation of that person's effort is a positive exercise that can be repeated with different individuals so that all contributions are acknowledged. The physicality of this acknowledgment can also be documented in a photo and gifted to both supervisor and supervisee.

Team Sculpting

Family sculpting (Duhl, Kantor, & Duhl, 1973) is another activity that can be utilized in group/peer supervision. Team members (in pairs) are asked to sculpt how they see the connections on the team, without judgment. After a few minutes, another pair can repeat the exercise in a different way. The discussion that follows will explore the participants' observations. Before this exercise, clear safety rules must be established.

Team Recognition

Every week, a team member may be assigned the responsibility of highlighting another team member's accomplishments and to meet with that member to discuss these.

Share Leadership

A team could engage in a discussion about sharing leadership during team meetings. Some topics to address might be how to facilitate the team, to share agenda items, or to bring food. It is a way of identifying what works for the team as well as to honour the many roles that team members take on that contribute to overall team functioning.

Changing the Supervision Space

Traditionally, supervision happens at an office or workplace. A discussion among team members might include how the experience could be made more creative, such as exploring alternate locations, different ways of communicating, creative ways of facilitating, and so on. Brainstorming may yield ideas like writing a poem or song that describes team attributes or creating a team flag.

Discussion Opportunity 9:18

After reviewing the activities above, which ones might you want to try in supervision? Which ones do you feel might be challenging? Do you have other activity ideas?

Below is an example of a tool that can be utilized for supervision preparation. The supervisee can fill out this chart in advance of supervision: *Identifying content, themes, process, relational practice/competencies, strengths/resiliencies, vulnerabilities, child's view of the world,*

Table 7: Supervision Preparation

	Questions to Ask	Answers	Additional Resources
Content of Interaction/ Event to Discuss	What has been the content of interactions with children/youth/families/community?		
	What has been the content of interactions with peers/colleagues/community members?		
Themes	Are there themes that are showing up in your interactions with children/youth/families/communities since your last supervision or over a longer period of time?		
Theoretical Orientation/ Process	What theory or theories underpin your work?		
Relational Practices/ Competencies	Are there examples of the 25 characteristics of CYC (Garfat & Fulcher, 2012) that you can identify or need to work on?		
	What CYC competencies (skills) are you utilizing? What competencies do you need to be utilizing? How can you do this? Who can help you?		
Strengths, Resiliencies, and Vulnerabilities	What are the strengths and challenges of the children/youth/families/communities that you are working with?		For vulnerabilities, think of Maslow's hierarchy of needs, or adverse childhood reactions (Dube, Felitti, Dong, Chapman, Giles, & Anda, 2003). For strengths, think of developmental assets.
Child/Teen/ Family's View of the World	What relational practices are you using with the children/youth/family/community?		
Goals and Hypothesis	What goals do you have for yourself?		
	What goals have the children/youth/families/communities self-identified? How can these be communicated as SMART goals?		
Questions for Supervisor			Supervisor reflections on own practice

Source: Adapted from Gardner & Yasenik, 2012.

goals (areas for development), and specific questions for supervision. The supervisor can review this chart and then ascertain which activities might best illuminate greater understanding of the CYCCB competencies.

During supervision, supervisor and supervisee reflect on the impact of the example brought to the conversations (reciprocal supervision).

Chapter 9 Learning Outcomes Evaluation

- Can you explain what a developmental or discrimination model of CYC supervision would look like?
- Are you able to integrate the CYCCB domains of practice in supervision? Which ones are easiest to integrate? The most difficult?
- Can you identify and discuss activities that can be utilized in supervision in addition to talking about your CYC practice?
- Can you apply the domain and competencies to field examples?
- Can you identify personal areas of strength and development?

REFERENCES

Aten, J. D., Madson, M. B., & Kruse, S. J. (2008). The supervision genogram: A tool for preparing supervisors-in-training. *Psychotherapy: Theory, Research, Practice, Training, 45*(1), 111–116. doi:10.1037/0033-3204.45.1.111

Bernard, J. M. (1979). Supervisor training: A discrimination model. *Counselor Education and Supervision, 19*(1), 60–68. doi:10.1002/j.1556-6978.1979.tb00906.x

Bernard, J. M. (1997). The discrimination model. In C. E. Watkins, Jr. (Ed.), *Handbook of psychotherapy supervision* (pp. 310–327). New York, NY: Wiley.

Barnett, J. E., Erickson Cornish, J. A., Goodyear, R. K., & Lichtenberg, J. W. (2007). Commentaries on the ethical and effective practice of clinical supervision. *Professional Psychology: Research and Practice, 38*(3), 268–275. doi:10.1037/0735-7028.38.3.268

Bratton, S., Ceballos, P., & Sheely. A. (2008). Expressive arts in a humanistic approach to play therapy supervisions: Facilitating therapist self-awareness. In A. A. Drewes & J. A. Mullen (Eds.), *Supervision can be playful: Techniques for child and play therapist supervisors* (pp. 211–232). Lanham, MD: Jason Aronson.

Carroll, M. (2011). Supervision: A journey of lifelong learning. In R. Shohet (Ed.), *Supervision as Transformation: A passion for learning* (pp. 14–28). London, UK: Jessica Kingsley Publishers.

Charles, G., & Garfat, T. (2016). Supervision: A matter of mattering. In G. Charles, J. Freeman, & T. Garfat (Eds.), *Supervision in child and youth care practice* (pp. 22–27). Cape Town, South Africa: CYC-Net Press.

Delano, F., & Shah, J. (2015). Making the transition to being a supervisor: Foreseeing, understanding and navigating the road to supervisory excellence. *Relational Child & Youth Care Practice, 28*(1), 76–90.

Denborough, D. (2008). *Collective narrative practice: Responding to individuals, groups, and communities who have experienced trauma.* Adelaide, SA: Dulwich Centre Publications.

Denholm, C. J. (1990). Canadian child and youth care 1979–1989. *Youth Studies, 9*(2), 51–57.

Dong, M., Andra, R. F., Dube, S. R., Giles, W. H., Felitti, V. J. (2003). The relationship of exposure to childhood sexual abuse to other forms of abuse, neglect, and household dysfunction during childhood. *Childhood Abuse & Neglect,* 27(6), 625–639.

Drewes, A. (2008). In A. Drewes & J. A. Mullen (Eds.), *Supervision can be playful: Techniques for child and play therapist supervisors.* Lanham, MD: Jason Aronson.

Duhl, F. S., Kantor, D., & Duhl, B. S. (1973). Learning space and action in family therapy: A primer of sculpting. In D. Bloch (Ed.), *Techniques of family psychotherapy: A primer.* New York, NY: Grune & Stratton.

Fox, L. E. (2017). Unusual challenges in supervising child and youth care professionals. *CYC-Online: E-journal of the International Child and Youth Care Network (CYC-Net),* (223), 5–19. Retrieved January 1, 2018, from http://www.cyc-net.org/cyc-online/sep2017.pdf

Fraser, T. (2019). The accessibility of quality supervision: Competency based mentoring using technology. In J. Stone (Ed.), *Integrating technology into modern therapies: A clinician's guide to developments and interventions.* New York, NY: Routledge.

Fraser, T., & Ventrella, M. (2016, April). *Supervision workshop for practicum supervisors.* Sheridan College Continuing Education Workshop for Child and Youth Care Supervisors, Brampton, ON, Canada.

Fraser, T., & Ventrella, M. (2018, January). *Psychosocial training: Mental health response to critical events.* Five-day training for Whitehorse Community, Whitehorse, YT, Canada.

Gardner, K., & Yasenik, L. (2012, April). *Enhancing supervisee's awareness of use of self: Therapist immersion.* Calgary, AB: Canadian Association for Child and Play Therapy.

Garfat, T. (2001). Editorial: Congruence between supervision and practice. *Journal of Child and Youth Care, 15*(2), iii–iv.

Garfat, T. & Fulcher, L. C. (2012). Characteristics of a child and youth care approach. In L. C. Fulcher & T. Garfat (Eds.), *Child and youth care in practice* (pp. 5–24). Cape Town, South Africa: CYC Press.

Garfat, T., Fulcher, L., & Freeman, J. (2016). A daily life events approach to child and youth care supervision. In G. Charles, J. Freeman, & T. Garfat (Eds.), *Supervision in child and youth care practice* (pp. 28–47). Cape Town, South Africa: CYC-Net Press.

Gharabaghi, K., Trocme, N., & Newman, D. (2016). *Because young people matter: Report of the residential services review panel.* Toronto, ON: Government of Ontario.

Hartman, A. (1995). Diagrammatic assessment of family relationships. *Families in Society, 76*(2), 111–122.

Hawkins, P., Shohet, R., Ryde, J., & Wilmot, J. (2012). *Supervision in the helping professions*. London, UK: McGraw-Hill Education.

Kilminster, S. M., & Jolly, B. C. (2001). Effective supervision in clinical practice settings: A literature review. *Medical Education, 34*(10), 827–840. doi:10.1046/j.1365-2923.2000.00758.x

Maier, H. W. (1985). Teaching and training as a facet of supervision of care staff: An overview. *Journal of Child Care, 2*(4), 49–51.

McGoldrick, M., & Gerson, R. (1985). Genograms in family assessment. New York, NY: W. W. Norton.

Michael, J. (2005). Life-space supervision in child and youth care practice. In T. Garfat & B. Gannon (Eds.), *Aspects of child and youth care practice in the South African context* (pp. 49–62). Cape Town, South Africa: Pretext.

Morrison, M., & Homeyer, L. (2008). Supervision in the sand. In A. Drewes & J. A. Mullen (Eds.), *Supervision can be playful: Techniques for child and play therapist supervisors* (pp. 233–248). Lanham, MD: Jason Aronson.

Phelan, J. (2017). *Intentional CYC supervision: A developmental approach*. Cape Town, South Africa: CYC-Net Press.

Poole, J. (2010). Perspectives on supervision in human services: Gazing through critical and feminist lenses. *Michigan Family Review, 14*(1), 60–70. doi:10.3998/mfr.4919087.0014.107

Ranahan, P. (2007, February). Reaching beyond caring to loving in child and youth care practice. *CYC-Online: E-Journal of the International Child and Youth Care Network (CYC-Net)*, (97). Retrieved from http://www.cyc-net.org/cyc-online/cycol-0207-ranahan.html

Shapiro, F. (2001). *Eye movement desensitization and reprocessing: Basic principles, protocols, and procedures* (2nd ed.). New York, NY: Guildford Press.

Steele, W., & Kuban, C. (2013). *Working with grieving and traumatized children and adolescents: Discovering what matters most through evidence-based, sensory interventions*. Hoboken, NJ: John Wiley & Sons.

Steele, W., & Raider, M. (2001). *Structured sensory interventions for children, adolescents and parents (SITCAP)*. New York, NY: Edwin Mellen Press.

CHAPTER 10

The Growing Edge of the Child and Youth Care Practitioner and Profession

---

Learning Outcomes

- Brainstorm learning opportunities for the new and seasoned CYCPs.
- Investigate how CYCPs can be "loving" in our interactions in ways that are not romantic nor sexualized.
- Discuss the CYCCB certification process.

Newly graduated CYCPs will ponder, "What does it mean to enter this field, to remain in it, to think of and present myself as a youth worker if I lack the competence to respond effectively?" (Anderson-Nathe, 2008, p. 3).

This is our growing edge when we graduate. Are we ready? CYCPs are committed to lifelong learning, yet learning is incremental. In this text, we have already read that sometimes we are just planting seeds that will be cultivated later.

> Child and youth care workers may enter the field with an exaggerated sense of idealism that may turn to frustration and disappointment when the difficult reality of child and youth care work becomes apparent. Unsupportive supervisors, poor coping skills, and challenging clients may also add to the elevated burnout levels in beginning workers. (Barford & Whelton, 2010, p. 275)

CYCP mentors, elders, supervisors, and educators want to support your learning. We want you to have access to and utilize the supports available to you as you increase in your confidence and competence.

Discussion Opportunity 10:1

Discuss learning opportunities that you have identified after reading this book.

Brainstorm ways that students can learn more about the CYCP field outside of the classroom.

We want your work to be informed by praxis (practical application of theory). We want you to know why you chose to intervene in the way you did. What best practice or emerging practice informed your intervention? We do not want you to forget *that relational practice underpins all of our interactions.*

Discussion Opportunity 10:2

Discuss how relationship is important in our interactions with supervisors, each other, children, youth, families, and communities.

We want you to advocate with those you walk alongside, for yourself and for the field. This means standing up for what's right and challenging policies and practices that are not focused on children/youth, families, and communities. Dr. Kiaras Gharabaghi gave the closing presentation at the 2016 Canadian CYC Conference in Halifax. During his presentation, he talked about how systemic rules and culture communicate to youth that they do not matter. He provided examples where CYCPs are not demonstrating kindness or care by doing things like rationing shampoo for youth (Vachon, 2016).

It is our hope that growing CYCPs recognize that their understanding of praxis is developmental and their confidence and identity formation as a CYCP are developmental. We do not want new members of our profession to feel that they can and are required to do it all. They need to understand the theory that underpins intervention. Without praxis, "attempting to separate practice from theory, a worker can inadvertently perpetuate belief systems and power relations that operate directly against the interests of the worker and the young people they engage" (Skott-Myhre & Skott-Myhre, 2011).

With experience, CYCP mentors, a solid educational framework, and a good support system, the CYCP will increase their toolbox of competencies. In order to increase these, it is important to evaluate your toolbox regularly. What are areas of strength? What are areas of challenge/opportunity? How can you work on your goals? Your toolbox is full of skills, knowledge, and your relationship to self and relationship to others.

Please use the Competency Chart (Appendix A) as a way to track your progress to this point. Then revisit your chart and use the language of the competencies to create SMART goals that can be practised, reflected on, and evaluated. Make this process part of your supervisory relationship so you are intentional in not only meeting the needs of the children/youth and families you are in relationship with, but also being reflective about how you are meeting those needs for yourself.

Many regulated professions utilize competencies to assist members in determining entry to practice. In order to become certified, it is often required that applicants provide proof of competency development or attainment. Proof can include:

- Letters of endorsement by supervisors or colleagues
- Book reviews
- Flyers of facilitated programs
- Conference certificates or papers
- Training synopses
- Event artifacts

Discussion Opportunity 10:3

Brainstorm additional artifacts that can be gathered to symbolize learning experiences.

All of these can be evidence of the applicant being able to connect theory to practice. The competencies published by the Child and Youth Care Certification Board are organized under five domains. Each of these competencies can also be looked at as elements of your performance in your role as a CYCP. You can gather artifacts in a binder or create an online portfolio of evidence of your learning and achievements. Check with the CYCCB to ascertain which type of submission meets current criteria.

Appendix A is a place for you to identify competencies that are already strengths as well as competencies that are learning opportunities. In either case, ponder what evidence you can provide in your practice that affirms your competency or evidence that you would want to see to confirm you have achieved your goal!

PORTFOLIO

You can also review your portfolio as you apply for employment or prepare for a job interview. What a great way to answer an interview question!

For example:

Potential Employer:
Can you provide an example of an area of strength?

Potential Employee:
I have brought my portfolio with me today. I would like to draw your attention to a reflection I completed in my first placement. While engaging with a youth, I was tasked to identify a specific behaviour that was contributing to a conflict he was experiencing with his peers. It is hard to take on an authority role while guiding the youth's behaviour instead of managing it, but I was able to communicate with him in a way that was clear and respectful. I demonstrated this competency during my third-year placement as well. Consequently, I am comfortable taking on a staff role while encouraging youth to self-manage.

Using the language of the competencies in your supervision is an important way to maintain currency in your field. Your employer may be responsible for your job, but you are responsible for your career.

Child and Youth Care Practitioners need to be committed to ongoing training. We also have to be aware that demonstrating a competency with one population or in one milieu does not necessarily mean that we can also demonstrate the same competency with other populations. This is up to the CYCP to ascertain when and how they work on these to enhance the many tools in their toolbox. Having an experienced CYCP supervisor to help navigate your journey is a treasured resource. Regulated professions usually require ongoing supervision and evidence of the same.

Training opportunities can be found everywhere. There are CYC association conferences provincially, statewide, countrywide, and worldwide. Local agencies may also offer training, and there are many online training opportunities. Look for training opportunities that connect to domain competencies. We also need to encourage our colleagues to be open to sharing their expertise. CYCPs are often a humble bunch of professionals. CYCPs are stronger, wiser, and more relational when we share our expertise with each other. These relational opportunities subsequently benefit the children/youth/families and communities that CYCPs are privileged to walk alongside of.

We hope that, as you have read through this book, you have reflected on your personal journey as both a Child and Youth Care Practitioner and a human being.

When we live relationally in the life spaces of children/youth and families, it is not unusual that we will develop connections with all those we work alongside (and this includes our colleagues). This shows up in the supervisory relationship.

This connection can be loving and is often communicated by care. "Caring can be seen as 'a close attention, liking or regard, to protect or to look after' (Mayeroff, 1961, cited in Denholm, 1990; Ranahan, 2007). This caring can be felt by those children and youth who may have not experienced caring or love before in the same way as it has been communicated by a CYCP. Seeds can only grow after being planted with that thing called care. There's a popular line attributed to Maya Angelou that captures something we remind CYCPs of often: "People won't remember what you tell them and they may not remember what you did, but they will always remember how you made them feel."

Discussion Opportunity 10:4

Who is a CYCP role model for you? Who is someone who symbolizes the epitome of caring/love in your life?

Please ponder what it is about these individuals that makes you want to mirror their presentation with others. Please share these stories with group members/classmates.

We encourage you to continue to show and demonstrate love and care in the little things you do, such as sewing on a button, helping a child with a chore, or rubbing their back as they are throwing up when they have the flu. Caring is memorable, and once experienced, it is transferable so that the children/youth/families and communities that you are in relationship with will begin to create tapestries of their own competencies that have vibrant colours and warm fibres. These can be hung on their walls or wrapped around someone in their time of need.

Lastly, do not forget to *love*. Love is reciprocal. As a CYCP, you always get back way more than you ever give. Already quoted but worth repeating, the wise Mr. Rogers said, "The greatest thing we can do is go help somebody know that they are loved and capable of loving" (Neville, Ma, & Capotosto, 2018).

Chapter 10 Learning Outcomes Evaluation

- Are you able to identify learning opportunities for the new and seasoned CYCPs?
- Can you, in your role as a CYCP, be "loving" in a way that is clearly not romantic nor sexualized?
- Identify ways you could engage in the CYCCB certification process.

REFERENCES

Anderson-Nathe, B. (2008). Chapter 1: My stomach fell through the floor: The moment of not-knowing what to do. *Child & Youth Services, 30*(1–2), 1–9. doi:10.1080/01459350802156482

Barford, S. W., & Whelton, W. J. (2010). Understanding burnout in child and youth care workers. *Child and Youth Care Forum, 39*(4), 271–287.

Charles, G., & Garfat, T. (2016). In G. Charles, J. Freeman, & T. Garfat (Eds.), *Supervision in child and youth care practice.* Cape Town, South Africa: CYC-Net Press.

Denholm, C. J. (1990). Canadian child and youth care 1979–1989. *Youth Studies, 9*(2), 51–57.

Neville, M., Ma, N., Capotosto, C. (Producers), & Neville, M. (Director). (2018). *Won't you be my neighbor?* [Motion picture]. USA: Tremolo Productions.

Ranahan, P. (2007, February). Reaching beyond caring to loving in child and youth care practice. *CYC-Online: E-journal of the International Child and Youth Care Network (CYC-Net),* (97). Retrieved from http://www.cyc-net.org/cyc-online/cycol-0207-ranahan.html

Skott-Myhre, K., & Skott-Myhre, H. (2011). Theorizing and applying child and youth care praxis as politics of care. *Relational Child & Youth Care Practice, 24*(1–2), 42–43.

Vachon (Producer). (2016, August 31). *A last resort profession—Resisting the trend.* [Podcast]. Retrieved from https://www.podbean.com/media/share/pb-2iidt-619394

Appendix A

Table of National Child and Youth Care Certification Board Competencies

Below are the competencies from the Child and Youth Care Certification Board (CYCCB).

These are listed as elements of performance under each of the domains of practice. Students, front-line workers, and supervisors can use this checklist to track if a competency is an area of strength or an area of opportunity.

PROFESSIONALISM	Professional Competencies	Is skill observed?
Awareness of the Profession	Access the professional literature	
	Access information about local and national professional activities	
	Stay informed about current professional issues, future trends, and challenges in one's area of special interest	
	Contribute to the ongoing development of the field	
Professional Development and Behaviour	Value orientation	
	(1) State personal and professional values and their implications for practice, including how personal and professional beliefs, values, and attitudes influence interactions	
	(2) State a philosophy of practice that provides guiding principles for the design, delivery, and management of services	
	Reflection on one's practice and performance	
	(1) Evaluate own performance to identify needs for professional growth	
	(2) Give and receive constructive feedback	

PROFESSIONALISM	Professional Competencies	Is skill observed?
	Performance of organizational duties	
	(1) Demonstrate productive work habits	
	(a) Know and conform to workplace expectations relating to attendance, punctuality, sick and vacation time, and workload management	
	(b) Personal appearance and behaviour reflect an awareness of self as a professional as well as a representative of the organization	
	Professional boundaries	
	(1) Recognize and assess own needs and feelings and keep them in perspective when professionally engaged	
	(2) Model appropriate interpersonal boundaries	
	Staying current	
	(1) Keep up-to-date with developments in foundational and specialized areas of expertise	
	(2) Identify and participate in education and training opportunities	
Personal Development and Self-care	Self-awareness	
	(1) Recognize personal strengths and limitations, feelings, and needs	
	(2) Separate personal from professional issues	
	Self-care	
	(1) Incorporate "wellness" practices into own lifestyle	
	(2) Practise stress management	
	(3) Build and use a support network	
Professional Ethics	Describe the functions of professional ethics	
	Apply the process of ethical decision making in a proactive manner	
	Integrate specific principles and standards from relevant code of ethics to specific professional problems	
	Carries out work tasks in a way that conforms to professional ethical principles and standards	
Awareness of Law and Regulation	Access and apply relevant local, state/provincial, and federal laws; licensing regulations; and public policy	
	Describe the legal responsibility for reporting child abuse and neglect and the consequences of failure to report	
	Describe the meaning of informed consent and its application to a specific practice setting	

PROFESSIONALISM	Professional Competencies	Is skill observed?
	Use the proper procedures for reporting and correcting non-compliance	
Advocacy	Demonstrate knowledge and skills of advocacy	
	Access information on the rights of children, youth, and families, including the United Nations Convention on the Rights of the Child	
	Describe the rights of children, youth, and families in relevant settings and systems advocate for the rights of children, youth, and families in relevant settings and systems	
	Describe and advocate for safeguards for protection from abuse, including institutional abuse	
	Describe and advocate for safeguards for protection from abuse, including organizational or workplace abuse	
	Advocate for protection of children from systemic abuse, mistreatment, and exploitation	

CULTURAL AND HUMAN DIVERSITY

CULTURAL AND HUMAN DIVERSITY	Professional Competencies	Is skill observed?
Cultural Human Diversity Awareness and Inquiry	Describe own biases	
	Describe interaction between own cultural values and the cultural values of others	
	Describe own limitations in understanding and responding to cultural and human differences and seek assistance when needed	
	Recognize and prevent stereotyping while accessing and using cultural information	
	Access, and critically evaluate, resources that advance cultural understandings and appreciation of human diversity	
	Support children, youth, families, and programs in developing cultural competence and appreciation of human diversity	
	Support children, youth, families, and programs in overcoming cultural and diversity-based barriers to services	

CULTURAL AND HUMAN DIVERSITY	Professional Competencies	Is skill observed?
Relationship and Communication Sensitive to Cultural and Human Diversity	Adjust for the effects of age, cultural and human diversity, background, experience, and development on verbal and nonverbal communication	
	Describe the nonverbal and verbal communication between self and others (including supervisors, clients, or peer professionals)	
	Describe the role of cultural and human diversity in the development of healthy and productive relationships	
	Employ displays of affection and physical contact that reflect sensitivity for individuality, age, development, cultural and human diversity, as well as consideration of laws, regulations, policies, and risk	
	Include consideration of cultural and human diversity in providing for the participation of families in the planning, implementation, and evaluation of services impacting them	
	Give information in a manner sensitive to cultural and human diversity	
	Contribute to the maintenance of a professional environment sensitive to cultural and human diversity	
	Establish and maintain effective relationships within a team environment by:	
	(1) promoting and maintaining professional conduct;	
	(2) negotiating and resolving conflict;	
	(3) acknowledging and respecting cultural and human diversity; and	
	(4) supporting team members	
Developmental Practice Methods Sensitive to Cultural and Human Diversity	Integrate cultural and human diversity understandings and sensitivities in a broad range of circumstances	
	Design and implement programs and planned environments, which integrate developmental, preventive, and/or therapeutic objectives into the life space, through the use of methodologies and techniques sensitive to cultural and human diversity	
	(1) Provide materials sensitive to multicultural and human diversity	

CULTURAL AND HUMAN DIVERSITY	Professional Competencies	Is skill observed?
	(2) Provide an environment that celebrates the array of human diversity in the world through the arts, diversity of personnel, program materials, etc.	
	(3) Recognize and celebrate particular calendar events which are culturally specific	
	(4) Encourage the sharing of such culture-specific events among members of the various cultural groups	
	Design and implement group work, counselling, and behavioural guidance with sensitivity to the client's individuality, age, development, and culture and human diversity	
	Demonstrate an understanding of sensitive cultural and human diversity practice in setting appropriate boundaries and limits on behaviour, including risk-management decisions	

RELATIONSHIP AND COMMUNICATION

RELATIONSHIP AND COMMUNICATION	Professional Competencies	Is skill observed?
Interpersonal Communication	Adjust for the effects of age, cultural and human diversity, background, experience, and development of verbal and nonverbal communication	
	Demonstrate a variety of effective verbal and nonverbal communications skills, including	
	(1) Use of silence	
	(2) Appropriate nonverbal communication	
	(3) Active listening	
	(4) Empathy and reflection of feelings	
	(5) Questioning skills	
	(6) Use of door openers to invite communication, and paraphrasing and summarization to promote clear communication	
	(7) Awareness and avoidance of communication roadblocks	
	Recognize when a person may be experiencing problems in communication due to individual or cultural and human diversity history, and help clarify the meaning of that communication and to resolve misunderstandings	

RELATIONSHIP AND COMMUNICATION	Professional Competencies	Is skill observed?
	Assist clients (to a level consistent with their development, abilities, and receptiveness) to receive relevant information about legislation/regulations, policies/standards, and supports pertinent to the focus of service	
	Provide for the participation of children/youth and families in the planning, implementation, and evaluation of service impacting them	
	Set appropriate boundaries and limits on the behaviour using clear and respectful communication	
	Verbally and nonverbally de-escalate crisis situations in a manner that protects dignity and integrity	
Relationship Development	Assess the quality of relationships in an ongoing process of self-reflection about the impact of the self in relationship in order to maintain a full presence and an involved, strong, and healthy relationship	
	Form relationships through contact, communication, appreciation, shared interests, attentiveness, mutual respect, and empathy	
	Demonstrate the personal characteristics that foster and support relationship development	
	Ensure that, from the beginning of the relationship, applicable procedures regarding confidentiality, consent for release of information, and record keeping are explained and clearly understood by the parent/caregiver and by the child, as appropriate to developmental age. Follow those procedures in a caring and respectful manner	
	Develop relationships with children, youth, and families that are caring, purposeful, goal-directed, and rehabilitative in nature; limiting these relationships to the delivery of specific services	
	Set, maintain, and communicate appropriate personal and professional boundaries	
	Assist clients to identify personal issues and make choices about the delivery of service	
	Model appropriate interpersonal interactions while handling the activities and situation of the life space	
	Use structure, routines, and activities to promote effective relationships	

RELATIONSHIP AND COMMUNICATION	Professional Competencies	Is skill observed?
	Encourage children, youth, and families to contribute to programs, services, and support movements that affect their lives by sharing authority and responsibility	
	Develop and communicate an informed understanding of social trends, social change, and social institutions. Demonstrate an understanding of how social issues affect relationships between individuals, groups, and societies	
	Identify community standards and expectations for behaviour that enable children, youth, and families to maintain existing relationships in the community	
Family Communication	Identify relevant systems/components and describe the relationships, rules, and roles in the child/youth's social systems and develop connections among the people in various social systems	
	Recognize the influence of the child's relationship history, and help the child develop productive ways of relating to family and peers	
	Encourage children and families to share folklore and traditions related to family and cultural background. Employ strategies to connect children to their life history and relationships	
	Support parents to develop skills and attitudes which will help them to experience positive and healthy relationships with their children/youth	
Teamwork and Professional Communication Skills	Establish and maintain effective relationships within a team environment by promoting and maintaining professional conduct, negotiating and resolving conflict, acknowledging individual differences, and supporting team members	
	Explain and maintain appropriate boundaries with professional colleagues	
	Assume responsibility for collective duties and decisions, including responding to team member feedback	
	Use appropriate professional language in communication with other team members, consult with other team members to reach consensus on major decisions regarding services for children and youth and families	

RELATIONSHIP AND COMMUNICATION	Professional Competencies	Is skill observed?
	Build cohesion among team members through active participation in team-building initiatives	
	Collect, analyze, and present information in written and oral form by selecting and recording information according to identified needs, agency policies, and guidelines. Accurately record relevant interactions and issues in the relationship	
	Plan, organize, and evaluate interpersonal communications according to the identified need, context, goal of communication, laws/regulations, and ethics and involved. Choose an appropriate format, material, language, and style suitable to the audience	
	Acknowledge and respect other disciplines in program planning, communication, and report writing using multidisciplinary and interdisciplinary perspectives. Communicate the expertise of the profession to the team	
	Establish and maintain a connection, alliance, or association with other service providers for the exchange or information and to enhance the quality of service	
	Deliver effective oral and written presentations to a professional audience	
	Demonstrate proficiency in using information technology for communication, information access, and decision making	

DEVELOPMENTAL PRACTICE METHODS

DEVELOPMENTAL PRACTICE METHODS	Professional Competencies	Is skill observed?
Genuine Relationships	Recognize the critical importance of genuine relationships based on empathy and positive regard in promoting optimal development for children, youth, and families	
	Forming, maintaining, and building upon such relationships as a central change strategy	
Health Safety	Environmental safety	
	(1) Participate effectively in emergency procedures in a specific practice setting and carry them out in a developmentally appropriate manner	
	(2) Incorporate environmental safety into the arrangement of space, the storage of equipment and supplies, and the design and implementation of activities	

DEVELOPMENTAL PRACTICE METHODS	Professional Competencies	Is skill observed?
	Health	
	(1) Access the health and safety regulations applicable to a specific practice setting, including laws/regulations related to disability	
	(2) Use current health, hygiene, and nutrition practices to support healthy development and prevent illness	
	(3) Discuss health-related information with children, youth, and families as appropriate to a specific practice setting	
	Medications	
	(1) Access current information on medications taken by clients in a specific practice site	
	(2) Describe the medication effects relevant to practice	
	(3) Describe the rules and procedures for storage and administration of medication in a specific practice site, and participate as appropriate	
	Infectious Diseases	
	(1) Access current information on infectious diseases of concern in a specific practice setting	
	(2) Describe the components relevant to practice	
	(3) Employ appropriate infection control practices	
Intervention Planning	Assess strengths and needs	
	Plan goals and activities that take agency mission and group objectives, individual histories, and interests into account	
	Encourage child/youth and family participation in assessment and goal setting in intervention planning and the development of individual plans	
	Integrate client empowerment and support of strengths into conceptualizing and designing interventions	
	Develop and present a theoretical/empirical rational for a particular intervention or approach	
	Select and apply an appropriate planning model	
	Select appropriate goals or objectives from plans, and design activities, interactions, and management methods that support plans in an appropriate way	
	Work with client and team to assess and monitor progress and revise plan as needed	

DEVELOPMENTAL PRACTICE METHODS	Professional Competencies	Is skill observed?
Environmental Design and Maintenance	Recognize the messages conveyed by environment	
	Design and maintain planned environments which integrate developmental, preventive, and interventive requirements into the living space, through the use of developmentally and culturally sensitive methodologies and techniques	
	Arrange space, equipment, and activities in the environment to promote participation and prosocial behaviour, and to meet program goals	
	Involve children, youth, and families appropriately in space design and maintenance	
Program Planning and Activity Planning	Connect own childhood activity experiences and skills, and adult interests and skills, to current work	
	Teach skills in several different domains of leisure activity	
	Assist clients in identifying and developing their strengths through activities and other experiences	
	Design and implement programs and activities which integrate age, developmental, preventive, and/or interventive requirements and sensitivity to culture and diversity	
	Design and implement challenging age-, developmentally, and cultural and human diversity-appropriate activity programs	
	(1) Perform an activity analysis	
	(2) Assess clients' interests, knowledge of, and skill level in various activities	
	(3) Promote clients' participation in activity planning	
	(4) Select and obtain resources necessary to conduct a particular activity or activity program	
	(5) Perform ongoing (formative) and outcome (summative) evaluation of specific activities and activity programs	
	Adapt activities for particular individuals or groups	
	Locate and critically evaluate community resources for programs and activities, and connect children, youth, and families to them	

DEVELOPMENTAL PRACTICE METHODS	Professional Competencies	Is skill observed?
Activities of Daily Living	Integrate client's need for dignity, positive public image, nurturance, choice, self-management, and privacy into activities of daily living	
	Design and implement, and support family members and caregivers to implement, activities of daily living, which integrate age, developmental, preventive, and/or interventive requirements and sensitivity to culture and diversity	
	(1) Age- and cultural and human diversity appropriate clothing	
	(2) Pleasant and inviting eating times that encourage positive social interaction	
	(3) Age- and developmentally appropriate rest opportunities	
	(4) Clean and well-maintained bathroom facilities that allow age- and developmentally appropriate privacy and independence	
	(5) Personal space adequate for safe storage of personal belongings and for personal expression through decorations that do not exceed reasonable propriety	
	Design and maintain inviting, hygienic, and well-maintained physical environments and equipment and supplies, which positively support daily activities	
	Encourage development of skills in activities of daily living	
	(1) Personal hygiene and grooming skills	
	(2) Developing and maintaining of areas related to daily living (e.g., maintaining living space, preparing and serving meals, clean-up)	
	(3) Socially appropriate behaviour in activities of daily living: respecting others' privacy, expected grooming, and dress for various occasions	
Group Process	Assess the group development and dynamics of a specific group of children and youth	
	Use group process to promote program, group, and individual goals	
	Facilitate group sessions around specific topics/issues related to the needs of children/youth	
	Mediate in group process issues	

DEVELOPMENTAL PRACTICE METHODS	Professional Competencies	Is skill observed?
Counselling	Recognize the importance of relationships as a foundation for counselling with children, youth, and families	
	Has self-awareness and uses oneself appropriately in counselling activities	
	Able to assess a situation in the milieu or in individual interaction and select the appropriate medium and content for counselling	
	Able to make appropriate inquiry to determine meaning of a particular situation to a child	
	Assist other adults, staff, parents, and caregivers in learning and implementing appropriate behavioural support and instruction	
	Employ effective problem-solving and conflict resolution skills	
Behaviour Guidance	Assess client behaviour, including its meaning to the client	
	Design behavioural guidance around level of client's understanding	
	Assess the strengths and limitations of behavioural management methods	
	Employ selected behavioural management methods, where deemed appropriate	
	Assist other adults, staff, and parents and caregivers in learning and implementing appropriate behavioural guidance techniques and plans	
	Give clear, coherent, and consistent expectations; set appropriate boundaries	
	Evaluate and disengage from power struggles	
	Employ genuine relationship to promote positive behaviour	
	Employ developmental and cultural/diversity understandings to promote positive behaviour	
	Employ planned environment and activities to promote positive behaviour	
	Employ at least one method of conflict resolution	
	Employ principles of crisis management	
	(1) Describe personal response to crisis situations	
	(2) Describe personal strengths and limitations in responding to crisis situations	

DEVELOPMENTAL PRACTICE METHODS	Professional Competencies	Is skill observed?
	(3) Take self-protective steps to avoid unnecessary risks and confrontations	
	(4) Dress appropriately to the practice setting	
	(5) Employ a variety of interpersonal and verbal skills to defuse a crisis	
	(6) Describe the principles of physical interventions appropriate to the setting	
	(7) Conduct a life space interview or alternative reflective debriefing	
Family and Caregiver Engagement	Communicate effectively with family members	
	Partner with family in goal setting and designing and implementing developmental supports and/or interventions	
	Identify client and family needs for community resources and supports	
	Support family members in accessing and utilizing community resources	
	Advocate for and with family to secure and/or maintain proper services	
Community Engagement	Access up-to-date information about service systems; support and advocacy resources; and community resources, laws, regulations, and public policy	
	Develop and sustain collaborative relationships with organizations and people	
	Facilitate client contact with relevant community agencies	

APPLIED HUMAN DEVELOPMENT

APPLIED HUMAN DEVELOPMENT	Professional Competencies	Is skill observed?
Contextual-Developmental Assessment	Assess different domains of development across various contexts	
	Evaluate the developmental appropriateness of environments with regard to the individual needs of clients	
	Assess client and family needs in relation to community opportunities, resources, and supports	

APPLIED HUMAN DEVELOPMENT	Professional Competencies	Is skill observed?
Sensitivity to Contextual Development in Relationships and Communication	Adjust for the effects of age, culture, background, experience, and developmental status on verbal and nonverbal communication	
	Communicate with the client in a manner that is developmentally sensitive and that reflects the client's developmental strengths and needs	
	(1) Recognize the influence of the child/youth's relationship history on the development of current relationships	
	(2) Employ displays of affection and physical contact that reflect sensitivity for individuality, age, development, cultural and human diversity, as well as consideration of laws, regulations, policies, and risks	
	(3) Respond to behaviour while encouraging and promoting several alternatives for the healthy expression of needs and feelings	
	Give accurate developmental information in a manner that facilitates growth	
	Partner with family in goal setting and designing developmental supports and interventions	
	Assist clients (to a level consistent with their development, abilities, and receptiveness) to access relevant information about legislation/regulations, policies/standards, as well as additional supports and services	
Practice Methods Sensitive to Development and Context	Support development in a broad range of circumstances in different domains and contexts	
	Design and implement programs and planned environments, including activities of daily living, which integrate developmental, preventive, and/or therapeutic objectives into the life space through the use of developmentally sensitive methodologies and techniques	
	Individualize plans to reflect differences in culture/human diversity, background, temperament, personality, and differential rates of development across the domains of human development	
	Design and implement group work, counselling, and behavioural guidance, with sensitivity to the client's individuality, age, development, and culture	

APPLIED HUMAN DEVELOPMENT	Professional Competencies	Is skill observed?
	Employ developmentally sensitive expectations in setting appropriate boundaries and limits	
	Create and maintain a safe and growth-promoting environment	
	Make risk-management decisions that reflect sensitivity for individuality, age, development, culture and human diversity, while also ensuring a safe and growth-promoting environment	
Access Resources That Support Healthy Development	Locate and critically evaluate resources that support healthy development	
	Empower clients, and programs in gaining resources that support healthy development	

Source: Competencies were developed by the National Child and Youth Care Certification Board (CYCCB).

Appendix B

The LEAP Skills

This appendix reviews the LEAP skills developed by Torrance and Safter (1999) and further added to by Burnett and Figliotti (2015). Identify how you have applied each LEAP skill in your placement/practicum, workplace, or volunteer site.

Be original
Be flexible
Produce and consider many alternatives
Be aware of emotions
Elaborate—but not excessively
Combine and synthesize
Highlight the essence
Put your ideas in context
Stay open
Visualize it—richly and colourfully
Make it swing, make it ring
Look at it another way
Enjoy and use fantasy
Breaking through—expand the boundaries
Let humour flow and use it
Get glimpses of the future
Curiosity
Embrace the challenge
Mindfulness
Tolerate ambiguity

Author Biographies

Theresa Fraser is a CYC Practioner, an internationally renowned Play Therapist, and a published author. She is also an adult educator who is passionate about CYC education and her CYC students. In all her roles, Theresa embraces opportunities to demonstrate love and caring. She and her husband, Kevin, have been treatment foster parents to over 200 children and youth for the past 30 years. She is very proud of all her children. She is currently completing her PhD research, which involves the use of sandtray play therapy with older adults.

Mary Ventrella has a Child and Youth Worker Diploma from George Brown University, a B.A. in Child and Youth Counselling from the University of Victoria, an MA in Family Support Work from Nova Southeastern University, and a PhD in Counselling Studies at Capella University. She currently teaches and mentors at Georgian College in the Child and Youth Care program and runs a private practice. Mary facilitates training across Canada on mindfulness, attachment, trauma, psychosocial development, and the importance of play. She has worked with children and families for 30 years.

Glossary

Each term defined here is explored in more depth within the text. Chapter numbers are given in parentheses to help you locate these discussions.

absolute confidentiality—A guarantee between practitioner and client that information the client discloses will not be shared with anyone. An example would be a priest and confession. *See also* relative confidentiality (Chapter 5)

accreditation—A standard recognized by a regulatory body that identifies institutions that prepare students for the child and youth care field according to field expectations and best practices. (Chapter 1)

advocacy—Actions taken by CYCPs and other professionals to ensure needs are fulfilled. Advocacy can include speaking on behalf of a child, youth, or family, or supporting someone else as they make a case for the support they need. (Chapter 2)

aggression—The demonstration of feelings in ways that are verbally or physically hurtful to other beings. (Chapter 5)

anti-oppressive lens—An intersectional way of viewing situations and attempting to understand how systemic inequality affects people because of their race, age, sexual orientation, gender, class, and so on. (Chapter 3)

association committees—Professional groups that offer opportunities to learn, to challenge current practices, and to develop personally and professionally. (Chapter 2)

attachment style—In John Bowlby's attachment theory, the way a child or youth relates to a caregiver when separated can impact how the child/youth behaves in relationships later in life. The different ways of relating are known as attachment styles. There are four different attachment styles: secure, ambivalent, avoidant, and disorganized. (Chapter 5)

attitude—An enduring evaluation—positive or negative—of people, objects, and ideas. Attitude has three components: cognition, affection, and behaviour. (Chapter 2)

baseline—A standard or norm established by sampling. Baselines can then be used to compare a child or youth's current emotional or mental state and devise ways to help them return to their "normal." (Chapter 4)

behaviour guidance—A strength-based process through which a CYCP and the child/youth/family they are walking beside reflect on behaviour to find a path that builds on their abilities, aspirations, and needs. (Chapter 3, 6)

behaviour management methods—Extrinsic interventions aimed at creating an environment that promotes learning and teaching while preventing inappropriate behaviour. (Chapter 6)

behavioural guidance interventions—Methods a CYCP can use to guide children and youth so they can understand why rules, routines, and expectations are designed the way they are. (Chapter 6)

being in relationship—The essence of reciprocal, in-the-moment interactions that happen between the CYCP and children/youth/families and communities. (Chapter 5)

beliefs—Personal truths, which people hold at their cores. (Chapter 2)

best practices—Practices and methods that are recommended at the current time on the basis of research, evidence, and hoped-for outcomes. Best practices change as new theories and research emerge. (Chapter 2, 9)

bias—A belief, value, or thought that separates, judges, or marginalizes a person or group of people. (Chapter 3, 5)

body sensations—The sensory experiences (e.g., smell, hearing, taste, touch). (Chapter 1)

boundaries—Limits set within relationships to establish appropriate and inappropriate interactions. (Chapter 3, 4, 5, 6, 7)

certification—The process by which a child and youth care professional can become certified according to the standards and requirements developed by the Child and Youth Care Certification Board. (Chapter 1)

challenges and opportunities—Skills and knowledge a person hopes to develop. Once a CYCP identifies what skills or knowledge he/she/ze/they need to develop, he/she/ze/they can utilize this information to create goals. (Chapter 2)

child welfare agency—A government-sanctioned body involved in protecting the well-being of children. (Chapter 2)

child-centred approach—An approach to care that puts the child and his/her/hir/their communicated needs first. Child-centric approaches create dialogue with the child and approach with attention, respect, and empathy. (Chapter 5)

chronosystem—Environmental events and transitions in a child's life, including socio-historical events. It is one of five systems in the ecological systems theory. (Chapter 6)

code of ethics—A code that outlines ethical responsibilities and expectations of a practising professional, often agreed to formally by membership in a CYC association prior to professional practice as a student, graduate of a CYCP program, or certified professional. (Chapter 2)

cohesion—The process of coming together as a whole. (Chapter 5)

colonization—The process by which a migratory group settles among and establishes control over the indigenous peoples of the area. In most cases, this refers to the process of European immigration to other parts of the globe from the 15th century on. (Chapter 3)

community setting—A space within the community where a child, youth, or family lives or spends time. A community setting may be defined by a CYCP as a space where the CYCP works with children, youth, and families that is not an educational, residential, or justice setting. (Chapter 1)

competencies—The skills that Child and Youth Care Practitioners demonstrate and practice in their work with children/youth/families/communities. (Chapter 1, 10)

conflict resolution—The process of bringing a conflict to a safe conclusion for all parties involved. (Chapter 3, 5, 6)

constructive feedback—A kind and respectful response from others that provides information that can precipitate necessary change. (Chapter 7)

context—The circumstances that form the location or source for an interaction, event, or idea that impacts the meaning of these experiences. (Chapter 1, 4, 6)

continuous development—Life-long development, particularly in the professional field. Child and Youth Care practitioners recognize that their personal and professional development is life-long and informed by reflection, the relationships they share, and the training they participate in. (Chapter 2)

Convention on the Rights of the Child—An agreement signed by all United Nations member states (except the United States) regarding the care and treatment of children. (Chapter 2, 4, 5)

creativity—The ability to produce novel and useful ideas or solutions to everyday challenges. CYCPs should embrace creativity in every aspect of their practice. (Chapter 7)

crisis intervention—A method used to support individuals who experience an event that precipitates emotional, physical, or behavioural distress. (Chapter 6)

countertransference—A term coined by Dr. Sigmund Freud, which explains the reaction of the practitioner to the "client's" projection of unfinished business or feelings. *See also* transference (Chapter 5)

Crown wards—Children in state/province-managed residential care until they are considered legal adults. (Chapter 2)

cultural values—Values influenced by upbringing and how a child is socialized. Cultural values can impact many aspects of a child's life, including the clothing they wear and the people they associate with. *See also* values (Chapter 2, 3)

culture—The traditions, lifestyles, beliefs, and achievements of a people or social group, which inform how a person walks in the world, sees the world, and engages in the world. Culture is unique to the individual and can include ancestors and current family experiences. (Chapter 1, 2, 3)

CYCP conferences—Gatherings of child and youth care professionals, which present opportunities to connect with colleagues locally and from far away. (Chapter 2)

development—The stage of a person's mental, physical, emotional, spiritual, and social growth. (Chapter 1)

developmental model approach—An approach to supervisions that involves the supervisor assessing the current stage of practice of the supervisee as he/she/ze/they go through the process of learning. (Chapter 9)

developmental stage of functioning—The level of development at which a child seems to be able to function independently. CYCPs are aware that a child can function at different developmental stages in different contexts as a result of neglect and abuse. (Chapter 6)

developmental/ecological perspective—A framework that predicts and tries to precipitate unmet developmental needs in children and youth. (Chapter 2)

discrimination model—An approach to supervision in which the supervisor observes a student's intervention and discusses the student's observations. The supervisor encourages the supervisee to identify how he/she/ze/they can adapt to meet the needs of the children/youth/families communities, while understanding how all of this impacts him/her/hir/them. (Chapter 9)

diversity—A term recognizing that each individual within a population is unique, as there will be differences with regards to ethnicity, race, age, gender, sexual orientation, gender identity, ability, and so on. (Chapter 1)

domain of practice—Objectives or elements of performance that identify a variety of competencies, such as professionalism and applied human development, among others. (Chapter 1)

duty to report—A legislated requirement for any practitioner working with a minor to report situations of neglect or abuse. CYCPs have a responsibility to report institutional and workplace abuse, even if this is not mandated by legislation. (Chapter 2)

ecomap—A map or diagram, created by Dr. Anne Hartman, that illustrates the many social relationships that an individual/family/group is involved in. (Chapter 9)

ecological model—A framework developed by Urie Bronfenbrenner, which encourages understanding and working with children/youth/families by examining all of the systems they interact with. (Chapter 4)

educational setting—A space where a child/youth or adult learns skills and competencies, such as a school. (Chapter 1)

efficacy-based practice—Practice that is defined by its effectiveness or ability to achieve a desired result. (Chapter 2)

elaborating—The process of clearly explaining a situation or idea. CYCPs must strike a balance between giving clear details and giving too much information, as it can overwhelm listeners. (Chapter 7)

empathy—The ability to both understand and share or experience the feelings of another being. (Chapter 5)

empowerment—The process or action by which an individual or community can claim rights and voice. (Chapter 1, 6)

ethics—Principles that govern a professional's behaviour. (Chapter 2)

evidence-based practice—Practice supported by research and the evidence produced. (Chapter 1)

family sculpting—An exercise designed by David Kantor, Fred Duhl, and Bunny Duhl in which participants are asked to sculpt how they see the connections within the family, without judgment. The exercise can be modified to have participants' model team connections, supervision, and so on. (Chapter 9)

fight, flight, and freeze—The self-protective and automatic reactions to threat based on past trauma experiences. Most individuals experience one of the three in a given situation, although they may experience all three at different times. (Chapter 6)

folklore—Word-of-mouth stories, traditions, and customs. *See also* culture (Chapter 5)

genogram—A diagram created by Murray Bowen, which illustrates family systems (family tree). (Chapter 9)

Goal Attainment Scale—The scale used to measure a child or youth's progress toward a goal. The scale involves levels and allows the child/youth to verbalize how it feels to work toward the goal. (Chapter 6)

goal statement—Also known as a statement of purpose, an indication of one's goals and the steps to take to achieve it. (Chapter 2)

group intervention—An intentional interaction shared with a group in order to support or encourage change. (Chapter 3)

holistic assessment—Assessment of the whole picture, whole child, youth, family, or community. It includes all aspects of development. (Chapter 5)

inclusion—The action or experience of being added to a formal or informal group. (Chapter 3)

in relationship—The state of being connected through mutual commitment. (Chapter 2)

in-the-moment relational practices—Interactions that happen in the moments of everyday life, which provide opportunities to praise, provide feedback, enhance the relationship, and continue building skills. (Chapter 7)

informed consent—Consent obtained once a person has been provided with and understood all relevant information. If a person consents, but does not have all the information needed to make an informed decision, his/her/hir/their consent is not informed. Once made aware of the missing information, they may choose to withdraw their consent. (Chapter 2)

institutional abuse—Abuse that occurs in an institutional setting. The abuse or "damaging acts" can be inflicted through institutional policies as well. (Chapter 2)

intrinsic motivation—An internal factor that encourages a specific behaviour or action. *See also* extrinsic motivation (Chapter 6)

justice setting—A custody space a youth is sentenced to be in for a specific, court-ordered period. This includes follow-up spaces such as probation offices or attendance centres. (Chapter 1)

labelling—A form of identification based on assumptions of future behaviours. (Chapter 5)

LEAP skills—A set of skills associated with the Torrance Incubation Model (TIM) that promote creative teaching. LEAP skills can be implemented with children, youth, families, systems, and students. *See also* Torrance Incubation Model (TIM) (Chapter 7)

legislation—Laws created at the national, state, or local level. (Chapter 2)

life space—The physical and psychological environment that a child, youth, or family lives in. (Chapter 1, 6)

life space intervention—The therapeutic use of daily life events in settings where CYCPs share life space with clients. (Chapter 2)

love—Affection and positive regard for a person, which is a prerequisite of healthy development. (Chapter 1, 10)

meaning making—The process of understanding an interaction or experience, which is unique to the individual. People should be encouraged to reflect on the meaning they attach to the experiences. (Chapter 1)

mentor—An individual who supports the learning and professional development of the CYCP. (Chapter 9)

microaggressions—Forms of communication that reflect oppression, lack of cultural awareness, lack of cultural competency, and bias. (Chapter 3)

milieu—A setting where needs of children, youth, families, and communities are addressed. These needs can be physical, emotional, cultural, ideological, and social. (Chapter 1)

multidisciplinary team—A group of practitioners comprised of different disciplines (professions), working together. (Chapter 5)

needs—A motivating force that urges an individual or group to achieve a goal by engaging in behaviour. A need can be physiological, psychological, spiritual, or emotional. (Chapter 2)

networks—The connections shared with individuals and formal and informal groups, often for the benefit of supporting children/youth/families and communities. (Chapter 2)

non-compliance—Refusal or failure to comply with established rules or regulations. (Chapter 2)

nonverbal communication—Communication processed through the sending and receiving of wordless messages. Body language is an example. (Chapter 4)

open-ended questions—Questions that cannot be answered with a yes or no response. (Chapter 5)

organizational and workplace abuse—Abuse committed within the workplace or any organization, including oppression that might exist in educational and work spaces. (Chapter 2)

personal development—Growth through self-awareness of personal strengths, limitations, feelings, and needs. (Chapter 2)

policies and procedures—Rules set in place to inform caregivers of their responsibilities. They can include the reporting of expectations and investigative practices against allegations. (Chapter 2)

positive regard—An assurance that someone will continue to care for a person irrespective of what they say or do. The idea is derived from the work of Carl Rogers. (Chapter 6)

praxis—The application of theory or research to practice. (Chapter 1)

primary emotions—What someone feels in the moment. Beliefs, values, or thoughts precipitate these feelings. (Chapter 2)

productive work habits—Things people do on a daily (or shift-by-shift) basis that support their efficacy. (Chapter 2)

professional language—Written and spoken communication that employs words that adhere to the values and beliefs identified in a code of ethics. (Chapter 5)

rapid eye movement desensitization—A new, non-traditional form of psychotherapy where a patient's eye movements are used to lower the patient's distress during recollection of a traumatic event. (Chapter 9)

reflection-in-action—Self-reflection that occurs during the supervision process, when alone, or with colleagues. (Chapter 2)

reflection-on-action—Self-reflection that occurs after the supervision process, when alone, or with colleagues. (Chapter 2)

regulation—A process that supports having a legislative body for the profession, which then oversees and monitors the practice to ensure it meets standards. (Chapter 1)

relational practices—Approaches that CYCPs implement to meet the developmental needs of children, youth, and families. (Chapter 1, 2, 6, 7)

relational process—The supervisory process of assessing the developmental stages of a CYCP and providing support, skill, knowledge, and self-awareness so that the CYCP can continue his/her/hir/their professional development. (Chapter 1)

relative confidentiality—Information shared within the agency, outside the program agency with the client's permission, or in a court of laws when information is subpoenaed. Legislated "duty-to-report" falls into this category. *See also* absolute confidentiality (Chapter 5)

residential setting—Any space where a child has a bed to sleep in. (Chapter 1)

resources—Items or attributes that enhance functioning of an individual, family, group, or community. (Chapter 2, 6)

rights—A moral or legal entitlement that a person has. This can include the right to attend court, the right to contact family, or the right to read reports written about them. (Chapter 2)

risk factors—Anything that can increase the chances of harm to any member in a relationship. (Chapter 3)

roadblocks—Anything that stands in the way of effective communication. They can include social location or power imbalances. (Chapter 5)

routine—A sequence of activities that occurs regularly. (Chapter 5)

safe base—Support through healthy connections to one's community. Someone who lacks a safe base may not know where to turn for support or help. (Chapter 5)

safe space—A place where anyone can relax and fully express themselves, without fear of being made to feel uncomfortable, unwelcome, or unsafe on account of biological sex, race/ethnicity, sexual orientation, gender identity or expression, cultural background, religious affiliation, age, or physical or mental ability. (Chapter 3)

safeguards—Measures taken to protect someone or something. They can include rules or procedures intended to avoid an unpleasant outcome. (Chapter 2)

safety—A state of being when one is protected from danger, damage, or risk of injury. Safety includes psychological safety and social safety, as well as physical safety. (Chapter 6, 9)

scope of practice—The extent to which a CYCP can act within their role. (Chapter 5)

self—What we bring to the relationship, which encompasses the totality of the individual. The self is an integral part of the relationship. (Chapter 1)

self-care—Taking an active role in protecting your well-being and happiness. Being able to identify self-care needs will help CYCPs be ready to meet the needs of others. (Chapter 2, 7, 9)

self-care strategies—Processes or routines designed to maintain self-care. This can include exercise, getting proper sleep, and maintaining social support. (Chapter 2)

self-regulation—The ability to adapt emotions and actions when experiencing often unanticipated situational stressors. The process begins in the brain. (Chapter 4)

seven-generation principle—A philosophy that asks people to consider how every decision will impact the future, not just the present. People must think of the impacts on the next seven generations. This philosophy is referenced in the Great Binding Law of the Iroquois Nation and guides many Indigenous peoples. (Chapter 5)

sexual safety—Taking precautions to protect against STIs when engaging in sexual activity. (Chaper 6)

SMART goals—Goals that are structured in a way to make them more achievable. They are specific, measurable, attainable, realistic, and timely. (Chapter 2, 6)

social location—Where a person is situated socially. It includes gender, faith, sexuality, where a person grew up, and everything that contributes to someone's identity. (Chapter 3)

social trends—Short- or long-term changes in activities that most or all community members engage in. (Chapter 5)

standard precautions—An approach in infection control and safety, which involves precautions such as wearing gloves when handling bodily fluids. Originally designed for healthcare professionals, these precautions are important for everyone in a care setting to know. (Chapter 6)

stereotyping—The use of an oversimplified belief or image to represent or discuss a group of people, often harmful in nature. These beliefs are usually widely held. (Chapter 3)

strength-based practice—A practice that highlights the strengths of others at all times and in all spaces. (Chapter 1)

strengths—Tasks or actions that a person does well at. (Chapter 2)

stress—A normal psychological and physical reaction to the demands that people experience. When stress is chronic or overwhelming, it becomes damaging. (Chapter 2)

stress management strategies—Strategies used to limit and reduce stress experienced in daily interactions. They are essential to wellness. (Chapter 2)

structure—In child and youth care practice, the arrangement of the parts that create a predictable whole. (Chapter 5)

structured interventions—A therapeutic approach that creates scenarios to safely revisit and rework past trauma. (Chapter 9)

summative evaluation—Experiences or activities that formally or informally assess learning at the end of a period. (Chapter 6)

supervision—As defined by the CYCCB, the relationship of a person assigned the role of supervisor, mentor, or individual for the purpose of supporting another's development as a CYCP. (Chapter 9)

systemic relationships—Children develop directly and indirectly with every connection they have. The relationships create a bigger whole when combined. (Chapter 1)

tapestry—A textile art woven by hand on a loom. The threads are hidden, but are integrated relationally to the overall piece. We refer to CYCPs' "tapestry" as a cohesive whole woven of their experiences and relationships, which represent the "hidden" threads that create an overall piece. (Chapter 1)

teachable moment—A moment in time that allows for the teaching of a developmental skill, which then makes achievement in subsequent tasks possible. (Chapter 1)

team culture—The agreed-upon norms and expectations within a team. (Chapter 2)

Torrance Incubation Model (TIM)—A creative problem-solving method that teaches children, youth, families, and communities how to problem-solve before a situation becomes a crisis. TIM uses the LEAP skills to encourage creativity. (Chapter 7)

transference—A term coined by Dr. Sigmund Freud explaining the projection of unfinished business or feelings from one person or situation on to another. *See also* countertransference (Chapter 5)

triggers—Thoughts, experiences, emotions, or situations that precipitate a memory that reminds or causes a re-experiencing of an event defined as traumatic by the individual. (Chapter 5)

values—Ideas that help people to understand what is important to them. Values are informed by education and drive both the choices a person makes and how he/she/ze/they make those decisions. (Chapter 2)

vicarious trauma—The process of experiencing emotional and psychological impact through empathy toward someone who has gone through a traumatic event. (Chapter 2)

we-space—A space where communication between two people generates shared experiences and understanding, values, and meaning. (Chapter 3)

window of tolerance—A model that visualizes someone's ability to handle, manage, and incorporate moments in his/her/hir/their life. (Chapter 5)

work-integrated learning opportunities—Chances to apply academic or other forms of knowledge to practical experiences in the workplace. (Chapter 2)

workload management—Strategies designed to help people stay on top of responsibilities and tasks and maintain balance. (Chapter 2)